Abraham Lincoln

Abraham Lincoln

Twentieth-Century Popular Portrayals

Frank Thompson

Taylor Publishing Company
Dallas, Texas

Published by Taylor Publishing Company
1550 West Mockingbird Lane
Dallas, Texas 75235

Library of Congress Cataloging-in-Publication Data
Thompson, Frank T., 1952–
    Abraham Lincoln : twentieth-century popular portrayals / by Frank Thompson.
        p.   cm.
    Includes bibliographical references and index.
    "Abraham Lincoln filmography": p.
    ISBN 0-87833-241-3
    1. Lincoln, Abraham, 1809–1865—In motion pictures. 2. Lincoln, Abraham,
    1809–1865—In literature. I. Title.

PN1995.9.L53.T49   1999
810'.9351—dc21   99-045071

10   9   8   7   6   5   4   3   2   1

Printed in the United States of America

For Martha and Gerald

Contents

Contents

Acknowledgments

THIS BOOK has been brewing for almost a decade now, and over that time I have annoyed and imposed myself upon many people, nearly all of whom responded with kindness, assistance, information, friendship, and generosity of all sorts.

Of course, my deepest thanks goes to my miracle of a wife, Claire, who gives me total love and support. She isn't only the perfect wife, she's the perfect friend. Without her I wouldn't accomplish anything; indeed, I wouldn't see the point. She is, literally, everything to me.

If not for the interest and support of Mike Emmerich of Taylor Publishing, this book would have continued to be nothing more than a gleam in my eye. Mike's the best kind of editor—even when I was dangerously past my deadline, his calls were calm and infrequent, which was perfect since I was panicking enough for both of us.

I want to especially thank Sheryl O'Connell, who assisted me on my first trip to the Library of Congress when I started gathering material for this book. She was particularly helpful and supportive at a time when she would have been highly justified in being otherwise, and she will always have my love and gratitude.

Speaking of the Library of Congress, Madeline Matz and Brian Taves not only served as great sources of information during my research visit there, but extended hospitality and assistance above and beyond the call of duty. I look forward to my next Library of Congress visit, not only to take advantage of the incredible riches that the place holds, but also to enjoy the company of Madeline and Brian while I'm at it. Thanks to both of you.

As always, the staff of the Margaret Herrick Library was invaluably helpful, and as always, I must single out Stacey Endres for my most sincere gratitude. There is plenty of information in this book that wouldn't have made it in if Stacey hadn't pointed me toward it, and I thank her for it.

Claire, of Eddie Brandt's Saturday Matinee, performed heroic tasks in tracking down many of the photographs in this book, and thanks to the great staff there, I also had access to many Lincoln films I couldn't have found elsewhere. This place is one of the greatest resources I know of, and I like everything about it, except the fact that the doughnut boxes are invariably empty by the time I get there.

Jere Guldin of the UCLA Film and Television Archives went out of his way to make sure that I saw some great Lincoln stuff—and some that wasn't all that hot. Jere and I suffered a little heartbreak together when we carefully unspooled the last surviving fragment of *Lincoln's Thanksgiving Story* only to find that the ravages of nitrate decomposition had robbed even those few frames of any image whatsoever. It was another reminder—as if we needed it—of how much of our cinematic heritage we've lost and how uncertain the rest of it is.

Over on the campus of UCLA, I screened dozens of film and television productions. The staff there was unfailingly helpful, friendly, and professional and went out of their way to make sure I could sit at a monitor near an outlet so that I could plug in my laptop.

Leith Johnson and the great Jeanine Basinger at Wesleyan University Cinema Archives worked some of their magic for me at the eleventh hour. I want to especially thank Leith for going through the

Omnibus files when I couldn't, and for coming up with some great stills and some important information. And of course, thanks to Jeanine for her friendship and for being the model of what a film historian and writer should be.

The good folks at Larry Edmunds' Bookshop and Cinema Collectors in Hollywood, and Jerry Ohlinger's in New York, went through my 100-plus page filmography, helping me find stills, posters, and lobby cards. In each case, I walked away with some treasures.

My deepest thanks also go to the heroic and patient Mike and Nancy Boldt, who have learned to prepare a room for me at some point during the research of each of my books. I have so much fun there that I'm going to have to write more books in order to make my visits more frequent. Kidding. Don't change the locks.

I also want to thank Bob Birchard, Kevin Brownlow, Quince Buteau, Rob Dames, Donna and Mike Durrett, Scott Eyman, John Gallagher, Sam Gill, Tom Holland, Paul Hutton, Ronnie James, the legendary Lloyd Kaufman, David Pierce, Harry Ringel, Lennie Ripps, Fran Roy, David Shepard, John Tibbetts, Marc Wanamaker, and Sam Waterston.

My landlord and I want to thank Jay Renfroe, Matt Papish, and David Garfinkle of Gold Coast Television for giving me a job on *Fast Food Films*, which kept groceries on the table while this book was being completed. And I want to thank them for being such great guys to know and work with—even though that show *did* consistently rob me of valuable Abe Lincoln time. Still, would I have become so intimately acquainted with the Troma library otherwise? I think not.

And finally, much thanks to my helpful, sympathetic, and Lincolnesque pile of dogs: Jake the Rail-splitter; Honest Pete; and Molly, Friend of the People.

Abraham Lincoln

Introduction

A Jacklegged Lawyer from Springfield

Abe Lincoln of the Movies

IN JOHN FORD'S *Young Mr. Lincoln* (1939), we first glimpse the Great Emancipator as a gangly youth dressed in homespun clothes, rough boots, and suspenders. As he waits for a fellow Whig candidate to finish a flowery speech on the porch of a general store, Abe leans back in a chair, writing on a slate. Introduced, he untangles his long legs, slowly walks into the light, awkwardly fumbles for a place to put his hands, then looks out solemnly at the small crowd. "Gentlemen and fellow citizens," he says. "I presume you all know who I am."

They do. And so do we. Even before he introduces himself as "plain Abraham Lincoln," we recognize the deepset eyes, the prominent and slightly misshapen nose, the broad forehead topped by an unruly mass of black hair. Lincoln's face seems created to be carved into stone, impressed onto coins, engraved on currency. It is a primal landscape, one that every American recognizes. We know who he is because, in addition to the countless books written about him, there have been poems, plays, scores of films, and nearly as many television productions, that have used that mythic image, building upon it and adding to it. What the photographs of Mathew Brady

Henry Fonda as *Young Mr. Lincoln* (1939).
Courtesy of 20ᵗʰ Century-Fox

"A jacklegged lawyer from Springfield, Illinois, a gawky kid still wet behind the ears who rides a mule because he can't afford a horse." Henry Fonda in John Ford's *Young Mr. Lincoln* (1939).
Courtesy of 20ᵗʰ Century-Fox

and others did for Lincoln's image in the nineteenth century, the movies have done in the twentieth; his features—real and impersonated—are forever burned into our national consciousness.

Ironically, this monumental image of Lincoln's made actor Henry Fonda resist taking the part in *Young Mr. Lincoln.* He turned the role down more than once. Finally director John Ford called the actor into his office. "He looked at me for a long while," Fonda recalled. "Suddenly he sprang up and said, 'What's all this bullshit about you not wanting to play Abraham Lincoln? You're not playing the Great Emancipator! You're playing a jacklegged lawyer from Springfield, Illinois, a gawky kid still wet behind the ears who rides a mule because he can't afford a horse.' I couldn't believe it. But he was right. He was making me see the character for what he was. I had him on too high a pedestal."

Most filmmakers who have brought Lincoln to the screen from 1903 to the present have had similar trouble with that pedestal. Some, like John Ford, could see the character clearly enough to go past the marble statue in the public's mind. Others—many others—have been content to dress an actor up in the accepted Lincoln Memorial style and let him pose in tableau.

In fact, making an actor look reasonably like Lincoln is usually the easiest part of the process: virtually any tall, thin actor, with a Quaker beard, black clothes of the period, and a stovepipe hat can be an acceptable Lincoln. But resemblance is not enough. Waiter Nicholas Schroell looked so much like Lincoln that patrons often called him Abe. Actor Lionel Barrymore was a regular patron at Beefsteak Charlie's, the place where Schroell worked, and decided to cast the look-alike in a very brief role as the president in *The Copperhead* (1920), a Civil War drama in which Barrymore was the star. However, it soon became apparent that Schroell lacked the personality to fully inhabit the role. Some critics, in fact, weren't even all that impressed with his physical resemblance: "The brief part of Abraham Lincoln is played by N. Schroell, a restaurant waiter, selected for his supposed natural resemblance to the President, and,

Hal Holbrook undergoing his transformation into Abraham Lincoln for NBC's *Sandburg's Lincoln* (1974). *Courtesy of NBC Television Network*

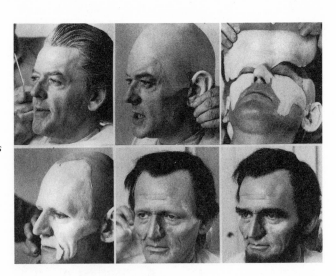

A Lincoln family portrait from *Gore Vidal's Lincoln* (1988). Mary Tyler Moore as Mary Todd Lincoln and Sam Waterston as Abraham Lincoln. *Courtesy of NBC Television Network*

in certain poses, he does strongly suggest Lincoln as known today in pictures, but at other times the suggestion is faintly, if at all, present."[1]

The *Variety* critic agreed. "The Lincoln of N. Schroell is not by any means qualified. His makeup is funny when the close-up reflects his features, and the conception of the features of Lincoln as they must seem to thousands will find this short bit discounted."[2]

Years later, in the David L. Wolper production *They've Killed President Lincoln!* (1971), another Lincoln look-alike failed to deliver the goods. Joseph Leisch Jr. possessed a passing resemblance to Abe, but his utter lack of expression made him nothing more than a wax figure that could unaccountably move about under its own steam.

Conversely, some actors who don't particularly look at all like Lincoln, create remarkable, vital portraits of the president. Sam Waterston put on the clothes and the beard for *Gore Vidal's Lincoln* (1987)—and still looked like Sam Waterston with a beard. Nevertheless, he found the essence of the character—and a harsh country voice that sounded just right—that brought his Lincoln to life.

"It was a combination of the practical and the artistic," Waterston explained recently. "Extensive makeup is time consuming and that means you'd have to take time away from something else. The director [Lamont Johnson] and makeup artists [Vince Callaghan and Coree Lear] were all very strongly in favor of creating an illusion with makeup but not to go the whole nine yards. I was very sceptical about that working, but I thought, in the finished film, there were moments where you had to look twice. The relative lack of makeup was liberating for the actor. On the artistic side it was terrific because things come through on your face; that can't happen quite so effectively if you're completely masked by makeup."[3]

Hal Holbrook also found a kind of whiny farmer's voice that added immeasurably to his several notable Lincoln performances: onstage in *Abe Lincoln in Illinois* (1963); and onscreen in *Sandburg's Lincoln* (1974–76), and in the first two "books" of *North and South*

Hal Holbrook in the "Prairie Lawyer" episode of
Sandburg's Lincoln (1975).
Courtesy of NBC Television Network

Lincoln (George A. Billings)
and his new whiskers prepare
to depart Washington, D. C.,
and destiny. *The Dramatic
Life of Abraham Lincoln*
(1924).
*Courtesy of the Academy of Motion
Picture Arts and Sciences*

(1985 and 1987). However, unlike Waterston, Holbrook went out of his way to alter his own appearance to match Lincoln's. The make-up is so heavy that his appearance is a little disconcerting at first, but he is so thoughtful about the character and infuses his performances with so much insight and intelligence that he truly inhabits the role, making the viewer believe inherently in both the sight and sound of the Lincoln on the screen.

In recreating Lincoln onscreen the voice may be more important than the face. George Billings so closely resembled Lincoln that he went on tour to give public appearances as the Great Emancipator. He was, apparently, quite convincing in the Rockett brothers' epic *The Dramatic Life of Abraham Lincoln* (1924)—the film is lost, but the stills are convincing—but when he spoke aloud, the illusion was gone. To be fair, Billings's voice was probably just what the public wanted to associate with Lincoln at the time: strong, deep, stentorian. But such an orator's voice robs Lincoln of the ingenuous country boy that must have always lurked just beneath the skin of the politician. In 1929 Billings delivered the Gettysburg Address in an odd and disjointed little sound film, and except for the novelty of hearing this otherwise silent actor speak, the performance is annoyingly bland, with none of the spark we imagine Lincoln must have given his public speech.

In "Lincoln Speaks for Himself," a 1955 episode of the religious show *The Christopher Program*, actor Reed Hadley makes the same mistake. He has a cultured, accentless voice—like a radio announcer. Nothing could be further from the spirit of Lincoln.

At the same time, Gregory Peck's beautiful and distinctive voice is probably as unlike Lincoln's as Peck's handsome features are unlike Lincoln's "ugly beauty." But in the miniseries *The Blue and the Gray*, Peck captures the man anyway—one icon portraying another. His delivery of the Gettysburg Address is one of the most thoughtful and affecting of any of the dozens of film and television versions of that famous speech.

Sam Waterston went looking for Lincoln's voice and found it in

Gregory Peck as
Lincoln in *The
Blue and the Gray.*
*Courtesy of CBS
Television Network*

Gregory Peck as Lincoln delivers the Gettysburg Address in the television
miniseries *The Blue and the Gray* (1982). Opposite, an artist's rendition of the
same moment in 1863.
Courtesy of CBS Television Network

a basement office at the Library of Congress. He recalls, "I was in Washington for another purpose and I had a half a day and I thought, 'Well I'll just go to the Library of Congress and see what they have on Lincoln.' And I was wandering around in the catalog room—a vast and beautiful place—and I told a librarian I was wondering what they had on Lincoln and that's when I found out the Library of Congress was the Lincoln library. I told her I was going to be playing Lincoln soon and she rolled her eyes and said, 'Oh dear,' because I was starting out with such colossal ignorance. So she got some people to help me, and I spent one of the most fascinating days of my life.

"As far as the voice is concerned, there is a guy down in the corner office in the basement who was in charge of the voice recording archives. [Someone] took me down to see him and he pulled some recordings and named one man who he thought from temperament and location was his favorite candidate. The recordings were from the WPA times of guys telling tales. Since these were the least touched accents in the mid-Atlantic states at that time, they were most likely the closest relatives to the language that led to Lincoln's language."[4]

Differences in voice and appearance aside, and despite the scores of actors who have played the part and the varying styles of the films themselves, the image of Abraham Lincoln on film hasn't changed much from 1903 to the present. In each film Lincoln is wise, world-weary, slyly humorous. He patiently endures the encroaching madness of his wife, Mary Todd, dotes on his small sons, and tells folksy little fables to his Cabinet and military leaders. The young Lincoln splits rails, does his sums on the back of a shovel, wins court cases, and mourns the loss of his true love, Ann Rutledge. Lincoln on film, as in life, is a sad man, weighed down with the deaths of so many that he loved, by the division of his country, and by his prescience of his own tragic end.

Because of the sheer number of times that Lincoln has been portrayed on stage and screen, he has probably been luckier than most historical characters in terms of authenticity. Certainly most screen and television writers have depended upon the standard Lincoln texts as a basis for their works. They write Lincoln characters that are strictly in accordance with the mutually accepted facts of his life— there is little or no historical revision in even the most cynical of these films. On the whole, the Lincoln of stage and screen exists very comfortably alongside the Lincoln of history.

And even when these two cannot comfortably coexist, truth may still be present. In writing notes for his brilliant play *Abe Lincoln in Illinois*, Robert E. Sherwood put it this way:

> The playwright's chief stock in trade is feelings, not facts. When he writes of a subject out of history, or out of today's news, he cannot be a scholarly recorder or a good reporter; he is, at best, an interpreter, with a certain facility for translating all that he has heard in a manner sufficiently dramatic to attract a crowd. He has been granted, by a tradition that goes back to the Kings of Thebes, considerable poetic license to distort and embellish the truth; and he generally takes advantage of far more license than he has been granted. The Cleopatra who actually existed may have borne no resemblance to the Cleopatra of Shakespeare's creation nor to the entirely different one of Shaw's, but no one now cares about that, even in Egypt."[5]

In reality Lincoln could occasionally be coarse and earthy, and his folksy behavior masked a sometimes ruthless sense of ambition. But on film these traits—which might be perceived as negative—are virtually never present. He is usually downright Christlike in his persona: kind, patient, merciful, and wise.

Indeed, Lincoln films rarely break new ground in Lincoln scholarship; rather they delight in rehearsing the elements of Lincoln's life that every schoolchild knows: his youth as a storekeeper, his facility as a rail-splitter, his melancholy courtship of Ann Rutledge, the debates with Stephen A. Douglas, his troubled marriage, his

Lincoln (Walter Huston) speaks of reconciliation as he arrives at his box in Ford's Theater. D. W. Griffith's *Abraham Lincoln* (1930).
Courtesy of United Artists

tumultuous presidency, the Emancipation Proclamation, the Gettysburg Address, and his assassination at Ford's Theater.

Lincoln's childhood—though a major element of his mythology—is actually included in only a very few films. In the Rockett brothers' *The Dramatic Life of Abraham Lincoln*, Lincoln is born in the requisite log cabin. His gruff father Tom takes one look at the newborn and says, "A rather homely little cuss, but I reckon there's nothin' radical wrong with him." The birth is more violent in James Agee's *Mr. Lincoln* (1952). His mother's labor is an agonizing one—unusual enough for a television production of the period—and to help the baby emerge, Tom (Crahan Denton) rams the foot of the bed with a plow in the folklore-born belief that this will "jar" the baby out—which, in fact, it does.

In *Mr. Lincoln* and Benjamin Chapin's *Son of Democracy* series

(1914–18), we are introduced to a boy Lincoln so desperate for knowledge that he will walk miles to borrow a book, or return one, and who does his arithmetic on the back of a shovel, writing with a piece of coal. In both cases, his mother, Nancy Hanks, and later his stepmother, Sarah Bush, are exceedingly proud of his thirst for learning, and father Tom is just as suspicious of it. In Chapin's *My Father*, Tom thinks that Abe neglects his chores and wastes his time with books, so he tosses Abe's precious volumes of Shakespeare and *Pilgrim's Progress* into a hollow stump. But later, in an episode that does not come from history, Tom has a change of heart. A shifty neighbor wants to buy a piece of land from Tom. Tom is just about to sign the contract with his "X" when Abe reads it and sees that the neighbor is actually purchasing the entire Lincoln farm for a small price. Tom says to the neighbor, "Either you or Abe is lying—and it ain't Abe." After this close call, Tom has reason to rethink his position on reading. He retrieves the books and returns them to his son.

Lincoln's youth as a storekeeper crops up a little more often on film. He stretches across the counter, reading a book and ignoring the customers in *Abraham Lincoln* (1930). And in *Young Mr. Lincoln*, he tells a family to go into the store and get what they need. When they protest that they can't pay him just yet, it doesn't matter—the whole business was founded on credit, Abe says; actual money has never really entered the equation.

The same movie concentrates on young Lincoln's career as a lawyer in Springfield, Illinois. He defends two brothers accused of murder and eventually acquits them by using an almanac to prove that the absence of moonlight would have made it impossible for a key witness to see what he claims he saw. His common sense wins another case in *Rock Island Trail* (1950). Lincoln (Jeff Corey) is trying a case about a boat wreck—which was actually sabotage. His opponents claim that the currents of the river are so strong that no boat could withstand the pull into the bridge pilings. But Abe finds a young boy fishing on the banks and questions him about the best place to catch fish. He brings the boy—named "Stinky"—into court

Abe Lincoln (Henry Fonda, center) defends two young men on trial for murder. Seated, second from right, is John Ford regular Ward Bond. *Young Mr. Lincoln* (1939).
Courtesy of 20ᵗʰ Century-Fox

The country lawyer. Young Abe Lincoln (Jeff Corey) presents a surprise witness named Stinky (Jimmy Hunt) to win a case against a crooked railroad magnate in *Rock Island Trail*.
Courtesy of Republic Pictures

as his surprise witness, the boy's testimony proves that the river is still and calm at that crucial place—and Abe wins his case.

These movies use Lincoln's childhood and youth as signposts to the greatness to come. His lackadaisical attitude toward storekeeping is never presented as laziness or sloth, but as a way of indicating his separation from—and superiority to—common attitudes of greed and acquisition. His attitude is simple: people need things from the store, and people should have what they need. Since he is in a position to help them, it is his duty to do so, regardless of worries about profit and loss.

Similarly, his passion for books sets him apart from the crude country folk who surround him. As Ann Rutledge says approvingly in *Young Mr. Lincoln*, "You've read the Bible and Shakespeare—and now the law." She knows that his reading indicates ambition as well as his need for an inner life of poetry and philosophy.

But the films are always careful to make sure that his love of learning does not make him seem elitist. His self-deprecating wit—as well as his brute strength and physicality—keep him firmly in the world of his peers. The simple people adore his simplicity, and even his rivals in politics—at first suspicious of what they consider to be his low-class ignorance—come to appreciate the intelligence and wisdom behind his country boy facade.

What may keep Lincoln so satisfyingly intriguing decade after decade is his ability to be all things to all people, even as he remained resolutely true to himself. He is truly a unique historical figure, yet he lived his life and dealt with others in a way that told them he was just a common man, like themselves.

At least, that is the way we see him in plays and films, poetry and novels. He is a real man who lived an actual life upon this earth, yet his character, personality, and actions present so many possible interpretations that he is as malleable as a fictional character. Perhaps by now, history and myth have become so inextricably entwined that we can never truly separate the two.

To Sam Waterston, who has played Lincoln memorably on several occasions, Lincoln's words are the key to the truth of his character. He says, "My theory about Lincoln is that you can have all the theories about Lincoln that you want and you can try to glue them on him. But if you simply say the words that he said, he will shake all theories off. I really think Lincoln's a man who's alive in his words."[6]

In the hundreds of productions in which Lincoln is a character, many biographical or behavioral episodes come up again and again. But one trait surfaces more often than any other—in the movies, Lincoln spares lives. Since the earliest days of the cinema, movie Lincolns have considered the case of a sentry about to be executed for falling asleep on duty, or a patriot who has been mistakenly condemned as a spy, or the lover of some winsome lass who deserves a brighter future. Lincoln comes up against soldier after soldier accused of cowardice or espionage or dereliction of duty. And he pardons all of them.

Based on Lincoln's actual tendency to pardon condemned men, this plot device has been endlessly interesting to filmmakers, particularly in the earliest years of the cinema. In *The Reprieve: An Episode in The Life of Abraham Lincoln* (1908), Lincoln pardons a sentry who fell asleep on duty. He saves other lucky sentries in *The Sleeping Sentinel* (1910), *When Lincoln Was President* (1913), *When Lincoln Paid* (1913), and *The Sleeping Sentinel* (1914).

He doesn't stop with sentries; once Lincoln gets a taste for saving doomed men in the movies, he just can't help himself. He pardons a Confederate officer in *One Flag at Last* (1911), *A Romance of the 60s* (1911), and *The Birth of a Nation* (1915). He grants mercy to the seventh son of a widow who has already lost six sons in the war in *The Seventh Son* (1912). And in more recent times, Lincoln pardons suspected spy John Boles after taking little Shirley Temple on his knee and hearing her heartfelt plea in *The Littlest Rebel* (1935). (Perhaps it's significant that in the 1914 version of *The Littlest Rebel*, the father is spared by General Grant not Lincoln.)

In John Drinkwater's famous play *Abraham Lincoln* (1919), Abe pardons William Scott, an exhausted soldier who took a friend's guard duty, then went to sleep. He meets with Scott in a tent, and the young man begins to weep with gratitude at the president's merciful gesture. Ironically, a few days later, Scott is killed in battle—a true hero of the Union. In the 1952 television adaptation of the play, with Robert Pastene as Lincoln, a young actor named James Dean took the brief but intense role of William Scott.

An interesting—if somewhat fantastic—variation on this theme of redemption comes in *The Toll of War* (1913). Here, Lincoln spares a Southern girl accused of spying. She is so moved by his merciful act that she decides to stay in Washington to be near the great man. On the night of April 14, 1865, when Lincoln is shot, his body is carried across the street to the house of—guess who? Lincoln dies in the bed of the woman he earlier saved.

Sometimes Lincoln's forgiveness was such a plot cliche that the filmmakers didn't even feel they had to be plausible about it. In *The Blue and the Grey or the Days of '61* (1908), two friends are separated when they find themselves on opposite sides of the conflict. When one hides the other in his home to save his life, he is sentenced to be shot at sunrise. "The youth with Southern sympathies loved the sister of his school fellow," explained a *Variety* reviewer. "This brought about the complications which are remedied in the nick of time by the sister obtaining a pardon from President Lincoln. There is a mass of detail to the series, which has been carefully planned and carried out. A Southern home is shown and the costuming is according to the early days, even to the dress of a little girl. Impersonations of Generals Grant and Lee are given, with one of President Lincoln as well. That of General Lee is much the better. In the detail, however, the pardon granted by the President is given in the picture without sufficient explanation by the girl for the Chief Executive to have known what the trouble was. A Field battle in which the soldiers apparently die without being shot is another shortcoming, but these are offset by the excellence of the subject as

Leopold Wharton in *Abraham Lincoln's Clemency* (1910). The film is based
on the true story of Lincoln's pardoning of a sentry caught sleeping on duty.
The film ends with a fantasy tableau showing Lincoln literally bringing
North and South together again.
Courtesy of the Academy of Motion Picture Arts and Sciences

a whole, including a chase, cross-country ride on horseback, and
pretty scenic effects, with the hunted soldier swimming a stream."[7]

The story of William Scott was told with a few flourishes in
Abraham Lincoln's Clemency (1910). Because the film appears to be
lost, it is worth quoting this synopsis from *The Nickelodeon* at some
length:

> The incidents in this film are founded on fact and relate to William
> Scott, a young soldier from the state of Vermont. Scott is on guard
> after a heavy day's march, and being found asleep is placed under

arrest. He is tried by court-martial and sentenced to death. Meantime we see President Lincoln in his study at the White House in deep thought, and seeing a vision of the Civil War and the sorrow caused by it. The vision disappears and he reads a letter from Mrs. Scott pleading for the pardon of her son. Deeply affected, he lays the letter down and sees another vision—that of the gray-haired mother and a nameless grave. We next see Scott being marched off to the spot where he is to be shot. All is in readiness for the fatal word of command to be given when through a cloud of dust a coach dashes up attended by outriders. The President steps out and pardons the prisoner, who falls on his knees and blesses him. The next scene is that of a battle with the Union soldiers retreating. The color-bearer falls, but William Scott rushes up, grasps the flag and rallies the Union troops, but amid the dreadful carnage he himself is shot. That night the doctors and ambulances are searching among the dead for the wounded who are still alive. They reach Scott. He is dying. A vision of the President appears before him, giving him a wreath of fame. Scott staggers to his feet, and as the vision fades away, drops dead. As a fitting climax we see a tableau of President Lincoln taking from a Union and a Confederate color-bearer their respective flags, rolling them together, and when they are unrolled displaying the Stars and Stripes.[8]

The same trade magazine called *Abraham Lincoln's Clemency* "full of patriotic thrills [and] promises to have a wholesome and beneficial effect wherever it goes. Films that foster patriotism, heroism and brother-love cannot be commended too highly. To carp and peck at little flaws of detail would here be foolish; the piece has a large message which would cover a multitude of faults, if present. The photography excels technically and several scenes rise to artistic heights—that one, for instance, which shows the battlefield of the dead, in moonlight. The impersonator of Abraham Lincoln bore a fair resemblance to the original but he lacked something of dignity and impressiveness. The temptation to strut and spout has been commendably avoided, however."[9]

In later films there weren't quite as many visions of Lincoln on the battlefield, but the president kept pardoning right along. Victor Kilian's Lincoln pardons Errol Flynn at the urging of Miriam Hopkins in *Virginia City* (1940), and Sam Waterston's Lincoln takes on a whole pile of cases—and pardons the whole bunch of them—in *Gore Vidal's Lincoln.*

Finally, the press materials for D. W. Griffith's *Abraham Lincoln* (1930) claim that the film's only fictional character is a "boy who is saved from a deserter's grave through the Liberator's sympathy for human frailties. [The] part was written into Stephen Vincent Benet's script for the purpose of epitomizing Lincoln's supreme charity."

In the movies, when Lincoln isn't exercising that "supreme charity," he might be found delivering the Gettysburg Address, a piece of Americana that has figured in films as early as *Scenes from the Battlefield of Gettysburg* (1908) and continues (to date) with Jason Robards's lovely treatment of the speech—and Lucas Haas's touching restatement—in the television movie *The Perfect Tribute* (1991).

This moment is so popular that several films have the same title: *Lincoln's Gettysburg Address.* These include a 1912 Ralph Ince version, an early (1922) experimental sound film starring Ellery Paine as Lincoln, another sound version in 1929 with George A. Billings, and a 1973 go-round starring Charlton Heston. The Gettysburg Address has been intoned in CinemaScope (*The Battle of Gettysburg,* 1956), in miniseries (*The Blue and the Gray,* 1982), and in episodic television (*You Are There: "The Gettysburg Address,"* 1953). The brief, deceptively simple little speech is a splendid gift to actors, and it is not surprising that so many have jumped at the chance to reinterpret those immortal words so often.

What is perhaps the most touching delivery of the speech doesn't come in a Lincoln film at all. Toward the end of the comedy *Ruggles of Red Gap,* former British butler Ruggles (Charles

Laughton) is at a bar with his raucous American friends. Talk gets around to the Gettysburg Address, and one by one, the Americans try to remember just how it goes. Ruggles turns out to be the only person in the room who remembers, and his quiet recitation brings the room to attention. Laughton later said that delivering the speech was his favorite moment in any of his films; he loved the Gettysburg Address so much, in fact, that he regularly performed it in personal appearances.

A third recurring theme in Lincoln movies is his idyllic, ill-fated romance with Ann Rutledge. This poignant episode in Lincoln's life, the truth of which historians continue to debate, is an important one to the motion picture Lincoln. It gives the ungainly, unattractive man a sense of romance; more important, it marks his character with an aura of tragedy that informs both his past and future.

In one of the earliest treatments of the theme, *Lincoln the Lover* (1914), an older Lincoln (Ralph Ince) sits before the fire in his study and thinks back to his precious moments with Ann (Anita Stewart). The film shows their early flirtation, her brief infatuation with another man, their reunion, and finally, her death. A scene showing a disconsolate Lincoln standing at Ann's graveside in a snowstorm slowly dissolves back to the present, where Lincoln stares sorrowfully into the firelight, pondering his great loss.

A somewhat stranger version of the story appeared in the stage play *The Spirit of Ann Rutledge* (1927) by Harold Winsor Gammons. He wrote the play, he said, in response to John Drinkwater's play *Abraham Lincoln*. "Why," he wondered, "should not an American write a play on our great President? It seemed to me that a number of other good plays might be written about him, so I began to think of a Lincoln play from an entirely different point of view. The influence of Ann Rutledge on Lincoln and Lincoln's belief in the spirit life appeared to me as a dominant motive for my work."

The play that resulted is essentially a ghost story, with Ann's spirit following Abe to the White House and advising him on the important actions of the war. Even John Wilkes Booth sees Ann's ghost in

Lincoln's box at Ford's Theater and quotes *Hamlet* in wonderment. The Lincolns' guests that night are not Major Rathbone and his fiancée, but William Rutledge, Ann's nephew, and a young lady, Miss Brunner. When Abe takes his place in the box, he obliges the crowd with a long speech. Then they settle in to watch, of all things, *The Intrusive Cousin*. After Booth kills Abe—which doesn't seem to have much effect on the audience—Lincoln's spirit joins with Ann's and they head off to a happy eternity together, leaving one to wonder how Mary Todd Lincoln was supposed to occupy herself in the afterlife.

Abe Lincoln in Illinois's Ann (Mary Howard) dies just as Abe wins his first election. In this case, her death is presented less as a tragedy in and of itself, but as a foreshadowing of the moment when Abe will become president, only to realize that his wife Mary (Ruth Gordon) has descended into a permanent resentful bitterness that will ruin their marriage.

In D. W. Griffith's *Abraham Lincoln* (1930), the Lincoln-Rutledge romance is rendered clumsily. The charming Una Merkel was seriously miscast as Ann, and Walter Huston's expressions of loss were directed in a ham-fisted manner by Griffith, who was clearly not comfortable with talking pictures. Lincoln is prone to holding Ann's portrait and moaning, "Ann . . . Ann . . . Ann . . . ."

John Ford got closer to the heart of the matter in *Young Mr. Lincoln*. Abe and Ann (Pauline Moore) stroll along a river (to the strains of an achingly beautiful musical score by Alfred Newman). They talk of his ambition and her college plans. He stops and looks seriously at her.

"You're mighty pretty, Ann," he says.

She replies, eyes downcast, "Some folks I know don't like red hair."

"I do."

"Do you, Abe?"

"I love red hair."

Abe (Walter Huston) at the deathbed of his beloved Ann Rutledge (Una Merkel). D. W. Griffith's *Abraham Lincoln.*
Courtesy of United Artists

"You're mighty pretty, Ann." The understated romance of Ann Rutledge and Abe Lincoln (Pauline Moore and Henry Fonda) consists only of a single scene in *Young Mr. Lincoln* (1939), but it casts an aura over the entire film and helps to define Lincoln's melancholy persona.
Courtesy of 20th Century-Fox

Abe Lincoln's last moments with his true love Ann Rutledge. George A. Billings and Ruth Clifford in *The Dramatic Life of Abraham Lincoln* (1924).
Courtesy of the Academy of Motion Picture Arts and Sciences

The idyllic, tragic romance of Abe Lincoln (George A. Billings) and Ann Rutledge (Ruth Clifford) will haunt him for the rest of his life. *The Dramatic Life of Abraham Lincoln* (1924).
Courtesy of the author

Mary Todd (Marjorie Weaver) tries her best to capture the attention of Abe Lincoln (Henry Fonda), but he is consumed with thoughts of the late Ann Rutledge.
Young Mr. Lincoln(1939).
Courtesy of 20ᵗʰ Century-Fox

They look at each other for a long moment, then she turns and walks slowly away. They haven't said much, but we have learned everything we need to know about their feelings for each other.

The scene then dissolves to the same location in the dead of winter. Abe has come back to visit Ann's snow-covered grave and to tell her about his confusion over his future. The scene is almost without sentiment, but Ann's musical theme is still there, providing a rare moment of companionship to the desolate Lincoln.

Later, Lincoln is invited to a fancy party at the home of Mary Todd (Marjorie Weaver). Mary is flirtatiously interested in this gangly young lawyer, and they step out on the veranda. There, his eyes are drawn to the river, and as he stares at the moonlit water, the

Abe Lincoln (Henry Fonda) meets a new face, Mary Todd (Marjorie Weaver), and an old rival, Stephen A. Douglas (Milburn Stone), at a party. Courted by the aristocratic Douglas, Mary will soon learn that there is more to Abe than meets the eye.
Courtesy of 20th Century-Fox

Rivals in love and politics. Stephen A. Douglas (William Humphrey) introduces Mary Todd (Nell Craig) to Abe Lincoln (George A. Billings) in *The Dramatic Life of Abraham Lincoln* (1924).
Courtesy of the author

strains of Ann's theme again rise up on the soundtrack. It is a moment of sadness we privately share with Abe—only we know what he's thinking—and so much more heart-wrenching than "Ann . . . Ann . . . Ann . . . ."

Possibly the best—certainly the most interesting—Lincoln-Rutledge relationship comes in James Agee's brilliant script for *Omnibus, Mr. Lincoln* (1952) with Royal Dano as Lincoln and Joanne Woodward as Ann. Because of her engagement to John McNeil, Ann discourages Abe's interest in her. Later, however, she comes to love him more than he loves her. Agee's Ann is not an idealized beauty who exists only to die in Abe's arms; she is a complex and intelligent character who wants to marry him. The ambivalence

The relationship between Ann Rutledge and Abe Lincoln in James Agee's *Omnibus* series *Mr. Lincoln* (1952–53) is as poignant as that in any film. But the romance is also laced with ambivalence and guilt. In our last view of Abe in the final episode, he rides out of New Salem past Ann's grave, without even looking at it.
Courtesy of Wesleyan Cinema Archives

In Robert E. Sherwood's original play, the death of Ann Rutledge takes place offstage. But Sherwood reconceived his treatment of Lincoln's painful loss in the film version. Here, Abe (Raymond Massey) grieves at Ann's (Mary Howard) deathbed.
Courtesy of RKO Pictures

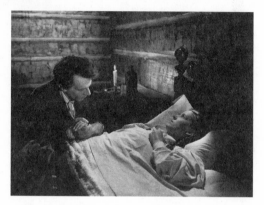

is all Lincoln's. After her death, wracked with guilt, Abe tells a friend that he once dreamed that she died, "And at first I didn't feel sorrow, I felt free."

Abe's relationship with Mary Todd is far more complicated—although filmmakers' views of Mary often are not. In the press materials for D. W. Griffith's *Abraham Lincoln,* we are told that "the task of [casting] a 'Mary Todd' was extremely difficult because history records Lincoln's wife as a peppery-tongued, scolding woman."

When Mary Todd is a full-fledged character in the films at all, "peppery-tongued and scolding" is usually the best that can be said of her. In *Lincoln in the White House* (1939), she angrily tells Lincoln to stop playing so vigorously with their son Tad. And in Sherwood's *Abe Lincoln in Illinois*—the play and film—she descends into bitterness and self-pity, regularly berating him until he breaks down on the night of the election:

> ABE: Damn you! Damn you for taking every opportunity you can to make a public fool of me—and yourself! It's bad enough, God knows, when you act like that in the privacy of our own home. But here—in front of people! You're not to do that again. Do you hear me? You're never to do that again!
>
> MARY: This is the night I dreamed about, when I was a child, when I was an excited young girl, and all the gay young gentlemen of Springfield were courting me, and I fell in love with the least likely of them. This is the night when I'm waiting to hear that my husband has become President of the United States. And even if he does—it's ruined for me. It's too late . . . .

Sada Thompson's Mary in *Sandburg's Lincoln* (1974–76) is also inclined toward vanity, extravagance, and bitter rages of jealousy. But her behavior is always tempered by an understanding of self, an understanding she occasionally loses sight of, but which Abe (Hal Holbrook), with his patience and love, can always help her retrieve. They are the most affectionate and loving of Lincolns on the screen, and possibly the most accurately depicted in that particular area. For all the reports on their marital problems and stormy relationship, one of the last things the historical Lincoln did on this earth was to take his wife's hand and hold it while watching *Our American Cousin*. When she asked, pleased and scandalized, what people would say about such a flagrant exhibition of affection, Abe smiled and said, "They won't think anything about it." If true, it means that his last words were ones of love and flirtatiousness—hardly the kind of thing a contentious and hateful husband would have said.

Mary Tyler Moore's Mary in *Gore Vidal's Lincoln* is touched by insanity, plagued by paralyzing migraines, opinionated, and strong. When she meets her new dressmaker, Elizabeth Keckley (Ruby

Abe and Mary (Hal Holbrook and Sada Thompson) are among the most loving and compatible of all screen Lincolns in the six-part series *Sandburg's Lincoln.*
Courtesy of NBC Television Network

As Mary and Abe Lincoln (Kay Hammond and Walter Huston) enjoy *Our American Cousin,* John Wilkes Booth (Ian Keith) prepares to change the play's ending. D. W. Griffith's *Abraham Lincoln* (1930).
Courtesy of 20th Century-Fox

Dee), Keckley warns her, "I am very political." "So am I," Mary replies, "So am I. The vampire press is always ready to spring at me." She and Abe are not affectionate at Ford's Theater; on the contrary, she is angry that General and Mrs. Grant refused their invitation to accompany them to the play. Still, Lincoln's death seems to rob her

Abraham Lincoln
(Willard Mack) delivers
the Gettysburg Address
against a backdrop of
the scrub-covered hills
of Malibu. Thomas
Ince's *The Battle of
Gettysburg.* (1913).
*Courtesy of Bison
Archives/Marc Wanamaker*

of rational thought. When we last see her, she complains that Abe wants to set up law practice again with his old partner Billy Herndon, as her sons Robert and Tad look at her with a mounting sense of horror.

Which of these Mary Todd Lincolns is most like the genuine article? For that matter, which of these Abes can truly represent the man as he lived and walked upon the earth? The answer is, probably, none. No life can be truly replicated in a work of drama. Too many contradictions, too many levels of behavior and personality, too many hidden motives and unspoken ideas exist in one life. Drama in any form can never recreate a person in all his or her dimensions, but it can bring an historical figure to life in a way that helps us form an emotional bond across the years. When someone's life has been dramatized as often as Lincoln's—and there are very, very few people who belong in his company in this sense—we can find pieces of the truth in countless places, but they are still only reflections of reality, not reality itself.

It is, finally, the human moments that truly bring Lincoln out of the dusty pages of history far more effectively than do speeches and declarations. We expect the "history book" in film scenes in which Abe solemnly intones how the Union must be preserved, when he says "Four score and seven years ago," when he signs the Emancipation Proclamation, and when he laughs his last laugh at Ford's Theater. But that poignant walk by the river with Ann Rutledge, that romp with little Tad, that determined boy writing on the back of a shovel in the golden light of the fireplace—these are the images that bring Abraham Lincoln to life and which help us bridge the century that looms between our lives and his. These are the moments that speak volumes about who this elusive man really was, how he fulfilled such a dark and powerful destiny, and how he came to be a part of our national consciousness.

It is the Lincoln of the Gettysburg Address whom we respect as a great leader. It is young Abe, bent with sorrow at a snow-covered grave, whom we take to our hearts.

NOTES

1. *New York Times*, February 9, 1920, p. 10.

2. *Variety*, December, 1919.

3. Author interview with Sam Waterston, June 16, 1999.

4. Ibid.

5. Robert E. Sherwood, "The Substance of Abe Lincoln in Illinois, from the published version of the play (Charles Scribner's Sons, 1939), pp. 189–190.

6. Author interview with Sam Waterston, June 16, 1999.

7. *Variety*, June 20, 1908.

8. *The Nickelodeon*, November 1, 1910, p. 257.

9. *The Nickelodeon*, November 15, 1910, p. 281.

Chapter One

A Remarkable Likeness

Lincoln of the Silent Screen

TODAY, ABRAHAM LINCOLN is a citizen of a lost world. Every person who walked the earth during the span of his life, from 1809 to 1865, is now dead. No one now alive was ever in his presence, ever heard his voice, ever witnessed his loping gait or saw his ironic smile.

But this was not the case in 1903 when the new medium of the moving picture first transformed Lincoln from a creature of flesh and blood to an image of light and fantasy. Only thirty-eight years elapsed between his death in Ford's Theater and his rebirth in the world's nickelodeons and moving picture emporiums (that's just two years longer than the period between the assassination of President John F. Kennedy in 1963 and the writing of this book in 1999). Lincoln was still a fresh and vital presence in the mind of audiences when these earliest films were produced; many observers not only had lived through Lincoln's presidency, but had known him personally. Actor Benjamin Chapin's remarkable impersonation of Lincoln on both stage and screen was complimented by several people who had been friends of the president's (see chapter 6). Sometimes the connections were deeper—or at least more gruesome—than that. According to an item in *The Moving Picture World*, W. J. Ferguson, an actor with the World Film company, had been present in Ford's Theater on the night of Lincoln's assassination:

> Mr. Lincoln, Mr. Ferguson states, took his reception at the hands of the great audiences very quietly. The President was an unostentatious man who did not care much for publicity and who avoided even the appearance of being attended by protective members of his suite told off to make his personal safety their object. On the fatal night, contrary to what has been stated, and even shown in motion pictures, the President had no bodyguard. Mr. Ferguson is positive that no man was detailed off to sit outside the President's box, and that Booth had no difficulty at all in finding his way into the box.
>
> A talk with Mr. Ferguson is an intellectual treat; he is one of the comparatively few living men who enjoyed the personal acquaintance of President Lincoln.[1]

Unfortunately, the article does not state exactly what form this "personal acquaintance" took, but the point remains that, to the Americans who lived during that period of motion picture history we refer to as the "silent era"—roughly, 1896–1928—Abraham Lincoln was not a remote historical figure, but a martyred president still vividly remembered and deeply mourned.

By 1924 when Al and Ray Rockett produced the first full-length motion picture biography of Lincoln, *The Dramatic Life of Abraham Lincoln*, the ranks had thinned. The film's press materials said, "The men and women still living who were first-hand witnesses of acts and words of Abraham Lincoln are now pitifully few and widely scattered and their testimony by these tokens has, therefore, taken upon itself the character of rich treasure, for the stature of Lincoln as a world figure grows mightier day by day and the simplest new fact appertaining to him and his events is precious beyond computation."

A unknown Lincoln portrayal from
The Overland Telegraph (1929).
*Courtesy of the Academy of Motion
Picture Arts and Sciences*

Francis Ford is a stern-
looking Lincoln in *On Secret
Service* (1912).
*Courtesy of the Academy of
Motion Picture Arts and Sciences*

Francis Ford as Lincoln in *On Secret Service* (1912).
Courtesy of the Academy of Motion Picture Arts and Sciences

The self-educator, George A. Billings's Lincoln pores over a late night volume in *The Dramatic Life of Abraham Lincoln* (1924). This Rockett Brothers' production was one of the few feature films that covered the whole of Lincoln's life, from birth to death.

Courtesy of the Academy of Motion Picture Arts and Sciences

Willard Mack is Lincoln in the lost Thomas Ince production, *The Battle of Gettysburg* (1913).

Courtesy of the author

An advertisement and a poster for Thomas Ince's *The Battle of Gettysburg* (1913). Oddly, although producer Ince's brother Ralph was one of the most famous Lincoln impersonators of the movies of this era, Willard Mack was chosen to play Lincoln in this production. No prints of *The Battle of Gettysburg* are known to exist.
Courtesy of the Robert S. Birchard Collection

The Rocketts, nevertheless, managed to interview several people who knew the president: Grace Bedell, who as a little girl had written the famous letter to Lincoln, urging him to grow whiskers; Paris Henderson, "at whose childhood home in Illinois Abraham Lincoln used to stop frequently as he rode the circuit in the old eighth Judicial district practicing law in the county seat towns"[2] ; Helen Truman Wyncoop, who had been a cast member of *Our American Cousin* at Ford's Theater on April 14, 1865; and Cornelius Cole, a 101-year-old former Senator, "a lifelong friend of Lincoln and his daily associate during Lincoln's life in Washington." Senator Cole "rode on the train with President Lincoln from Washington to Gettysburg and sat on the platform when Lincoln delivered the Gettysburg Address."[3]

Perhaps it was this proximity that suffused Lincoln with an aura of almost religious regard in the silent cinema—his memory was simply too fresh. Besides, it was a time when the great figures in history were held in almost unquestioned regard; the kind of cynical, myth-shattering revisionism that has become so much a part of the process of studying history today was virtually unknown then, at least in the popular media.

But the treatment of Lincoln in the silent film went far beyond mere respect for a great leader; his martyrdom imbued him with mystical (and mythical), almost Christlike qualities. Usually these manifested themselves in his many acts of mercy, as detailed in the previous chapter—Lincoln in the movies never saw a sentry he wouldn't pardon. These qualities created an aura of saintliness, a saintliness ever tinged with sadness.

In *Court Martial* (1928), Lincoln only has one scene: he's there just to get the plot started. Meeting with Union officer Captain Camden (Jack Holt) while a big society reception is going on, Lincoln (Frank Austin) asks Camden to go after a Confederate guerrilla leader named Belle Stone (Betty Compson). Lincoln never rises, merely talks for a moment, then shakes Camden's hand. When Camden leaves, Lincoln turns back to his desk, sighing heavily. Nothing in his brief scene indicates why he should have such a heavy heart—it is there as a kind of shared knowledge with the audience. Lincoln's melancholy is as much a part of his myth as is his mercy.

In D. W. Griffith's landmark film *The Birth of a Nation* (1915), Joseph Henabery's Lincoln is lethargic, like a statue constructed of respect instead of stone, but Sam D. Drane's Lincoln in *The Crisis* the following year can be downright jolly. The film begins with a stark tableau—right out of Griffith—of Lincoln striking the chains from a slave's legs, then putting his hand on the kneeling man's head. But when we see him next, on the night of his debate with Stephen A. Douglas, he is the most robust Lincoln on film to date, laughing uproariously while telling jokes, and playfully kicking a man when the man stands up.

Lincoln (Sam D. Drane) and his cabinet in *The Crisis* (1916). Barely visible in this photograph is a dispatch box, on the table behind a satchel. This was Lincoln's own box and was loaned to the production company by the Library of Congress.
Courtesy of the Academy of Motion Picture Arts and Sciences

Of course, *The Crisis* offers Lincoln his standard role as figure of mercy: Stephen Brice, a Union officer (Tom Santschi), asks him to pardon Clarence Colfax (Marshall Neilan), his rival in love, who is about to be shot as a spy. Lincoln, omniscient as always in the movies, knows all about their private lives, of course. While the officer is waiting in another room, the woman he loves, Virginia Carvel (Bessie Eyton), comes in to ask the same thing. Lincoln sits her down to talk with her, and she tells him that she is not in love with Colfax but with Stephen. Once again, Lincoln already knows this— he probably knew it before she did.

Lincoln calls Stephen into the room and unites the couple, explaining to Virginia that Stephen has also asked for Colfax's pardon, thus clearing the way for the two—a Northerner and a Southerner—to be united in love. And just as he has brought the lovers together, so can Lincoln now bring the country together. "I am

Lincoln (Sam D. Drane) promises a reunited country to Stephen Brice
(Tom Santschi), a Northerner, and Virginia Carvel (Bessie Eyton), a
Southerner. Just as he brings the United States back together again, so
does he help unite this couple, despite their political differences.
Courtesy of the Academy of Motion Picture Arts and Sciences

Abraham Lincoln (Sam D. Drane) gives a dangerous assignment to
Northern agent Stephen Brice (Tom Santschi). Widely praised for his
performance as Lincoln, Drane never had a chance to repeat the role.
He died of pneumonia in August, 1916, while *The Crisis* was still in
movie theaters.
Courtesy of the Academy of Motion Picture Arts and Sciences

sparing his life," Lincoln says, "because the time for which we have been waiting and longing is now at hand. The time to be merciful. Let us all thank God for it."

Virginia replies, "How I wish that all my people in the South might see you as I have seen you today."

"Virginia," Lincoln says, "I have not suffered by the South, I have suffered with the South. Your sorrow has been my sorrow, and your pain has been my pain."

Later, at film's end, Stephen and Virginia, now happily married, read of Lincoln's death. Together they go to his casket to pay homage. The film's last title card reads: "In the hush of the last night two united hearts, symbols of the reunited nation, bow down to the man of sorrows."

Before the film was released, an item appeared in one of the trade papers: "Sam D. Drane's characterization of Abraham Lincoln, in . . . *The Crisis*, is pronounced by those who have viewed private showings of the Abraham Lincoln scenes to be wonderful in every respect. Drane has spent the best years of his life studying Lincoln lore. He has visited all the localities that in any manner figured in the life history of Lincoln, has talked with Lincoln's son and has studied all the books in which the great emancipator is mentioned. He greatly resembles Lincoln and his make-up is the result of many years of careful study. It is believed that Drane will prove to be one of the greatest Lincolns that ever reached the screen. Drane never appeared in his world-famous Lincoln characterization in motion pictures before *The Crisis* was filmed."[4]

And Drane was never to portray Lincoln—or anybody else—in another film. On August 15, 1916, while *The Crisis* was still playing in movie theatres, Sam Drane died of pneumonia at the age of forty-seven. He apparently never even saw the film himself. In response to Drane's death, William N. Selig, the film's producer, recalled that he had actually held off producing *The Crisis* because he had so much trouble finding a convincing Lincoln—he must have felt that Ralph Ince, Francis Ford, Benjamin Chapin, and all the other great

Lincolns of the period were inadequate or too widely known. Selig went on to say, "Then one day Sam D. Drane was brought to my attention. I had carefully studied the capabilities of dozens of men willing to portray the historical character and had rejected them one by one. I confess that the Drane proposition did not appeal. However, I decided to meet Drane and wired him to come to Chicago. He came and his tests at the studio were marvelous. No other word will describe his makeup. I consider Drane's characterization of Abraham Lincoln to be wonderful in every detail. He looks like Lincoln, acts like Lincoln, and gives atmosphere to the story instead of detracting from the play as is so frequently the case in like instances."[5]

Lincoln's role is a similar mixture of the human and the mythical in John Ford's epic of the Transcontinental Railroad, *The Iron Horse* (1924). Ford's great admiration for Lincoln is evident in a number of his films, from the full-scale Lincoln portrait, *Young Mr. Lincoln* (1939), to the Lincoln-inspired drama *The Prisoner of Shark Island* (1936) to the poignant moment in *Cheyenne Autumn* (1964) in which Secretary of the Interior Carl Schwurz (Edward G. Robinson) talks to his "old friend's" picture on the wall, with Schwurz's image reflected in Lincoln's. That admiration manifests itself in *The Iron Horse* not only in the sensitive portrayal by Charles Edward Bull, but in Ford's decision to dedicate the film "to the ever living memory of Abraham Lincoln, the Builder—and of those dauntless engineers and toilers who fulfilled his dream of a greater nation."

The film's first title reads: "More than to any other man, the Nation owes gratitude to Abraham Lincoln, whose vision and resolution held the North and the South while moulding with blood and with iron the East and the West."

The Iron Horse begins with the ambitions of a man who longs to build a railroad from the East Coast to the West Coast. To that end, he is heading west with his young son. A young Abe, beardless but wearing a shawl, still a storekeeper, is a friend to the man and is moved by this pioneer's dream to unite the country with a single rail line. Lincoln, prescient in this as in everything (at least in the movies), knows instinctively how important such a railroad would be. "He feels the momentum of a great nation pushing westward," a title reads, "—he sees the inevitable."

Later, in 1862, Lincoln is now in the White House, but he hasn't given up on the idea. Although others think the transcontinental railroad is folly, Lincoln supports it. "We must not let problems of war blind us to greater problems of the peace to come," he says, "or we will have fought in vain." He signs the bill authorizing the beginning of construction. A title tells us: "The far-seeing wisdom of the great rail-splitter President is the beginning of the Empire of the West."

Charles Edward Bull is a dead ringer for Lincoln and, thanks possibly to Ford's affection for the character, also finds much of Lincoln's whimsical spirit, as well as his aura of destiny. "It is believed," wrote one trade paper, "that Mr. Bull is the closest counterpart of the great Emancipator ever found."[6] He was not, however, the most prolific Lincoln of the movies. Bull only made one more appearance on film as Lincoln, in the 1927 production *The Heart of Maryland*.

By the time John Ford produced *The Iron Horse* in 1924, Abraham Lincoln had figured in some sixty films, either as a main character or as a peripheral figure. But even though several biographical movies had been made about him, no one had made a full-scale, feature-length film on Lincoln's life. Over a decade earlier, W. Stephen Bush had urged filmmakers to consider making the cinema's first "biographic masterpiece" about Lincoln—"the idol of the American people. The eagerness of our people to learn all they can about Lincoln is little short of marvelous. The man who writes or speaks about Lincoln is immediately sure of his audience. If the chance is offered why not perpetuate the personality and the great deeds of Lincoln in motion pictures. We have had glimpses of Lincoln in motion pictures, but no attempt has been made to give to the American public such a series of pictures in motion as would at least come near doing justice to the subject."[7]

George A. Billings and Nell Craig as Abe and Mary Lincoln in
The Dramatic Life of Abraham Lincoln (1924).
Courtesy of the author

Benjamin Chapin's important series, alternately called *The Lincoln Cycle* and *Son of Democracy,* answered the call, in a sense. The ten films that made up the cycle were the most serious and in-depth portrait of Lincoln ever attempted, but with its mixture of historical and fictional elements and with its stress on Lincoln's pre-history—including stories about his father and grandfather and their struggles in the wilderness—*Son of Democracy* could not really be considered the full-scale biography that W. Stephen Bush had requested.

But that biography was on its way. In the summer of 1922, it was announced that the Rockett-Naylor Company had received permission from the Springfield, Illinois, Chamber of Commerce to build a stage in which to film interior scenes for a motion picture they were planning: *The Life of Abraham Lincoln.*[8] By the time the film actually went into production, in January 1923, the producing company was called the Rockett-Lincoln Company and the title of the film had been changed to *The Dramatic Life of Abraham Lincoln.*

The Rockett-Lincoln Company was owned by two enthusiastic brothers, Al and Ray Rockett. Active in the motion picture industry for about a decade, the young brothers had already tried their hands at producing films, with *Keeping Up With Lizzie* (1921) starring Enid Bennett and *Handle With Care* (1922) with Grace Darmand and Harry Myers. But they had made their fortunes in other fields: Ray through the Missouri Pacific Railroad and Al with the American Smelting and Refining Company. Their publicity for the film claimed that *The Dramatic Life of Abraham Lincoln* was "a life-long dream" and that, in making it, they "have pioneered into regions never before explored by the cinema, deliberately selecting a subject from the real life of the past, and have reincarnated it in pictures, to the end that 'government of the people, by the people, for the people, shall not perish from the earth.'" Which is a lot to hope for one single movie.

To help them along in their dream, the Rocketts approached screenwriter Frances Marion. She, too, had been in the movie business for about a decade and had been incredibly prolific over that span, having written or cowritten nearly ninety produced film scripts between 1915 and 1923. Most notably, Marion had written many of Mary Pickford's best and most profitable films—among them *Rebecca of Sunnybrook Farm* (1917), *The Little Princess* (1917), *Stella Maris* (1918), and *Pollyanna* (1920).

The Rockett brothers told Marion that since they were funding the Lincoln picture out of their own pockets, they could not afford to meet her regular salary requirements. But after meeting them and sifting through the mountain of research materials they had accumulated, Marion came to believe in both the producers and their film. According to Marion biographer Cari Beauchamp, "[Marion] agreed to take no money up front and to write the script for a portion of future profits. In addition, she invested $50,000 of her own money to the film."[9]

The next big hurdle for the Rocketts was one of casting. Like William Selig before them, they did not want to choose their Abe

Lincoln from the pool of available impersonators. They felt that they had to offer an unknown actor in the part, so that the audience would believe totally in their illusion of authenticity. They seem to have made a concerted effort to *keep* him unknown, for after casting George Billings, the brothers seem to have gone out of their way to keep his name out of the publicity. In the souvenir book, which features profiles of the Rocketts and Frances Marion, a detailed synopsis of the film, an interview with 101-year-old Senator Cornelius Cole, and numerous anecdotes, excerpts from speeches, and raves from critics, Billings is never mentioned. Neither does Al Rockett mention his name in the long foreword he wrote for the Photoplay Edition of *The Dramatic Life of Abraham Lincoln* by A. M. R. Wright. Even their press releases tended to skirt the issue: "It is stated that the company has discovered an actor well suited to portray Lincoln, and one who measures up to the ideal in spirit, feeling and intelligence as well as in physique and physiognomy."[10]

Only after the release of the film did Billings get the praise his performance deserved: "In the selection of George Billings as Lincoln the Rocketts dug up a find. If the story that is told is true, that he had never played a single role on either stage or screen prior to his advent in this picture, it is all the more remarkable that they selected him, but Billings is a born actor, at least he was in the role of Lincoln."[11]

While much of the film was shot in Los Angeles, the Rockett-Lincoln company traveled to Springfield and New Salem, Illinois, and Washington, D. C., for certain scenes. The fragments of surviving footage and the many photographs from the production indicate that the Rockett brothers' passion for accuracy resulted in an unusually convincing sense of period.

Production of the film took nearly five months, a very long time for the era. In October 1923 the Rocketts and their director Phil Rosen took a print to the Garden Theater in Burlingame, near San Francisco, to give it a sneak preview. There was no publicity, but according to the *New York Morning Telegraph*, "The news spread and two thousand people were turned away, only to demand a second running of the film at nearly midnight."[12]

For the first time, Lincoln's entire life had been captured in a single feature film. The result received reserved enthusiasm from critics, who responded to the film's beauty and patriotic power but complained that it tried to do too much in too short a time—even with a running time of well over two hours. By trying to hit every dramatic point in Lincoln's life, from the moment he entered the world in a little cabin in the wilderness until he left it in a stranger's bed across the street from Ford's Theater, the film reportedly had the feeling of a highlight reel. "The picture is naturally sketchy," one critic wrote. "It had to be to contain the incidents in his life. The sponsors have aimed in painting him an abolitionist—and have missed in establishing that he was a man of destiny—moved by but one spirit—the preservation of the Union. Which leads us to remark that the picture could have been more dramatic had they started with his nomination. Much more could have been made of the Civil War episodes. It has to include so much in his life that many of the scenes are no more than illustrations. . . ."[13]

In his introduction to the Photoplay Edition of the film, Al Rockett made a claim that now seems unusually poignant: "Professor Hitchens of Ansco Film Laboratory is working on a film of this picture that is expected and hoped to last forever. With the approbation of the authorities it is to be placed in the Smithsonian Institution at Washington, D. C., and to be opened on the three hundredth anniversary of Lincoln's birth [on February 12, 2109]."[14]

Despite the work of Professor Hitchens, there was not, and is not, a film stock that will "last forever." *The Dramatic Life of Abraham Lincoln* didn't even last as long as most. In the early thirties, a pair of educational one-reel shorts were made using the Rockett brothers' footage: *Abraham Lincoln the Pioneer* and *Abraham Lincoln the Statesman*. These two little films are even more straightforward in their telling of the events of Lincoln's life than even the original picture reportedly was. They give us a hint—and only a hint—of the original's grandeur, with sweeping battle scenes and remarkably convincing settings and costumes. They also show us a little of the film's heart: Abe enjoying a rousing pillow fight with Tad and Willie; Lincoln's pardoning of a sentry, who falls weeping to his knees; and a touching moment when Abe, on the platform of the train that is taking him to Washington, bids his friends of Springfield farewell and an old woman who has knitted him a shawl gives it to him, gently kissing it beforehand.

Abraham Lincoln the Pioneer has brief scenes of young Abe writing on a shovel, touches upon his father's distrust for books, and shows Abe clerking at the store (here we see a glimpse of Ann Rutledge) and dancing awkwardly with Mary. It features his first speech ("If elected, I'll be grateful. If not it will be all the same") as well as his debates with Stephen A. Douglas.

Abraham Lincoln the Statesman takes us on a whirlwind tour of his life in the White House: the firing on Fort Sumter, a visit to a battlefield hospital, the Emancipation Proclamation ("Gentlemen, I am about to free 4,000,000 slaves"), the Gettysburg Address, Lee's surrender to Grant, and the moment when Lincoln asks the band to play "Dixie." Finally, we see Lincoln at Ford's Theater. He doesn't seem to react much when Booth's bullet hits him; he simply slumps forward. Then Stanton says, in a slight misquote, "He belongs to the ages now," at which point the film—like so many Lincoln films—dissolves to a final image: the Lincoln Memorial.

These two short reels are only a digest of the original *Dramatic Life of Abraham Lincoln*, but they seem quite precious nonetheless, containing as they do the only surviving footage of the Rockett brothers' "life-long dream." The film that they expected to outlive them—indeed, that they expected citizens of the twenty-second century to enjoy—didn't even make it past World War II.

The movie career of George Billings didn't survive even into the thirties. (A child actor with the same name confuses the issue a bit; that George Billings was very active during the thirties.) He was asked to reprise his Lincoln impersonation in three more feature

This Abe Lincoln is as in need of identification as he is in need of a haircut. Although these two poses are obviously behind-the-scenes, this unknown actor is in makeup for his role as the Great Emancipator in the Col. Tim McCoy western, *The Overland Telegraph* (1929).
Courtesy of the author

films: *Barbara Frietchie* (1924), *The Man Without a Country* (1925), and *Hands Up* (1926). These were no more than cameo appearances. In the last one, a terrific comedy starring the unjustly forgotten Raymond Griffith, Billings's Lincoln serves in his familiar role of getting the plot started. Indicative of how revered Lincoln was during this period, and how unwilling anyone was to appear to make fun of him, his scenes in this otherwise delightfully funny film are dead serious. One critic thought that was just the way things should be: "There is a foreword on the film leader stating that certain liberties have been taken with historical facts which removes criticism through the use of the character of Abraham Lincoln. A clever touch in casting was registered here for they placed George Billings in the role of the president, the character he achieved fame in in *Abraham Lincoln* and the scenes in which he appears are shot with all seriousness."

When screen roles as Lincoln stopped coming his way, George Billings took the character on the road, doing live performances of Lincoln all over the United States. He brought with him a few cast members and created significant scenes from Lincoln's life for the stage. One of the young actors who traveled with Billings in the late twenties was Henry Fonda—later to become one of the motion picture screen's best, most memorable Lincolns, in John Ford's masterpiece, *Young Mr. Lincoln* (1939).

George Billings's last screen appearance came in an odd little sound short in 1929 called, simply, *Abraham Lincoln*. This rather disjointed one-reeler intermixes modern documentary shots of the Gettysburg battlefield and other historic sites with a few dramatized moments. Early on, Billings, dressed as Lincoln, steps up to recite the Gettysburg Address in deep, stentorian tones. The camera doesn't move throughout the recitation, keeping Billings in a single medium shot against a black background. At the end of the address, "taps" is played.

After more modern views of the Gettysburg battleground, a quartet of Union soldiers sings "Tenting Tonight (on the Old Camp Ground)," which in turn leads to more shots of statues and other monuments of the Civil War.

The film closes on a series of significant Lincoln sights: we are shown an aerial shot of the Lincoln Memorial and footage of the president's son Robert Lincoln attending the dedication in 1922. Then we move on to several Lincoln landmarks in Springfield, including his store and his tomb. And then back to George Billings, making his last appearance as Lincoln on film, solemnly intoning, "that the government of the people, by the people, and for the people, shall not perish from the earth."

With those words, spoken with a theatrical sense of melodrama that the real Lincoln would not have recognized as his, the era of Lincoln in the silent film ended. Billings was not the first Lincoln to perform for the talkies—both Frank McGlynn Sr. and Ellery Paine had spoken Lincoln's words in experimental sound films. But he was the Lincoln associated with the biggest, most thorough Lincoln movie biography of his era: indeed, the most significant such film that would exist until the late thirties brought along *Young Mr. Lincoln* (1939) and *Abe Lincoln in Illinois* (1940). Billings was one of the great silent Lincolns, and when he said his few words, he was bidding farewell to more than an era. He was saying his good-byes to a point of view, an attitude of reverence and awe, a respect for Lincoln—and other major characters in the pageant of American history—that would never again be quite so unwavering, so unquestioning, so pure.

NOTES

1. *The Moving Picture World*, June 19, 1915, p. 1951.

2. A. L. Rockett, foreword to *The Dramatic Life of Abraham Lincoln*, by A. M. R. Wright (Grosset & Dunlap, 1924), pp. viii–ix.

3. Ibid.

4. *The Moving Picture World*, July 1, 1916, p. 78.

5. *The Moving Picture World*, September 16, 1916, p. 1845.

6. *The Moving Picture World*, May 14, 1927, p. 11.

7. *The Moving Picture World*, February 1, 1913, p. 443.

8. *New York Morning Telegraph*, June 23, 1922.

9. Cari Beauchamp, *Without Lying Down: Frances Marion and the Powerful Women of Early Hollywood* (Scribner, 1997), p. 144.

10. *New York Morning Telegraph*, December 24, 1922.

11. *Weekly Variety*, January 24, 1924.

12. *New York Morning Telegraph*, October 14, 1923.

13. Laurence Reid, *Motion Picture News*, February 2, 1924.

14. A. L. Rockett, foreword to *The Dramatic Life of Abraham Lincoln*, by A. M. R. Wright (Grosset & Dunlap, 1924), p. x.

Chapter Two

The Reverence of a Dramatic Moment

Lincoln on Television in the Fifties

THE SILENT ERA was a time that seemed particularly suited to Lincoln movies. Between 1903, when Abe Lincoln appeared in a tableau at the end of Edison's *Uncle Tom's Cabin,* and 1928, when he set the plot in motion in *Court Martial,* the character of Lincoln figured in nearly one hundred films. Like Jesus Christ, Lincoln became something like a stock character, always dependable, always welcome.

Lincoln has continued to appear sporadically in feature films up to the present day, but for the really important Lincoln productions since the fifties, one must look to television. A feature like *The Dramatic Life of Abraham Lincoln* could do blockbuster business in theatres in 1924. But the major Lincoln portraits of our time—*Sandburg's Lincoln* (1974–76), *Gore Vidal's Lincoln* (1988), *The Day Lincoln Was Shot* (1998)—could only have been produced for the small screen. Once considered the movies' poor cousin, television has now become the place to make movies about serious issues or to film historical subjects; with very rare exceptions, the big screen is just not interested in such fare.

Just as the early days of the cinema seemed particularly receptive to Lincoln (there were at least eight Lincoln movies in 1911 alone), so did the so-called "Golden Age of Television"—the fifties— embrace the Great Emancipator.

Some of these productions were primitive, others were silly, and others were passably entertaining. But some of them were first-rate productions, and one of them—the five-part *Omnibus* series *Mr. Lincoln*—was among the finest pieces ever produced for television.

Lincoln was on television, in fact, when virtually no one *had* a television. A production of Robert E. Sherwood's *Abe Lincoln in Illinois* played out over three nights beginning in April 1945 (to put this in historical perspective, this is four months before World War II ended). *Variety* claimed that it was "undoubtedly one of the most ambitious shows since the advent of video"[1]—which doesn't seem like much of a stretch.

There were several programs in the early fifties in which Lincoln didn't actually appear but on which he exerted considerable influence. A charming little episode of the *Fireside Theater* series called *Joe Giordano and Mr. Lincoln* (1954) concerns the troubles that befall Joe, an Italian immigrant grocer (Mario Siletti), when Dominic, his son (Peter Price), is chosen to deliver the Gettysburg Address at his school's Lincoln Day celebration. The rest of Dominic's rather stereotyped family is proud, except for Joe, who's suspicious. Dominic is sent to buy shoes, and when he spends too much, Papa goes berserk. Mama (Argentina Brunetti) buys him a new suit, but it, too, is far too expensive for Joe's taste. He gets so angry about the extravagance, in fact, that he refuses to go to the Lincoln Day ceremonies.

Mama says to him sternly, "Something is wrong when family argue over Lincoln. He stand-a for bringing people together in love and harmony. It's not right when he split the family apart like that. Not right!"

Dominic's uncle (Frank Yaconelli) is fed up with Joe's stingy attitude and says he's quitting. He tells Joe that Mama took back all the new suit, and that Dominic is going to make the speech in his old ragged clothes. That's when Joe Giordano sees the error of his Scroogelike ways. After a series of misadventures, he manages to repurchase the suit, get to the school, and get Dominic to change in the nick of time. Dominic delivers the Gettysburg Address to an enthusiastic audience and a beaming family.

The spirit of Lincoln inhabits another little boy in the magically simple children's show *Mr. I. Magination* (1953). In this determinedly low-tech program, host Paul Tripp helps kids use their imagination to entertain themselves or learn new things. In one episode, his pal Don (Donald Harris), unsure of what he wants to be when he grows up, thinks that he might aim at being president. Mr. I. Magination agrees that this is a fine idea and suggests that Don pattern himself after Abraham Lincoln.

Don pretends to be Abe, and the longer he pretends, the more he immerses himself in Lincoln's life and times, in effect "becoming" Lincoln. He goes to the "School of Experience" and starts doing his sums on a shovel with a chunk of coal. He splits rails. He opens a store "because womenfolk are always wantin' to buy something or other." Indeed, a woman does come in immediately and starts buying things. Don/Abe gives her the wrong change and has to chase her for "nigh onto a mile" to give her the two cents he owes her. Pretty soon the whole town starts calling him Honest Abe. He starts studying law and goes into politics. He wins a court case based on the almanac that proves that the moon wasn't shining when the defendant says it was (shades of John Ford's *Young Mr. Lincoln*).

Having gone this far into Lincoln's life, Don keeps imagining. He goes over to see Mary Todd (an adult) and proposes. When she notes how much taller she is than he, Mr. I. Magination gives him a stovepipe hat to kind of even things up. Don debates Stephen A. Douglas, is elected president, and meets General Grant. Finally, with Mr. I.'s help, Don/Abe writes the Gettysburg Address. And as he is reciting it, the scene dissolves to a picture of the Lincoln Memorial.

There were in the fifties two treatments of Louise Kennedy Mabie's comic story *A Kiss for Mr. Lincoln*. The first aired on February 22, 1951, and starred Richard Greene as Henry Kenneth and Grace Kelly as his wife Delight. Kenneth is a banker who has invited Mr. Murdock, a big railroad man, and his wife to dinner. Kenneth hopes to put together a business deal, but he also wants to sway Murdock's vote toward presidential candidate Abraham Lincoln, whom Kenneth heartily supports.

Kenneth is also neglecting his wife, who's hot to trot, and when Murdock arrives and starts flirting openly with her, she responds to him. Kenneth and Murdock argue politics throughout dinner, but Murdock always wants to swing the conversation away from Lincoln and toward Mrs. Kenneth. Finally, Murdock tells Kenneth that he expects to be bribed if Kenneth wants his vote. When the railroad man finds himself alone with the banker's wife, he tells her that the bribe doesn't necessarily have to be cash. He tells her that he wants a kiss —and she kisses him. Kenneth happens in just at the moment and punches Murdock and throws him out.

But Delight is far from ashamed of her indiscretion. She angrily tells her husband that she loved being kissed—the way a man kisses a woman, not the way a bank president kisses one of his liquid assets. "The kiss was for Mr. Lincoln. It wasn't for Mr. Murdock or against you or for me or anyone else. Only for Mr. Lincoln." Her husband finally admits that he has put her on a pedestal and has been treating her too reverentially. She replies that she doesn't want reverence, but love. He finally kisses her in a way that leaves no room to doubt his enthusiasm, and they head upstairs. "For Mr. Lincoln?" he asks. "No," she says, "for Mr. Kenneth."

This slightly racy story was remade for *Star Performance Theater* in 1956, this time starring Joanne Dru as Delight, Robert Cornthwaite as her husband, and Dick Foran as Mr. Murdock. The plot is the same, but the attitude is a little different. Where Grace Kelly's Delight was a childlike beauty, starved for love, Joanne Dru plays her as more sophisticated, but just as frustrated. She just can't understand why her husband won't let go—and why he wears a beard that makes him look much older than he is. "I'm a banker," he explains. "Bankers wear beards." Dru's Delight is known for being indecorous, for saying and acting exactly how she pleases no matter the circumstances. She is also not nearly as intimidated by her husband, and she's puzzled why they don't share a bedroom.

When Mr. Murdock asks to kiss her—at an earlier point in the story than in the previous version—Delight immediately closes her eyes and waits for it. She's not only ready to stray, she's eager. But instead, he escorts her into dinner. The kiss doesn't come until later.

After her husband has kicked Murdock out of the house for his indiscretion, Delight is defiant about the kiss. They finally come to the same understanding as Grace Kelly and Richard Greene did, and as they start to kiss passionately, Delight sighs, "Oh, thank you, Mr. Lincoln. Thank you!"

Sometimes Lincoln himself could be in on the silliness. "Lincoln's Doctor's Dog" (1955) was a story spun out of whole cloth about a time when Lincoln (Robert Ryan) is sick and confined to bed. His doctor (Charles Bickford) gives him a dog to help get him up and around again. As it turns out, the dog not only gets Lincoln back on his feet but helps to resolve a conflict in the Cabinet.

Variety called the production an "innocuous, turtle-tempoed, mediocre character study of Lincoln, indelible proof that it's still a good idea to have a story. For virtually all of the 26 minutes running time, Robert Ryan, as Lincoln, is ill in bed, delivering homespun humor and exuding kindliness. This may be all well and good in reading a book on Lincoln, but it's deadly dull on the visual medium."[2]

The ground-breaking CBS series *You Are There* came a bit closer to the mark when it visited the Lincoln theme at least three times in the fifties: "The Capture of John Wilkes Booth" and "The Gettysburg Address" in 1953 and "The Emancipation Proclamation" in 1955. The premise of the show was a mixture of fact and fantasy: *You Are There* looked at historical events as though they were breaking news stories. Host Walter Cronkite served as the news anchor, and other reporters—actual CBS reporters—would show up to interview Lincoln, John Wilkes Booth, and many of the other participants in the story. "The Capture of John Wilkes Booth" begins as sorrow-stricken citizens file past Lincoln's bier. One woman pauses to cry out, "Are you really dead? What kind of person could do such a thing?" To get the full picture, Edwin Booth (Richard Waring) is interviewed backstage at the theater. "I voted for Mr. Lincoln," he says sadly. "I considered him a wise and noble man." On a gunboat, two of the alleged conspirators, Mrs. Mary Surratt and David Arnold, are interrogated. Arnold is angry about being duped by Booth. Mrs. Surratt protests her innocence and calls Booth a "Southern gentleman."

Then there's a breaking news story at a barn in Virginia. One observer tells the reporter that Booth (David Stewart) is trapped inside: "That's Booth all right, sounds just like an actor." Booth invites the reporter in, saying, "The world should know the truth." He rants and raves. "I did it alone! They always said I couldn't work alone—without my father, without my brother." He complains that the people "always hated me and loved him" and hints that he was striking back at his father. "I tried to serve a degenerate people, unable to see what I had done for them. No one ever committed a more selfless act. History will be my judge."

Booth is brought down by a single shot, but it is unclear whether he shot himself or was hit by a soldier who claims "I killed him for the snake he really was." The captain in command (Darren McGavin) believes Booth shot himself. "He didn't know how to live and he didn't know how to die. Except as a coward." Booth dies saying, "Useless . . . useless."

The episodes of *You Are There* were scrupulously researched, even if their production values did not always allow for a feeling of true authenticity. Sometimes self-conscious, often a little silly, the series remains one of television's best attempts to interpret historical events for modern audiences. The segment on the Gettysburg

Address, which aired on November 29, 1953, "lacked drama," according to *Variety*, but "it was extremely well done and held fascination for anyone interested in the Civil War period and Abraham Lincoln." The address itself, the reviewer said, was "delivered effectively and in unvarying closeup for a sock finish. *You Are There* might have concentrated a little less on the broad issues and a little more on the intimate details of which people have less of a chance to learn in the history books. Be that as it may, the Sunday show still held plenty of strong interest."[3]

Throughout the decade, Lincoln appeared on television as regularly as clockwork. *Westinghouse Studio One* presented a condensed version of John Drinkwater's famous play *Abraham Lincoln* in 1952, starring Robert Pastene as Lincoln, and *The Cavalcade of America* offered a portrait of Lincoln's struggles in the White House during the Civil War in "One Nation Indivisible" in 1953.

One of the most complex Lincoln programs of the time was a live broadcast of *Kraft Television Theater* called *The Thinking Heart—A Lincoln Biography*, which aired in February 1954. Described by one reviewer as "a sort of 'documentary drama,'" *The Thinking Heart* told Lincoln's story through "scattered but chronological vignettes with a multiplicity of sets and a huge cast [and] emerged as refreshing and intelligent TV fare, endowed with what was the most fluid production the J. Walter Thompson agency crew has brought forth on the three-months-old ABC segment."[4]

The Thinking Heart featured Andrew Duggan as Lincoln in a script that combined historical fact and dramatic invention. It followed Lincoln through his general store days, through the presidency, and to his assassination, using a "series of sketches, some light, some serious, but all designed to give insight into Lincoln's background, his personality and his intensity."[5] The sketches were linked by narration, delivered by Anthony Ross, and adapted from the works of the "Lincoln poets" (Sandburg, Markham, Whitman, and others). However, what seemed most impressive to critics at the time was the remarkable facility of the cast and crew who mounted this ambitious production. In live television, sets had to be lit, cameras moved, and costumes changed with speed and precision; there were no second takes. A production such as *The Thinking Heart*, with its many sets and shifting time periods, offered a daunting challenge—a challenge that was apparently admirably met. *Variety* called it "a generally superior production job" and singled out for praise "a highly literary and fluent script by George H. Faulkner and a solidly etched performance by Andrew Duggan as Lincoln. The complexities of the production were secondary to the script and the central portrayal and in fact were necessitated by the very format of the script itself—the various vignettes showing Lincoln at different times and places. Actually, it's a credit to the script, the dynamic performance by Duggan, and the production know-how of the agency boys that the many sets and extras didn't clutter the screen or detract from the impact of the production."[6]

The anthology program *Robert Montgomery Presents* offered Lincoln from a child's point of view in *Good Friday, 1865*. It was based on a true story by William J. Ferguson, whose autobiography, *I Saw Booth Shoot Lincoln*, served as the basis for John Lewellen's teleplay. Broadcast in color—still something of a novelty in 1956—*Good Friday, 1965* was pretty close to an epic by the standards of live television. There were nearly one hundred people in the cast, a company that, according to one review, "very nearly supplied the illusion of 'cast of thousands.'"[7]

The story followed young Billy Ferguson's frustrating attempts to get a look at Lincoln over the course of a couple of years. First, he managed to be at Gettysburg when Lincoln delivered the address, but was unable to work his way through the crowd to see the president. Then he was fortunate enough to get a job as a callboy and prompter at Ford's Theater, where he finally saw Lincoln—just not under the best circumstances.

"Not structurally from the top shelf," a critic wrote, "the play had a number of moving and expertly staged scenes— the crowd at Gettysburg for the Address; the playout of "Our America Cousin," as seen from the wings of Ford's Theater; [Lincoln's] body being borne out of the theater, and most particularly, the all-night vigil outside the house where Lincoln lay dying. As young Ferguson, Michael Allen played it simply and well, with a natural style in a role that could easily have gone overboard in sentiment."[8]

Lincoln Speaks for Himself, a 1955 episode of the religious show *The Christopher Program,* was not nearly as interesting or as satisfying. The idea was a good one: to sketch out the important moments in Lincoln's life using only his own words from speeches and other writings. But actor Reed Hadley, with his sonorous radio announcer's voice, gave no sense of the wit or sorrow or humble humanity of the real Lincoln. It doesn't take much to make just about any tall, thin actor resemble Lincoln, but without any insight into his character or into the words Lincoln spoke, such an actor is no more than a mannequin.

Another problem with the program is that it lacked any kind of narrative structure; it simply meandered from speech to speech— and they all started to sound the same after awhile. Hadley was filmed on stark, artificial sets with one or two extras at most; these flimsy scenes were intercut with crowd scenes from *Abe Lincoln in Illinois*, which only served to make the TV footage look even less adequate.

Lincoln Speaks for Himself, shot on cheap sets with flat lighting, is the kind of production we too often associate with the early days of television. But there were remarkable things being done in those "primitive" days. In fact, one Lincoln production from 1952 still stands as one of television's finest achievements—and certainly one of the greatest dramatic works ever based upon his life. This production was *Mr. Lincoln*, a five-part series written by James Agee and starring Royal Dano as Lincoln and Joanne Woodward as Ann Rutledge.

Mr. Lincoln was created for *Omnibus*, the legendary program that became virtually synonymous with "quality television." There was no set format for *Omnibus*: any given episode might include a

Behind the scenes on location in Kentucky filming the *Mr. Lincoln* series for *Omnibus*. At left is cameraman Marcel Rebiere and at right, script clerk Sasha Lawrence. Between them is a young man who would soon be making his own remarkable films, assistant to the producer Stanley Kubrick.
Courtesy of the Wesleyan Cinema Archive

jazz combo, a ballet performance, a puppet show, or a documentary on plastics. The only thing that viewers could count on was that— whatever the content—*Omnibus* would offer something special, something wonderful.

James Agee, in addition to his poetry and books like *A Death in the Family* (1957) and *Let Us Now Praise Famous Men* (1941, with photographs by Walker Evans), was also a screenwriter of note, with classics like *The African Queen* (1951) and *Night of the Hunter* (1955) to his credit. Agee had a lifelong fascination with Lincoln, and when he was offered the chance to write a five-part film based on Lincoln's youth, he happily agreed. The scripts reflect a unique mixture of several of his gifts, resulting in screenplay that is poetry. As Agee biographer Laurence Bergreen has pointed out, "From the outset, Agee decided that his Lincoln would be a poet's Lincoln, not a historian's. As his primary source of biographical information, he turned to the first volume of Carl Sandburg's majestic but suspect work on the subject, *Abraham Lincoln: The Prairie Years.*"[9]

Agee himself wrote that he wanted the programs to show "how a child born into the humblest depth . . . began to ripen into one of the greatest men who ever lived . . . and how many of the things . . . which gave him his shape, were new in the world, and unique to this nation."[10]

Live broadcast was still by far the most common method of production for new television shows in 1952. But *Mr. Lincoln* was shot on film and on location—the very places, when possible, where the story took place. Director Norman Lloyd took his crew (including a young production assistant named Stanley Kubrick) to Kentucky, Indiana, and Illinois. The result is a remarkable, evocative song of Lincoln's youth, not bound by history but infused with a sense of authenticity. Long, slow passages celebrate the day-to-day duties, rituals, and pleasures of a poor family on the frontier—there is more insight here on what kind of people the Lincolns were, and what their lives must have been like, than in any other Lincoln film ever made.

More important, Agee's script is filled with an understanding of Lincoln's melancholy—perhaps because it is one trait that Agee shared with Abe. This Abe doesn't merely grieve over the death of Ann Rutledge, he holds himself personally accountable for it. On the night she dies, Abe asks his friends Mr. and Mrs. Jack Armstrong, "How many people have you killed?" They say they have never killed anyone. Abe replies, "I have. Three. [His sister] Sarah, my mother and Ann—the three people I loved most in the world, they died."

He continues, "I got an idea how I killed Ann. I didn't really want to marry her. I was scared. Even after we was engaged, something kept telling me, we won't ever come to it." Once, he tells the Armstrongs, he dreamed that she died, "and at first I didn't feel sorrow, I felt free."

Abe Lincoln (Royal Dano) talks about philosophy, poetry, and liquor with his friend Jack Kelso in the fourth installment of James Agee's *Omnibus* series *Mr. Lincoln: New Sale* (1953). Kelso was portrayed by Agee himself, who wrote some tender—self-mocking—dialogue for the character defending the excessive use of alcohol.
Courtesy of the Wesleyan Cinema Archive

Abe's reaction to Ann's death also reveals to him—to his great dismay—his own dogged, nearly ruthless, sense of his own destiny. His friend Bowling Green suggests that Abe never married Ann because he knew that she didn't have the stamina to stick with him in the life he saw for himself. "Cold ambition," Bowling Green calls it. "Well, now you've lost Ann, so you'd better use that ambition. It's all you have."

Agee's personal involvement in the story even included writing a part for himself. He appears in the fourth episode as Jack Kelso, a New Salem man with a love of Shakespeare and a passion for liquor. Kelso is puzzled by Abe's attendance at temperance meetings, and Abe replies, "I sort of like knowing people that take a thing so much to heart." But at the next temperance gathering, Abe makes it a point to defend those who drink, a point of view that, predictably,

Abe and Mary Lincoln (Royal Dano and Joanna Roos) are having
an enjoyable evening in the theater—for the moment—in the
Omnibus production of *Mr. Lincoln: The End and
the Beginning* (1952).
Courtesy of the Wesleyan Cinema Archive

angers most present, but endears Abe to Ann's father, Mr. Rutledge,
who says Abe spoke "like a true Christian."

Although *Mr. Lincoln* concentrates on events in Lincoln's childhood and youth, ending as he leaves New Salem for Springfield, the
first episode—appropriately titled "The Beginning and the End"—
starts with Lincoln's last days. We first see him only from behind,
having a photographic portrait taken by Alexander Gardner (Richard
Purdy). Gardner notes that it's the first time he has ever seen Lincoln smile for a picture and attributes his mood to the fact that the
war is finally over.

But Lincoln is not entirely carefree. "Something's awfully heavy
on your mind," Mary (Joanna Roos) says to him. He tells her about
the disturbing dream he had the night before, the one ending with
the question, "Who is dead in the White House?" He makes light of

The deathbed vigil from James Agee's *Omnibus* production *Mr. Lincoln: The End and the Beginning* (1952). Royal Dano plays the dying President.
Courtesy of the Wesleyan Cinema Archive

it, but the dream frightens Mary. "That is horrid! I wish you hadn't told it."

That night, at Ford's Theater, the audience is laughing uproariously. We can barely hear any dialogue from the stage—until the laugh line "you sockdologizing old mantrap." The pistol is aimed at Lincoln's head and fired. We don't see Booth, only his legs entering the box, then running away. Then we cut to the floor—Abe's glasses hit the floor first, then the playbill that he has been reading.

The vigil at Lincoln's deathbed is shown in a long, quiet scene with virtually no dialogue; only Lincoln's labored breathing, rising and falling. The sun rises, the cock crows. As the bells toll seven, the breathing changes. He is pronounced dead at 7:22, and the men kneel in prayer. Mary rushes in and kneels beside her husband. "Oh my God! And I am given my husband to die! Why didn't they kill me instead?" They place coins on his eyes and pull a sheet over his face. Stanton utters, "Now he belongs to the ages."

Two soldiers bring in a wooden casket and place Lincoln's sheet-covered body in it. Everything is slow and deliberate, a compelling cross between documentary realism and the eerie slow motion of a dream. A Union officer methodically gathers Lincoln's clothes and boots. The last man to leave the room is Dr. Charles Leale, who, through narration, mentions his bloodstained cuffs. "I knew I would keep them forever."

The next passage is also without dialogue; Lincoln's funeral train travels across the countryside as narrator Martin Gabel reads from Walt Whitman's poem "When Lilacs Last in the Dooryard Bloom'd":

> Over the breast of spring, the land, amid cities,
> Amid lanes and through old woods, where lately the violets peep'd from
>   the ground, spotting the grey debris,
> Amid the grass in the fields each side of the lanes, passing the endless
>   grass,
> Passing the yellow-spear'd wheat, every grain from its shroud in the dark
>   brown fields uprisen,
> Passing the apple-tree blows of white and pink in the orchards.
> Carrying a corpse to where it shall rest in the grave, Night and day
>   journeys a coffin.

There is no music, only Whitman's words and the puff and rattle of the old train clacking along tracks of wood and steel. Every once in a while, someone will step to the side of the track and wave respectfully as the train passes. People enter the railroad car to file past the coffin as Gabel continues reading from Whitman:

> Coffin that passes through lanes and streets,
> Through day and night with the great cloud darkening the land,

With the pomp of the inloop'd flags with the cities draped in black,
With the show of the States themselves as the crape-veil'd women
  standing,
With processions long and winding and the flambeaus of the night,
With the countless torches lit, with the silent sea of faces and the
  unbared heads,
With the waiting depot, the arriving coffin, and the sombre faces,
With dirges through the night, with the thousand voices rising strong
  and solemn,
With all the mournful voices of the dirges pour'd around the coffin,
The dim-lit churches and the shuddering organs—where amid these you
  journey,
With the tolling tolling bells perpetual clang,
Here, coffin that slowly passes, I give you my sprig of lilac.

As the train travels from Washington, D.C., back to Springfield, so does the scene travel from the present to the past, February 12, 1809, in a small cabin in Kentucky as Lincoln's mother, Nancy Hanks (Marian Seldes), is giving birth to him. The midwife (Doris Rich) is chanting harshly, "Bear down, bear down. . . . " Because Nancy is having trouble with the birth, husband Tom Lincoln (Crahan Denton[11]) relies on an old folk remedy: he rams the bed with a plow to help jar the baby out. It works. Nancy screams in pain and little Abraham Lincoln is born as the episode ends.

According to Agee biographer Bergreen, the network was troubled by a passage in the script that called for the camera to "lunge toward the bed, then drop, 'as a primitive ploughshare, grating on the floor, is thrust violently beneath the foot of the bed.' This graphic display of mountain folkways caused concern at CBS, where an executive overseeing the program, Hubbell Robinson, demanded it be excised. It was."[12] In fact, it wasn't. The scene—still rather painful to watch—remains in existing prints of "The Beginning and the End."

"It was a piece of pure film poetry," wrote one critic. "Long

Nancy and Tom Hanks
(Marian Seldes and
Crahan Denton) endure
the hardships of pioneer
life in the second
episode of James Agee's
Omnibus series *Mr.
Lincoln: Nancy Hanks*
(1952).
*Courtesy of the Wesleyan
Cinema Archive*

stretches were without dialog or narration . . . but the visual images were more potent than any spoken word. The scene in which the martyred President's body was removed from the house opposite the Booth [sic] Theater in D. C. had striking impact the understated detailing of the event silently but powerfully creating the reverence of a dramatic moment."[13]

The paucity of dialogue continued in the second episode, which begins in a kind of loving tribute to the pleasures and toils of Abe's childhood. The film luxuriates in the day-to-day workings of the Lincoln farm, in long pastoral scenes not only of work but of quiet moments—the family sitting outside gazing at the sunset, Abe sitting beside his mother as she sings.

But their lives, and the tone of the show, change when restless Tom moves them from Kentucky to a rude, three-sided shack, and then to a fine new log cabin. There has been no dialogue in the episode so far, until Tom says of his new cabin, "It ain't much and it ain't that good."

Nancy, herself uneducated, is determined to send Abe and his sister Sarah to school against Tom's wishes. He's furious and "aims to skin them alive" when they get home. But Nancy is getting ill and Tom is immediately contrite. Agee doesn't linger over Nancy Hanks's death; she merely dies, leaving Abe and Sarah to sit forlornly under a tree while Sarah sings her mother's song.

Tom, having matter-of-factly lost one wife, just as sentimentally goes after another. He remembers a woman back in Kentucky who once indicated that she wouldn't mind marrying him, so he goes there, reintroduces himself, and proposes on the spot. Sarah Bush Johnston is a widow with three children. Abe is reluctant to accept her as his new mother, but when Sally supports his plan to have a circuit preacher come around to preach a funeral over Nancy's grave, he begins to feel some affection for her.

Midway through the series, in the third episode, "Growing Up," Agee took a break from chronology to mediate on various aspects of young Abe's developing character. At the Blab School, the teacher tries to teach him etiquette, but the other kids laugh at Abe and mock his shyness. Shy or not, he's remarkably confident in his opinions and challenges his teacher to a debate. The teacher refuses, but does encourage Abe's love of learning, even though, he says Sarah learns for the love of learning but Abe learns to help put it over on people.

Abe's strength—and his unwillingness to settle things with violence—is exhibited when a bully keeps ragging him and, in order to make him stop, Abe picks up an outhouse—with a boy inside. The other students are impressed, and pretty Mary Lamar allows him to carry her book home from school.

His increasing affection for stepmother Sarah is shown by his good-natured teasing. After she scolds him for tracking mud across the floor—and also tells him to keep his head clean, so he won't mess up the rafters—he and his stepbrother put muddy footprints on the ceiling.

The third episode becomes dreamlike with characters, dead and alive, coming forth to recall significant moments in Abe's life. Sarah dies in childbirth, leaving Abe to say mournfully, "Seems like I'm just naturally haunted by dyin'. Everyone I love best in the world, they die for sure."

And in the most touching sequence, Abe and Tom—now both dead and recalling their lives—talk about their slightly dysfunctional relationship. Abe assures Tom that he always loved and respected him, though Tom is convinced that his son never liked him much.

In ways like these, Agee could mix hard facts, speculation, folklore, and poetry to convey the Lincoln of Agee's own imagination. There is not much historical basis to the belief that Ann Rutledge was really the love of Lincoln's life, and Agee was well aware that this fourth episode smacked more of legend than of history. But to him, the legend was just as crucial as fact in our understanding of a powerful, nearly mythical figure such as Lincoln. He made their doomed romance the centerpiece of his drama, and the sadness and disappointment the episode inspired in Lincoln would reverberate throughout his life. Certainly, *something* is at the heart of Lincoln's incurable melancholy, and the tragedy of a lost love struck Agee—as it has struck many Lincoln scholars—as the perfect, inescapable source of that sadness.

Ann Rutledge is played by a very young Joanne Woodward, whose beauty is given dimension by the native wisdom in her eyes and her unadorned view of life. Abe is, of course, struck by her immediately, even though he can barely force himself to look her in the eye at first. As storekeeper, Abe sells two spools of thread to Ann and puts them on the counter rather than risk touching her hand. But she makes a point of putting the money directly in his palm, her fingers lingering there.

He falls in love with Ann, and down by the mill pond, he nearly declares that love. But she stops him and says that she has promised to marry John McNeil. Nevertheless, she wants Abe for a friend.

But she almost immediately writes to McNeil, breaking the engagement—news that, Abe says, "sorta knocks the wind outa me." This is virtually the only depiction of their romance—which has shown up in dozens of films and television productions—that actually includes a kiss. She wants to marry, but he thinks that would be the wrong thing for his destiny. She agrees to wait until his debts are paid off. "We have a world of time ahead of us," he says. "The rest of our lives."

Of course they don't have the rest of their lives; they have hardly any life together left at all. With Ann's death, Abe is compelled to leave New Salem for the greener pastures of Springfield. But her death also frees him to funnel his ambition toward the greatness he knows is within him. The final image of this extraordinary series is of Abe and Ann, yet of Abe alone. Leaving New Salem, he rides his horse slowly past Ann's grave, but doesn't give it even a glance.

Mr. Lincoln was received rapturously by critics and audiences. There was even talk for awhile of condensing the episodes—which would run about two and a half hours if played in one sitting—and converting them into a feature film. "According to Richard de Rochemont, who produced the series and was instrumental in cutting it to its present length," claimed a *New York Times* article, "[composer] 'Virgil Thomson saw the film and liked it and says he would consider doing a score for it.' Although one independent distributor already has evinced interest in the picture, de Rochemont is not certain just what attitude exhibitors will take toward 'something which has already been seen on TV. Of course,' he added, 'it did not have a normal TV distribution since it was not shown every week but on Nov. 16, Nov. 30, Dec. 14, Jan. 11 and Feb. 5, so exhibitors can't really compare it to the usual TV series.'"[14] As promising as the idea was, and as tantalizing as a new Virgil Thomson score sounds, the plan was finally abandoned. That's a pity, since a feature version might have gained a longer life for this beautiful work. Today, if it is known at all, *Mr. Lincoln* is probably considered nothing more than an early, probably dull and primitive, television production. In fact, it is among the finest—perhaps it is *the* finest—film about Abraham Lincoln ever made.

NOTES

1. *Variety*, April 18, 1945.

2. *Variety*, December 12, 1955.

3. *Variety*, December 9, 1953.

4. *Variety*, February 17, 1954.

5. Ibid.

6. Ibid.

7. *Variety,* February 8, 1956.

8. Ibid.

9. Laurence Bergreen, *James Agee: A Life* (E. P. Dutton, 1984), p. 369.

10. Victor A. Kramer, *James Agee* (Twayne Publishers, 1975), p. 124.

11. Crahan Denton, who played Tom Lincoln, played Abe Lincoln himself on two television productions: *The Election of Abraham Lincoln* (1952) and *Lincoln's Little Correspondent* (1953).

12. Laurence Bergreen, *James Agee: A Life* (E. P. Dutton, 1984), p. 371.

13. *Variety*, November 19, 1952.

14. *New York Times*, April 26, 1953.

Chapter Three
The Perfect Tribute
Latter-Day Television Lincolns

JAMES AGEE'S *Mr. Lincoln* may have been the definitive poetic treatment of Lincoln's early years, but actors have continued to find a way to put their own imprint on the role—or, perhaps, to have Lincoln make his imprint on them. Since the early seventies, there have been at least two full-scale Lincoln biographies produced for television, both from well-respected literary sources: *Sandburg's Lincoln*, starring Hal Holbrook, was a six-part series that played out over a period of two years; and *Gore Vidal's Lincoln*, starring Sam Waterston, covered somewhat less of Lincoln's life, but got the job done in a mere two evenings.

The eighties also brought two epic miniseries about the Civil War: *The Blue and the Gray* (1982) and *North and South*, which was actually three miniseries in a row, the first airing in 1985; Book II airing in 1986; and the final installment, *Heaven and Hell: North and South Book III*, in 1994. Each of these long, long works had a Lincoln of note—Gregory Peck in *The Blue and the Gray* and Hal Holbrook in the first two installments of *North and South*.

Since the sixties, many of America's heroes and icons have been reevaluated, often in quite a harsh light. General George Armstrong Custer, once considered a heroic martyr through his death at the Little Big Horn in 1876, is now just as widely considered an evil, even maniacal practitioner of genocide. Davy Crockett, worshipped by kids in the fifties as the King of the Wild Frontier and nearly deified as one of the heroes of the Alamo, is now believed by many to have surrendered at that fight, a controversy that has drawn battle lines among historians.

But for some reason, Abraham Lincoln—at least as an image of popular culture—has never undergone that kind of revisionism. The Lincolns of Holbrook and Waterston are more complex and conflicted than, for instance, Frank McGlynn's in *Lincoln in the White House* (1939) but, in terms of the broad outlines of character and event, not much has changed. In early 1999, a newly discovered diary created rumors about Lincoln's sexual preferences, a giddy story that immediately made it into the monologues of late-night talk show hosts, but which is unlikely to have real impact on Lincoln's image or reputation. Though it's difficult to imagine someone actually dramatizing the rumor in a film, it is, sadly, not impossible.

But in the Lincoln television portraits of the seventies, eighties, and nineties, Abe is as honest and admirable and forthright as in the simplest one-reeler from 1908. His image seems as unchanging, as unchangeable, on film as it is on the penny.

THE GREAT MAN'S WHISKERS/THE GRATE MANS WISKURS

One of the lighter moments in the Lincoln story came in October 1860, when he received a letter from Grace Bedell, a little girl from Westfield, New York. Grace had seen Lincoln's campaign posters and decided that his face, though striking, lacked one crucial element:

Hon A B Lincoln . . .

Dear Sir

My father has just come from the fair and brought home your picture and Mr. Hamlin's. I am a little girl only 11 years old, but want you should be President of the United States very much so I hope you wont think me very bold to write to such a great man as you are. Have you any little girls about as large as I am if so give them my love and tell her to write to me if you cannot answer this letter. I have got 4 brothers and part of them will vote for you any way and if you let your whiskers grow I will try and get the rest of them to vote for you you would look a great deal better for your face is so thin. All the ladies like whiskers and they would tease their husbands to vote for you and then you would be President. My father is going to vote for you and if I was a man I would vote for you to but I will try to get every one to vote for you that I can I think that rail fence around your picture makes it look very pretty I have got a little baby sister she is nine weeks old and is just as cunning as can be. When you direct your letter direct to Grace Bedell Westfield Chatauque County New York I must not write any more answer this letter right off.

Good bye

Grace Bedell

On October 19, Lincoln replied to her letter:

Miss Grace Bedell

My dear little Miss Your very agreeable letter of the 15th is received—I regret the necessity of saying I have no daughters—I have three sons—one seventeen, one nine, and one seven years of age—They, with their mother, constitute my whole family—As to the whiskers, having never worn any, do you not think people would call it a piece of silly affection if I were to begin it now? Your very sincere well wisher

A. Lincoln

James Cooper (Dean Jones) and Catherine Winfield (Beth Brickell) anticipate a visit from President-elect Lincoln (Dennis Weaver) in *The Grate Mans Wiskurs* (1971). This comedy was based on the true story of Grace Biddell, the little girl who wrote to Lincoln suggesting that he would look better with a beard. *Courtesy of Universal Television*

Of course, as it turned out, Lincoln took Grace's advice. When he was traveling through Westfield on his way to Washington for the inauguration, he called out to the crowd to see if his "little correspondent" was there. Grace came to the platform, where Lincoln kissed her and thanked her for the idea.

This charming little story inevitably appealed to dramatists and authors who wanted to further humanize Lincoln. On a 1955 episode of *The Hallmark Hall of Fame*, Grace's story was dramatized as *Lincoln's Little Correspondent*. As the story opens, Grace Bedell is arguing with her classmates about presidential candidate Lincoln. The other children insist that he's too ugly for the job—"A scarecrow president?"—but Grace tells her teacher, "I think he's beautiful."

Back at the Bedell home, Grace's family argues constantly about Lincoln and the issue of slavery. When her father quotes, "A house divided against itself cannot stand," Grace asks, "Father, does he mean our house, too?" The next day she writes her famous letter. She asks her servant to mail it. "It's the most important letter of my life. It might change the whole world."

For the next few days, Grace haunts the post office, hoping for her reply from Lincoln. She's even kept after school for being late, so even when the letter does arrive, she can't pick it up until the next day. When she reads it, she's upset. Lincoln replies that he isn't inclined to grow whiskers.

Nevertheless, Grace is excited to learn that her entire family plans to go see President-elect Lincoln's train when it comes through town. When it does, Lincoln (Crahan Denton) comes out to address the crowd and introduce the public to his new whiskers. He asks to meet Grace, and she is passed up to the platform, where he kisses her on the forehead. As the show ends, Grace is beaming with pride.

In a captivating epilogue, hostess Sarah Churchill introduces us to a little girl who, we are informed, is Grace Bedell's great granddaughter.

Playwright Adrian Scott had turned the story into something rather more fanciful a few years earlier in the play *The Great Man's Whiskers* (1947). In this comic two-act play James Cooper—described as about forty, "a pompous, would-be politician" who is "sturdy, righteous"—and his "nondescript" wife, Martha, have their hands full with their spirited daughter, Pippa, "even-tempered, violent-tempered, lovable, spiteful, and charming." Pippa, who is "six, almost seven," has a vivid imagination, a gift she shares with her invisible, extremely mischievous friend Jacalina.

Cooper, anxious to be named the town's postmaster, is attempting to make a little political hay by delivering a welcoming speech when president-elect Lincoln's train comes through town. Pippa has other ideas about the President. She has bought him a brush with which to keep his beard neat—the beard that she is certain he has grown since she wrote to him suggesting it.

When Cooper learns of this letter, he fears that he will be embarrassed in front of Lincoln and orders Pippa to stay home with the maid, Ella. Pippa is completely crushed.

Lincoln's train, however, breaks down just outside of town. As the large delegation cools its heels at the train station, waiting for him, Lincoln walks into town, asking for directions to Pippa's house. Once there—Pippa isn't particularly surprised to see him— they enjoy cocoa and cookies and Lincoln reads over Cooper's speech, suggesting that there are good things in it, but far too many com-promised ideas.

When Cooper returns home, he won't believe that Lincoln was there, thinking that, like Jacalina, the president has simply been conjured from Pippa's fertile imagination. But when the truth is confirmed, he apologizes to his daughter. Because the town fathers have learned of Cooper's "relationship" with Lincoln, he is now a shoo-in for the job of postmaster.

In 1971 this whimsical little tale was made longer, and slightly less whimsical, as a television movie called, for reasons best known to the producers, *The Grate Mans Wiskurs*. Here James Cooper (Dean Jones) is a widowed music teacher who has no particular political ambitions but would like the postmaster job to better sup-port his daughter Elizabeth (not Pippa; her invisible friend's name has been changed, too, to Mary Ann Hazelmeyer) and marry his girl friend (Beth Brickell). When it becomes known that Lincoln is stop-ping in their town specifically to come to the Coopers' home, every-one assumes he's a friend of James's, even though Abe really just wants to see his "little correspondent."

Without warning, James finds himself launched suddenly on a political career, but in the meantime, he loses his job as a school-teacher and finds himself increasingly estranged from his daughter, fiancée, and housekeeper Ella (Isabel Sanford). Politico John McGiver keeps urging him to compromise all of his views and make sure that he never says anything to offend anyone.

In the play, we never see Lincoln at all, but he actually shows up in the film in the person of Dennis Weaver. Actually, Lincoln is revealed rather gradually. We see Lincoln sitting for a portrait at the beginning of the film, but only from the back. Then, before his train arrives, we see a blurred Lincoln superimposed over the crowd heading for the station.

Only when he actually walks across town to the Coopers' house do we see the face full on. When Elizabeth announces him to Ella and asks Ella to make cocoa for them, the housekeeper assumes that Lincoln is just another one of Elizabeth's imaginary friends. Lincoln sits down in the parlor and immediately asks if it's all right if he takes off his shoes. "I let Mrs. Lincoln pick them out for me but she underestimated me a little." Ella brings in imaginary cocoa, and when she sees Lincoln, she nearly collapses. Lincoln "catches" the cups and has an imaginary drink with them—even giving a cup to the invisible Mary Ann Hazelmeyer. Finally, he leaves, almost forgetting his shoes.

The film ends essentially the way the play does, but with the added pomp of a triumphant parade to Cooper's door to celebrate his new position as postmaster.

Dennis Weaver makes a fine Lincoln in *The Grate Mans Wiskurs*. His distinctive twang of a voice—for years a favorite of impressionists due to his stint as "Mr. Dillon's" sidekick Chester in the TV western *Gunsmoke*—is believable, and he carries himself like someone who is used to wearing boots that are too tight and entering rooms where the doorways are too short. We know, too, that Lincoln was very fond of children, and his interaction with Elizabeth has the essential elements of gravity and silliness. He isn't thrown for a second when he is served imaginary cocoa. Instead, he takes to the game right away. More important, he talks to Elizabeth with respect for her ideas, without condescension—of which she gets plenty from the other adults in her life. Weaver's is not the sad Lincoln of war and loss and death, but the homespun friend of the people, always ready to make room in his busy day for a little yarn spinning—and some imaginary cocoa.

Left, Dennis Weaver as he appeard in his hit television show of the sixties and seventies *McCloud* and, right, in makeup as Abraham Lincoln in the made-for-television comedy *The Grate Mans Wiskurs* (1971).
Courtesy of Universal Television

Mr. Lincoln (Dennis Weaver) comes to call upon the little girl (Cindy Eilbacher, center) who wrote to him asking him to grow whiskers in *The Grate Mans Wiskurs* (1971). Also greeting the President are Ella, the housekeeper (Isabel Sanford), and her daughter Pearl (Nicole Meggerson).
Courtesy of Universal Television

Jason Robards in a "Hallmark Hall of Fame" production of
Robert E. Sherwood's *Abe Lincoln in Illinois*, which first aired on
February 5, 1964. Robards played Lincoln two other times: in a
1955 television production called *Flame and Ice* and in a 1991
television movie, *The Perfect Tribute*.
Courtesy of NBC Television Network

SANDBURG'S LINCOLN

Producer David L. Wolper conceived a multipart biography of
Lincoln to air as part of America's Bicentennial Celebration in 1976.
Lincoln was obviously a character for whom Wolper felt some spe-
cial affinity; he had already produced at least two television docu-
dramas on the subject: *They've Killed President Lincoln!* (1971) and
Lincoln: Trial by Fire (1974), both starring John Anderson as Lin-
coln. Wolper also later produced *North and South*—Books I, II, *and*
III.

The director of *Sandburg's Lincoln* was veteran George Schaefer.
Schaefer was a prolific and respected director of drama and had to
his credit scores of plays, television movies, and many installments
of the *Hallmark Hall of Fame* as well as a few highly regarded fea-

The Lincoln-Douglas Debates formed the basis for the drama *The Rivalry*, which aired as a "Hallmark Hall of Fame" production on December 12, 1975. Charles Durning, left, played Stephen A. Douglas and Arthur Hill portrayed Lincoln. The play had been introduced a few years earlier with Raymond Massey as Lincoln.
Courtesy of NBC Television Network

ture films such as *An Enemy of the People* (1977), starring Steve McQueen.

Like Wolper, Schaefer returned to the subject of Abraham Lincoln more than once. In 1964 he directed the *Hallmark Hall of Fame* production of Sherwood's *Abe Lincoln in Illinois*, starring Jason Robards Jr. In 1975, in the midst of the *Sandburg's Lincoln* series, he directed Julie Harris in *The Last of Mrs. Lincoln* by James Prideaux (who also wrote the first installment of *Sandburg's Lincoln*) for PBS. Schaefer had also directed Harris in the stage version of Prideaux's play.

According to Schaefer, Wolper put him in complete charge of the operation. "[Wolper] invited me to produce, pick writers, set up the whole operation, and direct. It would take a year, maybe a year and a half, and I liked everything about it."[1]

Schaefer chose Hal Holbrook to play Lincoln in a role that would take Abe from his days as a young lawyer in Springfield all the way to Ford's Theater. Holbrook, too, came to the project with some Lincoln experience under his belt. In 1963 he had played the title role in *Abe Lincoln in Illinois* in a Broadway revival. Of that performance, the *New York Times's* Howard Taubman wrote: "Thanks to the art of makeup, Mr. Holbrook's face bears a striking resemblance to Lincoln's. His voice is pitched higher and its accents call to mind a rustic seated with his cronies around a cracker barrel. In his plug hat, black suit and soiled boots, this Lincoln might be a figure in an old tintype come to life. The outward similarity has its value, but the inner glow makes one believe in Mr. Holbrook's Lincoln."[2]

Much the same can be said for his performance in this series. Whereas some actors are content to add just enough makeup to suggest a resemblance to Lincoln—Henry Fonda and Sam Waterston, for example—Holbrook elected to completely transform himself, a decision that turned out to be a little controversial. On the airing of the fourth installment, "The Unwilling Warrior," columnist Cecil Smith wrote, "Holbrook's elaborate makeup to transform his round face into the long, mournful countenance of the pennies and the stamps turned some viewers off in the early plays of the Sandburg series. I doubt the makeup will bother you tonight because 'The Unwilling Warrior' is a much better play than those that preceded it, the best I've seen in the series."[3]

Because Schaefer and Wolper decided to spread the six parts out over a two-year period, the episodes don't run in strictly chronological order; each was designed to stand alone as an hour-long special. The series began with "Mrs. Lincoln's Husband," which covered the controversy over Mary Todd Lincoln's sister—a Southern widow—visiting the White House, Mary's extravagance with money, Lincoln's battles with his Cabinet, and the death of their son Willie.

The hour doesn't contain a plot, exactly, just a series of events that serve to illustrate and illuminate the Lincolns' marriage. For instance, faced with a mountain of bills, Abe confronts Mary. Her

Hal Holbrook in "Mrs. Lincoln's Husband," the first of six specials on *Sandburg's Lincoln* that aired on NBC (1974). *Courtesy of NBC Television Network*

Hal Holbrook, as Lincoln, pauses on the White House steps to announce that the first officer to die in the Civil War was his own military aide and family friend in "The Unwilling Warrior." *Courtesy of NBC Television Network*

Before leaving for Washington, Lincoln (Holbrook) and the
beloved woman who raised him, stepmother Sarah Bush Lincoln
(Beulah Bondi), drive out for a final visit to his father's grave in
"Crossing Fox River."
Courtesy of NBC Television Network

Holbrook with John
Levin, as Lincoln's
youngest son, in the
final episode of
Sandburg's Lincoln,
"The Last Days."
*Courtesy of NBC
Television Network*

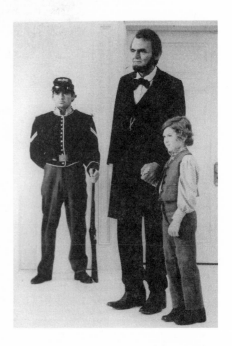

response: "You don't love me. I've been living with a man all these years who doesn't love me." He immediately sets out to make her feel better and brings her a bunch of posies in apology. They embrace. Later Lincoln rhapsodizes to his secretary John Nicolay about how Mary impressed him when they first met and how much in love with her he remains. When a committee has appointed itself to look into her financial dealings, Lincoln walks in, unexpectedly and uninvited, and offers to give testimony. He defuses the situation, and the subcommittee disbands. Then he goes home to a small party that Mrs. Lincoln is giving, ever the loving, supportive husband.

But perhaps the most telling moment about their relationship comes near the end of the segment. Mary and John Nicolay are rushing toward an army camp in a carriage, fearing that they'll be late for a ceremony over which Abe is presiding. When they are in fact late, Mary is furious to see that a general's wife has been riding in the procession with Abe. Mary confronts the startled woman and says that she's no better than a lady in the street. As Abe tries to calm her down, Mary gets ever more hysterical, threatening to pack and leave if her husband prefers younger women.

Abe takes her into a tent to calm her down. Angry at first, he says that he will not allow her to humiliate him in public. She sags, in humiliation and sorrow. "I want Willie here. I look for kindness and all I seem to find is hate everywhere I turn." This Mary is not insane, nor a harpy; just a woman battered by self-doubts and the suspicions of others. Abe comforts and compliments her; they are by far the most affectionate Lincolns in film.

The next segment, "Sad Figure Laughing," concerns Lincoln's famous wit and his propensity to explain a point with a funny, seemingly irrelevant story—and how much his opponents hated that sense of humor, using it to paint him as a buffoon ("He is an embarrassment sometimes, isn't he?" says one Cabinet member). The episode after that, "Prairie Lawyer," harks back to his days in

Springfield, where Abe squares off against Stephen A. Douglas in a murder case and tries to sort out his love life.

Dramatic productions about Lincoln deal only with two women when it comes to his love life: Ann Rutledge and Mary Todd. But there was a woman in the middle, also named Mary, to whom Lincoln was briefly engaged. Of the hundreds of movies and television programs about Lincoln, "Prairie Lawyer" is the only one in which that relationship forms the focal point of the plot.

Abe is kind of engaged to Mary Owens but isn't altogether pleased at the prospect. When he visits her, she makes a place for him on the couch, but he sits in a chair across the room. He masks his shyness and discomfort with jokes and a few quotes from *Richard II* and finally takes his place beside her on the couch, holding her hand. He asks her to play and sing and suggests that "Frog Went Courtin'" would be most appropriate.

Mary Owen is intelligent and pleasant, and Abe can't quite figure out why he feels so reluctant about marrying her. She saves him from having to act on the matter by breaking off their engagement herself. When she does, he tells her how much he loves her. "Like a true lawyer," Mary says, "even though you've lost your case you continue to plead, even though you know in your heart you're relieved."

After Abe wins his trial—something else he's ambivalent about, sensing that his client is actually guilty—he is invited to a party to welcome a visitor to town: Mary Todd. As the episode ends, he is telling Mary, "I would like to dance with you—in the worst way." And he does.

In "The Unwilling Warrior," time shifts forward again. Lincoln has just been elected, and a group of conspirators are trying to decide whether to murder or kidnap him as he passes through Baltimore. "Kill the ape," says one. Another agrees: "That gorilla must not take the oath of office."

Meanwhile, in Springfield, Abe is milking the cow for the last time. His son Tad asks, "Pa, does a cow have a north and a south?"

"Guess that depends which way she's pointed," Abe says. "Doesn't make much difference unless you cut her in two. Then there's no milk and no moo."

Allan Pinkerton joins the train at Harrisburg. He has a thick Scot accent. He tells Lincoln that there is an assassination plot in Baltimore. "If I ran from every threat they'd call me a rabbit instead of a baboon," Lincoln replies.

At first Lincoln discounts Pinkerton's warning but then remembers "my shadow's a little longer than it was" and decides to cooperate. He changes hats and changes trains, posing as the invalid brother to a female agent.

In Baltimore people rush the train and tear off the banners. A man bearing a knife gets into Lincoln's compartment but finds it empty. Lincoln arrives in Washington at night, welcomed by only one man. He hates the secrecy surrounding his arrival.

Time shifts again. The war is now well underway. Desperate for a general who can win the conflict, Abe decides to appoint McClellan the head of the army, despite protests that he's a popinjay and snob. "Lop an inch off McClellan and you'll have an American Napoleon." Lincoln visits McClellan at the front to assail him for his reluctance to do anything. "You said you could enter Richmond in ten days and that was ten months ago."

He fires McClellan and puts Grant in charge. Soon enough, Richmond falls. Lincoln comes over by longboat to tour the ruins with Tad. He makes it a point to arrive in broad daylight, still smarting from his secret entrance to Washington four years earlier. He sits in what was, until a few days earlier, Jefferson Davis's chair. "Old Jeff," he says. "We served in Congress together. Do you realize how close he came to sitting in my chair?" He holds Tad on his lap and says softly, "It's over."

In episode five, "Crossing Fox River," we are back in Springfield on the day that Lincoln learns he is the presidential nominee of the Republican Party. When he wins the election, he sets about saying farewell to his home of so many years. He rides out to visit his stepmother, Sarah Bush (Beulah Bondi). "Nancy birthed me, made me alive," Abe tells her. "But you made me human." They visit the grave of Abe's father, Tom Lincoln. Sarah asks, "Did you weep when he died?"

"I must have."

Bidding farewell to his friend and law partner, William Herndon, Abe says, "Being elected President makes no difference to the firm of Lincoln and Herndon. If I live I'll be back. Just keep on practicing until I come back."

Herndon says jovially, "We'll sit and visit in the White House."

But Abe isn't feeling jovial. "I shudder at what's ahead," he says.

As well he should. The final episode, broadcast on the 111th anniversary of Lincoln's assassination, finds a jubilant country at war's end. At the White House, Mary is concerned that Robert still might be involved in fighting. Southern General Johnson hasn't yet surrendered and Jefferson Davis is still at large. A mob comes to the White House. Abe tries to talk to them, but they're too happy and loud. Mary says they think of him as a kind of Moses. "This country's going to have to be reconstructed a great deal before it's any kind of promised land."

Mary asks him not to go outside, but he wants to talk to the people. He reassures her, "There'll be guards around somewhere. Anyway I expect after the good news today everybody in Washington is the president's friend—for this week, anyway." He steps out onto the front portico. "General Grant will be in the city presently and I suggest that you save your cheers for him." A drunken man brandishes a Bowie knife and says that Lincoln should use it on Davis. Tad unfurls a rebel flag from a window. Before the crowd can turn ugly at the sight of it, Lincoln says, "That flag and everything in it belongs to the United States. It's the first one taken down in the war. Taking it down, [Lincoln's friend] Col. Ellsworth was killed." He calls for the band to play Dixie. They do and the crowd starts singing along.

Lincoln is eager to get to the work of healing the country. He says that now he has the leisure to work out a complete plan for

A dramatic scene from "The Last Days."
Courtesy of NBC Television Network

reconstruction, since Congress is in recess until December. "For once, I have time. I have time. Die when I must I want it said of me by those who knew me best that I always plucked a thistle and planted a flower when I thought a flower would grow."

That night he dreams the ominous dream. Hearing a wailing outside, he gets out of bed, wraps a shawl around his shoulders, and walks down the hall and down the stairs. "Who is dead in the White House?" he calls. "The President," answers a shadowy figure. "He was killed by an assassin."

On the last afternoon, Abe and Mary go for their carriage ride. She says he looks fevered, and she hasn't seen him look that way since Willie died. "That's odd because I'm supremely happy." He says they should be more cheerful from now on. They stroll down to the riverside. He teasingly says they should go out to California and pan for gold. They plan a trip to Europe. He says that he hopes to see all the places Shakespeare wrote about but never got to see himself—Rome, Calais, Elsinore. But especially he wants to visit the Holy Land and "walk where the Savior walked. I think more than anything, I'd like to do that." Mary says, "Soon." He feels a sudden chill, and they decide to head back to the White House. Mary says, "Goodness, it is getting late. We must get ready for tonight." As the carriage heads back to Washington a title card tells us: "That Night Abraham Lincoln was Assassinated. The Prairie Years, The War Years Were Over."

Sandburg's Lincoln does not exactly serve as an in-depth biography of the president, but in its leisurely pace and nearly plotless structure, it allows for glimpses into corners of Lincoln's life that seldom crop up in movies about him. He weeps pitifully when his friend Elmer Ellsworth is killed capturing a rebel flag, and he lets his anger out at full force against the plodding pace of McClellan or the dishonest dealings of a Cabinet member.

But perhaps the freshest aspect of *Sandburg's Lincoln* is its sympathetic portrait of Mary. Without sugar-coating her occasional pettiness, her wild extravagance, or her deep-seated jealousy, she is still treated as a fully dimensional woman with good traits as well as bad, a woman married to Abe Lincoln because she truly loves him and believes in him. There is a charming scene in her bedroom before the Lincolns move on to Washington. In it, Sada Thompson beautifully reveals Mary's sincerity as well as her vanity. "I should have elegant things, shouldn't I?" she says. "You want me to. I want you to have pride in me. I want to be a help to you if you'll let me. I worry about your cabinet. I worry about my family in Kentucky. How I understand the Southern heart and fear what they'll do."

Other Lincolns hate their Marys or merely make the best of a bad situation. But there is genuine affection between these two, and that helps to make *Sandburg's Lincoln* among the most endearing of Lincoln portraits.

Hal Holbrook received an Emmy nomination for his performance, and Schaefer was nominated by the Directors Guild of America. "My only regrets about this project," Schaefer wrote, "are that David [Wolper] insisted we shoot it in 16mm instead of 35. It saved about $10,000 a show, but the prints have faded and turned brown. Moreover, the impact would have been greater had it been shown on six consecutive weeks."[4]

Even as Schaefer was directing Sada Thompson in her powerful and insightful performance as Mary Todd, he was working with another great actress to tell a different part of the First Lady's story: Julie Harris in *The Last of Mrs. Lincoln*. Producing this work on the New York stage was, Schaefer wrote, "a truly satisfying experience."[5] The play tells of the bitter final years of Mary Todd, the death of her son Tad, and her estrangement from her eldest son, Robert. She seeks peace in Europe and under assumed names but is under continued threat from poverty, the press, and her own mental problems. Julie Harris won a Tony Award for her performance, as did Leora Dana, who played her sister Elizabeth.

The television version was filmed for the PBS series *Hollywood Television Theater* and starred, in addition to Julie Harris, Robbie Benson as Tad, Patrick Duffy as Mary's nephew Lewis Baker, and Priscilla Morrill as Elizabeth Edwards. The cast included at least two actors with other Lincoln connections: Michael Cristofer, who played Mary's eldest son Robert, was also working with Schaefer at the same time, playing Lincoln's secretary, John Nicolay, in *Sandburg's Lincoln*. And Ford Rainey, cast here as Mary's brother-in-law, Ninian Edwards, portrayed Lincoln on the screen several times, including the Sunn Classics feature *Guardian of the Wilderness* (1977) and in *The Death Trap*, an episode of the science fiction series *The Time Tunnel* (1966).

THE EPIC MINISERIES

Good ideas in Hollywood seem to arrive in pairs. After years in which the Civil War remained virtually untouched as a movie or television subject, the 1980s suddenly presented television viewers with almost more Civil War than they could handle. Two major miniseries were put into production: *The Blue and the Gray* (1982) and *North and South*, the first installment of which had its debut in

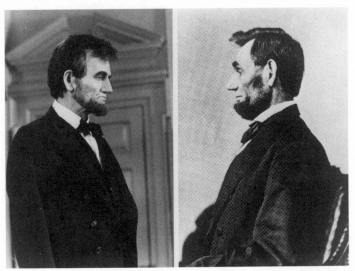

The actor faces the real thing. Hal Holbrook in makeup, created by
Dick Smith, for the epic miniseries *North and South* (1985).
Courtesy of ABC Television Network

1985. Both miniseries aimed at telling the story of the war through
the eyes of many characters on both sides of the conflict. Both were
sprawling epics with enormous casts of characters and soap opera
plots. And each had its own Abraham Lincoln.

In *North and South*, Hal Holbrook returned to the role he had
played a decade earlier. But although *North and South* was many
times longer than *Sandburg's Lincoln*, Holbrook found himself with
much less to do. His Lincoln exists on the edges of the plot; he's
there for historical purposes, not for dramatic ones.

Lincoln, in fact, doesn't show up until episode six, which opens
on the day of his inauguration. Our first look at Lincoln has him
reading a selection from his speech to Secretary of State Seward,
who says he's glad Abe left out any mention of his pledge to recap-
ture all Southern forts. Seward pleads with Lincoln to make more
concessions to the South, but Lincoln replies, "I believe it's time the
South learned to compromise, also. I intend to be president of all
the United States."

On the way to take the oath of office, Abe and Mary get into a carriage, prompting a woman (Morgan Fairchild) to say, "Don't you think he's impressive?"

Her companion replies with a sneer, "Impressive? The man is incompetent."

The man is also out of the story until . . .

NORTH AND SOUTH BOOK II

When Abe returns to *North and South*, he is battling with his Cabinet over the preferred way of bringing the South to its knees. Members of the Cabinet suggest another blockade, but Lincoln disagrees: "The Southern hotheads hooted my blockade as loudly as they questioned my ancestry. We cannot expect a blockade to bring them down." Holbrook is a more serious Abe than his previous incarnation in *Sandburg's Lincoln*. He has a way of underplaying a joke that doesn't violate his essential gravity. Even his voice is lower than before, but still flavored with that nasal, midwestern twang that reviewers of *Abe Lincoln in Illinois* mentioned.

But he has very little more to contribute to this oversized series: he mourns the loss of 25,000 dead at Antietam, and decides to appoint Grant the head of the army. "If it's God's will that we prevail, it's more than just a war we'll win. We'll secure freedom for all our people." He reads the Emancipation Proclamation to the Cabinet and gets furious when General Meade lets Lee slip from his grasp again. "The victory at Gettysburg seems so hollow now," he says gravely. "God knows, I never wanted this conflict. But I have sounded the trumpet and I can never call retreat. I must endure this fiery trial. I must go on."

But Hal Holbrook's Abe Lincoln does not go on—not in *North and South*, anyway. That's the last we see of him.

THE BLUE AND THE GRAY

Gregory Peck's Lincoln in *The Blue and the Gray* is a far more integrated one. He knows some of the characters and steps out of his historical role to interact with them. As a consequence, he seems much more like an actual participant in the story, instead of a remote icon.

The Blue and the Gray is about families torn apart by the war. One Southerner, John Geyser (John Hammond), becomes a newspaper artist as a way of removing himself from the conflict. His friend Jonas Steele (Stacey Keach) is a Secret Serviceman and friend of Lincoln's.

As Lincoln's train passes through town, Abe steps out on the platform to speak to the crowd of well-wishers. Some call out that they want to see Mary (Janice Carroll), too, so Abe brings her out to stand beside him. Referring to the disparity in their heights, Abe says. "I determined to give you the long and the short of it." The crowd is delighted; Mary is not amused.

Abe notices that John Geyser is sketching him and asks to see him after the speech. In the railroad car, John shows Lincoln the drawing; he has captured "the long and the short of it" and Lincoln laughs with delight. While John sketches out a more formal portrait, they chat about the war. Abe asks what the sentiments of the South are, and John replies that his brothers can't wait for secession. He says he won't fight for the South, however. "Nor for the North," Abe says, adding that he has sized John up as a man who wouldn't take up arms against his brothers. Abe suggests that John look to his talents to solve the dilemma of how to be a part of the upcoming historic event without taking up arms; he says that John should be a war correspondent. "You'd be making a contribution, too. You'd show the folks back home the face of war." Abe looks at John's portrait and says, "You see more than other men."

The next time we see Abe, he is with Jonas, trying out a new

Gregory Peck as Lincoln in
The Blue and the Gray.
(1982).
*Courtesy of CBS Television
Network*

John Hammond, left,
as a young
artist/correspondent for
Harpers Weekly, and
Stacey Keach as the
mysterious goverment
agent who befriends him
in *The Blue and the Gray.*
Courtesy of the author

repeating rifle which the inventor hopes to sell to the army. Learning that Jonas is about to be married, he gives the repeating rifle to him as a gift.

Later Seward urges Lincoln to sign the Emancipation Proclamation, to take advantage of the North's upper hand because of the victory at Antietam. Lincoln tells the story about the two men who are chased by a hog. One climbs a tree and the other grabs the hog by the tail and is dragged around and around the tree. Finally he calls up to his pal, "Come down and help me leave go of this hog." Lincoln laughs and acts out the story as he tells it, and the Cabinet laughs along with him—they don't seem to resent his digression, particularly when his face grows sober and he says, "That's what I need—somebody to help me leave go of this hog."

After reading an amended paragraph of the Proclamation, he sits down to sign it. "Bear me witness, Gentlemen. I hereby fulfill my promise to my country and to my maker." He signs. "It is done. Gentlemen, it is my hope that in giving freedom to the slaves we assure freedom to the free, and hasten the day when once more we shall be one nation."

Unlike poor Hal Holbrook, who never—in his multiple outings as Lincoln—got to deliver the Gettysburg Address, Gregory Peck is given the opportunity to give the famous speech and takes full advantage of it. It starts as a voiceover, as Jonas Steele rides through a battlefield littered with bodies, having just buried his wife. From this scene of carnage, we return to that platform in Gettysburg, where Lincoln infuses the words with urgency, as though desperate for people to understand what he is saying, even as he fears they do not. When he finishes, the crowd is silent as he folds the paper, picks up his hat, and starts to walk off stage. Only then do they applaud politely.

After the surrender, Grant meets with Lincoln and the Cabinet. Lincoln tells them, "Last night I had a good omen—a dream. I'm in a mysterious sort of vessel rowing across a hazy sea toward a dark, indefinite shore." He says the dream has always preceded some great event. "It must refer to Johnson's surrender; that's the only great event likely to occur."

Meanwhile Jonas has a vision himself. He sees Lincoln in that vessel, which crashes against the rocks, throwing Abe overboard. Jonas tries to save him, but he sees Lincoln lying on the beach with coins on his eyes. Jonas awakens and rides in a frenzy to warn Abe. When he arrives at Ford's Theater, Lincoln has already been shot. Both Jonas and John Geyser accompany Stanton to the house across the street.

Mary, Robert, and the others stand vigil at the bedside, where Mary cries, "Oh my God. I have given my husband to die." Lincoln lies on a blood-stained pillow. He is pronounced dead at 7:22 and 2 seconds. Stanton, Jonas, and John enter. "Now he belongs to the ages." Coins are placed on Lincoln's eyes, just as in the vision.

The Blue and the Gray ends with John Geyser's wedding, an event that reunites members of the family who were fighting only months before. As we hear Lincoln's voice—"With malice toward none, with charity for all"—the camera pans across photographs of all the film's characters who have died.

GORE VIDAL'S LINCOLN

Gregory Peck is in *The Blue and the Gray* for only a few minutes of its running time, but even in that brief span, he is allowed to hit several highlights of Lincoln's time in the White House. Curiously, Sam Waterston is not so lucky in the two-part adaptation of the best-selling biography, *Gore Vidal's Lincoln*. The Emancipation Proclamation and the Gettysburg Address are mentioned in passing, but they don't occupy a place of any importance in the film. Sam Waterston believes that their omission helped the viewer to focus on less apparent truths. "We are familiar with these big moments," Waterston says, "and what's curious and interesting is what they came out of, I think. Their context is less familiar to us than the words themselves."[6]

Mary Tyler Moore and Sam Waterston as the Lincolns in *Gore Vidal's Lincoln* (1988). Although Sam Waterston believes that the film offers a plausible account of Abe and Mary's marriage, "I think it's an imagined relationship," he says, "because nobody really knows what they were truly like together. Certainly he thought of marriage as a profoundly important thing to do. He must have meant seriously to make the most of it that he could. There are all the jokes that he told that imply she was a handful but that he had great affection for her. In her case, Mary didn't leave behind a lot of words to defend herself with, so everything else is pure speculation."
[interview with the author, June 16, 1999]
Courtesy of NBC Television Network

Neither does Gore Vidal's Abe split a rail or speak lovingly about the lost Ann Rutledge or comfort a condemned sentry. (He does, however, pardon many of them. In one batch, Lincoln receives 147 death sentences for his review. "I'll see how many of these I can squeak by with a pardon," he says. "Maybe I can convince Stanton that we need their votes in the election." He says that fleeing in the face of gunfire seems like a sensible reaction and that, faced with the situation, he might "find a nice tree to rest behind.")

In short, Vidal's and Waterston's Lincoln avoids the comfort zones and the cliches, allowing the film to hit upon aspects of his character—and that of his wife (played with brittle brilliance by Mary Tyler Moore)—that don't quite make it into more conventional biographies. This Abe is a scrapper, bracingly intelligent and sometimes brusque; there is never any doubt that he consciously puts on the backwoods character when it serves his purpose, but as one character says, "I'm sure he split a rail or two in his youth but he's been a lawyer and a politician ever since. Don't underestimate him."

Gore Vidal's Lincoln contains, by far, the most dysfunctional of Lincoln families: Mary is high-strung and bad tempered and tortured by choices she might have made. She is also vain, sneaky, and in almost constant agony from migraine headaches. Their oldest son Robert is embarrassed by his father and complains bitterly of how he was ridiculed at Harvard and Phillips Exeter Academy at his father's expense. Willie and Tad are tireless hell-raisers.

Lincoln is also a fatalist, keenly aware of his upcoming death, an event that doesn't seem to hold much terror for him. He says, "Sometimes I think there really is such a thing as hell. But we live in it before we die, not after."

And later he says to a senator who is urging him to step aside and support Grant for president, "Senator, there are those who say that I prolonged the war because I lust for power. I may have once wanted—lusted for power. But all that has been burned away. There is nothing left of me. But there is still the work I have been chosen to do. After that is done you are welcome to my dangerous place. In fact, you can come to my funeral. For I have known for some time now that once this conflict is over, I end."

"This is after the fact," Sam Waterston says of this aspect of Lincoln's character, "but I've come to believe that he had a sort of old-fashioned attitude towards the world—it was composed of skepticism on one hand and faith on the other. He's a cousin of Shakespeare and Montaigne with a real modesty about what a man can know for sure and a fatalism about duty and obligation. People wonder whether Lincoln's faith was political or sincere. To me it's impossible that anybody who wasn't sincere about faith could have written the Second Inaugural Address. The other thing that is really intriguing about him is the whole fascination with death—opening his son's [Willie] mausoleum and sitting in there—really crawly stuff."[7]

At the heart of *Gore Vidal's Lincoln* is Abe's tempestuous relationship with Mary. When the stacks of bills—the result of her compulsive acquisitiveness—are brought before him, he erupts in anger. She wilts before his fury and says that she can't seem to help herself; it's like she has to spend money.

At other times he treats her with affection or pity or disgust. After the death of their son Willie, he refuses to comfort her, retreating into his own work. Over a week later, he goes to her room, penitent. "I have left you alone too much with this thing. I had no choice. I suppose in a way it's been easier for me. I have the war. I have no time to mourn. I've let you do my mourning for me. But it is too much for you. Mother, you must save yourself." Suddenly angry, he drags her to the window. "Do you see that building on the ridge? That is the new asylum for the insane. If you do not pull yourself together, we will have to send you there!"

But later, talking with Secretary of State Seward (Richard Mulligan), Lincoln says sadly, "You did not know Mrs. Lincoln in years past, Mr. Seward. She was a gay and spirited young girl. I've often wondered if I did her a service by yoking her to such a galled and festering soul as mine. I have not been an easy man. You know I never discuss personal matters with anyone, for they are very painful to me and I see no need to share the pain. But I think I should give you my view of all this. And that is that these caprices of Mrs. Lincoln's are the result of partial insanity."

The incident at the army camp, when Mary berates an officer's wife for riding with Lincoln in the procession, calling her a whore and a camp follower, is used in other films as a sign of Mary's jealousy or perhaps insanity. But here, it is attributed to her migraines. After the outburst, Mary turns to Mrs. Grant and says in horror, "Your hair is on fire. I can see it." Then she wilts, suddenly realizing what she has been saying. She says softly, "I have a headache."

It is only after Lincoln's death that she seems to descend into a deep confusion that might foreshadow madness. As Robert and Tad solemnly discuss why their father has been killed, Mary says, "It had to happen. You know the South had every right to leave the Union. But Mr. Lincoln said no, this Union can never be broken. Now that was a terrible responsibility for one man to take but he took it, knowing he would be obliged to fight the greatest war in human history, which he fought and which he won. So he not only put the Union back together again, he made an entirely new country, and all in his own image."

She starts unpacking the trunks that have just been packed for their move out of the White House. Robert asks what she's doing, but she ignores him. "Your father means to set up practice in Springfield, with that dreadful Billy Herndon. Well, I will not have it. Your father is not an easy man."

For a film that resolutely avoids the "big moments," *Gore Vidal's Lincoln* accumulates a great deal of power and leaves the viewer with the impression of having seen an Abraham Lincoln that is not quite like any other ever committed to film. The show doesn't have the emotion of some or the sheer scope of others, but Sam Waterston and Mary Tyler Moore give it authenticity—of character, if not necessarily of history.

NOTES

1. George Schaefer, *From Live to Tape to Film: Sixty Years of Directing* (Directors Guild of America Publication, 1996), pp. 144–146.

2. *New York Times*, January 23, 1963.

3. *Los Angeles Times*, September 3, 1975.

4. George Schaefer, *From Live to Tape to Film: Sixty Years of Directing* (Directors Guild of America Publication, 1996), p. 146.

5. Ibid., p. 189.

6. Author interview with Sam Waterston, June 16, 1999.

7. Ibid.

Chapter Four
Robot Abes and Aliens
Lincoln in Comedy and Fantasy

ABRAHAM LINCOLN was treated with reverence in films of the pre-teens, teens, and twenties. Throughout that era, Lincoln was perceived as a Christlike figure of mercy, compassion, and wisdom. In fact, simply having an actor pretend to be Lincoln was already veering toward the edge of bad taste in the opinion of some critics. A reviewer for the *New York Times*, in discussing Benjamin Chapin's *Son of Democracy*, wrote, "Mr. Chapin appears in his impersonation only briefly . . . posing during most of their course as Tom Lincoln. In this character he is more successful, for there is never the feeling of irreverence that always attaches to the impersonation of a great character no matter how reverently it is done."[1]

The folksy wit that was so much a part of Lincoln's character in real life is barely in evidence in films of this time; if it surfaces at all, it is in low-key, mildly amusing exchanges such as occurs in Chapin's *Son of Democracy* entry *Native State* (1918). In this one Secretary of War Edwin Stanton has ordered the seizure of the property belonging to Southern sympathisers in Washington D. C. Lincoln objects to the order in general and to the seizure of one old man's property in particular. The old man is the grandson of Daniel Boone, who was a friend of Lincoln's grandfather, Abraham. The president sends an officer to Stanton with a note rescinding the order. When the officer returns, Abe asks if he gave Stanton his note and what Stanton's reply was. The officer says, "He told me to go to the Devil." Lincoln looks at him with shocked amusement and replies, "What? And you come to me?"

This, however, is about as lighthearted as Abraham Lincoln gets in films of the silent era. The reverence afforded him might have been due in part to proximity. In the 1900s to the 1920s, after all, there were still many thousands of people who had been alive in Lincoln's time. The *New York Dramatic Mirror* of July 22, 1916, wrote of "an unusual coincidence" that occurred when D. W. Griffith's Civil War epic *The Birth of a Nation* opened in London: "William Henry Hall, eighty-two years old, who was one of the four men who carried Abraham Lincoln from the box at Ford's Theater, Washington, on the night of his assassination by Wilkes Booth, lives at Bede House, South Shields." Having heard that *The Birth of a Nation* depicted incidents that he had experienced firsthand, Mr. Hall decided to attend his first movie: "[He] . . . accompanied by his wife, was invited to a seat in the front row of the dress circle, where, with the aid of a pair of opera glasses, he saw the pictures and read the captions with ease."

But as the years passed and the country's personal connection to Lincoln became more abstract, filmmakers began taking more liberties with his image. Lincoln has frequently appeared as a figure of fun in films and television productions—many of which treat the Great Emancipator with a sarcastic, sometimes nasty humor that would have been unthinkable to Benjamin Chapin's generation. Other productions have used Lincoln as an unlikely character in fantasy—and even in science fiction.

In Tay Garnet's *Stand-In* (1937), an accountant, Atterbury Dodd (Leslie Howard), has come to Hollywood to try and revive the fortunes of a failing movie studio. Having become acquainted with

Miss Plum, an attractive stand-in (Joan Blondell)—a stand-in is a person who takes the place of a movie star during the tedious process of lighting a scene—Dodd decides to move into her boardinghouse and experience the "real" Hollywood, not the Hollywood of highly paid executives and movie star glamour, but of the bit players and technicians. When he goes to Miss Plum's boardinghouse for the first time, the door is answered by—Abraham Lincoln. Of course, it's an actor dressed as Lincoln. He has been perfecting the outfit and the attitude for years, just in case a Lincoln movie comes along. He tells Dodd that a Battle of Gettysburg movie has been announced, and he starts reciting the Gettysburg Address. Unfortunately, he can't quite remember how it goes, and Dodd has to prompt him twice. This shakes Mr. Lincoln to his core. "I've been waiting for this chance for six years," he says, shaking his head sadly, "I thought I was ready. And now. . . ."

For movie buffs, this little joke is heightened by the fact that the ersatz Lincoln is portrayed by Charles Middleton. Middleton had already played Lincoln in a fantasy sequence in George M. Cohan's comedy *The Phantom President* (1932) and, at about the same time *Stand-In* was being filmed, was portraying Lincoln again in the Technicolor Warner Brothers two-reeler *The Man Without a Country* (1937). Though he never played Abraham Lincoln after that, he came close a few times, appearing as Abe's father, Tom Lincoln, in *Abe Lincoln in Illinois* (1940) and as Jefferson Davis in the Errol Flynn Western *Virginia City* (1940). However, no matter how frequently he wore the beard and stovepipe hat, Middleton is best remembered today as the evil Ming the Merciless in the *Flash Gordon* serials of the thirties.

After *Stand-In*, oddly enough, there were no more comic Lincolns in feature films for decades. Apparently the pressure was building, for there was an explosion of them in the eighties—even though most of these Lincoln gags came in sequences even briefer than Middleton's scene in *Stand-In*.

In the surreal and slapstick television series *Police Squad* (1982), starring Leslie Nielsen as the dull-witted detective Frank Drebbin, the action-packed credit sequence always included, ". . . and Rex Hamilton as Abraham Lincoln." Abe and Mary are seated in their box at Ford's Theater when a shot blows Abe's stovepipe hat off. But this is one Lincoln who doesn't take things lying down. He immediately crouches behind his rocking chair, pulls out an automatic pistol, and returns fire.

Two of the briefest, and most inexplicable, Lincoln comedy cameos come in the low-budget satire *Two Idiots in Hollywood* (1988) and the Adam Sandler golf comedy *Happy Gilmore* (1996). In both films, Abe appears at the very end as an escort for one of the movie's characters who has died. In *Two Idiots in Hollywood*, Abe is just some tall guy in a Lincoln mask; he ushers the ghost of a man into a courtroom to clear up the facts in his murder case. In *Happy Gilmore*, Abe, played by professional Lincoln impersonator Charles L. Brame, appears in a cloud with Happy's deceased mentor Chubbs (Carl Weathers), and the crocodile who had terrorized Chubbs for years and who Happy killed. The three of them wave to Happy, signaling that all is well in the afterlife and, we assume, that Lincoln has helped to reconcile the former enemies. In neither *Two Idiots in Hollywood* nor in *Happy Gilmore* does the gag amount to much; Lincoln is just a benign emissary from the netherworld with nothing to say.

A more proactive Lincoln appears in the teen hit *Bill and Ted's Excellent Adventure* (1989), starring Keanu Reeves and Alex Winter. Set in the picturesque little town of San Dimas, California, in 1988, the movie concerns Bill and Ted, two sweet-natured dim bulbs who dream of rock stardom but don't have much of a grasp on history. They think, for instance, that Joan of Arc is Noah's wife. Their teacher (Bernie Casey) warns them that they're about to flunk out unless they can come up with a very special history report. Worse, if they flunk, Ted gets sent to military school in Alaska.

Luckily for the boys, the citizens of some future world—whose entire civilization is somehow based on Bill and Ted—send Rufus (comedian George Carlin) back in time (in a time-traveling telephone booth) to help them with their history report. Otherwise, of course, they'll flunk out and will never be able to found their new future world.

Bill and Ted are delighted by the prospect of ping-ponging through time, conducting a kind of scavenger hunt for historical characters. First they meet Napoleon, who accidentally gets brought forward to San Dimas, where he is introduced to the joys of the water slide (at a theme park called Waterloo). Then they gather Billy the Kid, Socrates, Sigmund Freud, Beethoven, Joan of Arc (who, as it turns out, *isn't* Noah's wife), Genghis Khan (whom they lure into the phone booth with a Twinkie), and finally, Abe Lincoln.

Bill and Ted bring all their new friends back to San Dimas, where they all chip in on Ted's chores (Abe does the ironing). Then the boys introduce them to the wonders of the shopping mall, from slushies to escalators. ("Socrates, watch out for your robe, dude.") Socrates and Billy the Kid try to pick up a couple of cute chicks, while Freud enjoys a corn dog. Abe gets his photo taken, and can't understand why the kid wants the hat and the "phony beard" back. Joan of Arc leads an aerobics class as Beethoven makes the leap from conventional piano to electronic keyboads and Genghis Khan goes berserk in a sporting goods store. Naturally, they're all arrested. Only Abe protests as he is dragged off to his cell: "I *am* a lawyer, you know!"

Naturally, Bill and Ted rescue the prisoners and bring them to the school at the last minute, offering them to an amazed student body. Freud psychoanalyzes Ted ("Whoa!"), Socrates admits his newfound love of baseball, Joan of Arc shows the students how to fight with a broadsword, and Napoleon explains battle theories.

Finally they bring Abe up, to riotous applause. He hooks his hand in his lapel, in patented fashion, and delivers a most Lincoln-esque speech: "Four score and seven minutes ago we, your forefathers, were brought forth upon a most excellent adventure, conceived by our new friends, Bill and Ted. These two great gentlemen are dedicated to a proposition which was true in my time, just as it's true today: be excellent to each other. And party on, Dudes!"

In *The Big Picture* (1989), Kevin Bacon plays Nick Chapman, an aspiring filmmaker who finds that his big breakthrough movie is collapsing. Desperate to get another project going, he visits a low-budget film producer who has a great idea for a movie. "Do you know who the most popular historical characters are?" the producer asks. "Abraham Lincoln and Babe Ruth." He wants to make a movie called *Abe and the Babe*, and Nick immediately conjures up an idea of how it would play out. We see Abe and the Babe at a log cabin set in a bucolic wilderness. Abe is at work with his axe, not splitting rails, but putting the finishing touches on a new bat. He gives the bat to Babe, then winds up for the pitch. Babe says he can hit some great home runs with this bat and Abe smiles. "Just make sure the Yankees win," he says.

A robot Lincoln gets back to his lawyer roots in the animated feature *Bebe's Kids* (1992), based on the comedy of Robin Harris. In this one, Robin has agreed to take a bunch of kids to a Disneyland-like theme park in order to endear himself to the beautiful mother of one of them. Naturally, he spends so much time making time with the young woman that the kids are able to run wild around the park, getting into all kinds of mischief. They find themselves backstage at one of the animatronic attractions and are captured and placed on trial by some of the malevolent machines. Luckily, one of the animatronic characters is Abe Lincoln, who believes in fair treatment for all and who takes the kids' case. He wins, naturally enough, after an impassioned speech.

Heavenly Abes, baseball pitching Abes, or robot Abes are still relatively benign comic inventions. This was not the case in the short-lived and controversial television series *The Secret Diary of Desmond Pfeiffer* (1998). As portrayed by Dann Florek, this Abe Lincoln is stupid and sex-crazed—although not so sex-crazed that he doesn't constantly fend off the advances of his gluttonous and love-starved wife, Mary, played by Christine Estabrook ("The Civil War, the Civil War. What about *my* needs? When do I get the attention of the—Executive *Branch*?").

Before *The Secret Diary of Desmond Pfeiffer* even began airing on the UPN Network in October 1998, protestors were working to make sure it never aired at all. But the protestors weren't worried about the highly unflattering portraits of Abe, Mary, or a drunken and lascivious U. S. Grant (Kelly Connell). Instead, they believed that the show was finding fun in the subject of slavery.

The premise of *The Secret Diary of Desmond Pfeiffer* was that a highly intelligent and articulate black Englishman, Desmond Pfeiffer ("pronounced P-feiffer. The P isn't silent"), played by Chi McBride, becomes butler and advisor to Lincoln during the Civil War. That Pfeiffer was the only fully functioning, reasoning adult on the show did not matter much to those who saw the show as racist and offensive. The protestors were particularly incensed by a scene in the show's pilot—which never aired—showing two lynching victims in England (they are hooded and so their race is not revealed), and by certain lines such as when a white character who finds Pfeiffer with his feet propped up on a table tells him to get his feet down "because slavery isn't over yet."

A campaign was launched to keep the series from being televised. Three hundred people, led by the Brotherhood Crusade and the Beverly Hills/Hollywood chapter of the National Association for the Advancement of Colored People, picketed Paramount Studios. Some of them carried signs with slogans such as "Slavery is not funny." The protest did not keep the show off the air, but the protestors soon felt vindicated anyway. When the *The Secret Diary of Desmond Pfeiffer* debuted on October 5, 1998, it made a miserable showing in the ratings and was generally despised by the few who saw it, garnering reactions like "feeble," "tawdry," "silly," and "in very bad taste."

The producers of the show didn't respond to charges that they had made a comedy without laughs, but they continued to insist that *The Secret Diary of Desmond Pfeiffer* did not make fun of slavery; that, in fact, it was a thinly veiled satire of the Clinton administration.

The only inaccurate part of their argument was the term "thinly veiled." *Desmond Pfeiffer's* slaps at the Clinton presidency were overt, obvious, and numerous—though rarely funny. In the first episode that aired, Lincoln secrets himself in the Oval Office and has "telegraph sex" with an unidentified woman—who, in accordance with the unbreakable rules of the sitcom, turns out to be Mary. In another episode, a flirtatious intern sits on Lincoln's desk. In his enthusiasm, he overturns an ink pot. "Oh!" he says, "I've stained your dress!"

Abe and Mary are constantly at odds with each other. He makes fat jokes about her, and she retorts with lines like, "Shove it up your stovepipe, Abe." Abe wearily shakes his head and says, "I can't believe the war is the *easy* part of my day."

Sometimes the references touched on other cultural aspects of the 1990s. Abe and Desmond accidentally get launched in a balloon. Abe is terrified until Desmond convinces him to close his eyes and hold his arms outward in a parody of Kate Winslet and Leonardo DiCaprio's famous pose from *Titanic* (1997). Opening his eyes, Abe is delighted. "I'm flying! I'm King of the World! And President!"

But mostly the plot kept revolving around incidents that allowed the writers to take swipes at the Clinton White House. When Abe is slathering over his unidentified telegraph sex partner, Desmond chastises him: "This is the Oval Office. You're the president. And if I may be so bold, sir, you're acting no better than a horny hillbilly from Arkansas."

Only three episodes of *The Secret Diary of Desmond Pfeiffer* aired before it was unceremoniously canceled; the final show aired on October 19, 1998. Danny Bakewell, president of the Brotherhood Crusade, claimed victory. "This is a tremendous victory for African Americans and other good, decent people who supported our rallying cry that slavery is not funny," he said. "UPN needed to understand that we were very passionate about this, and how their arrogance awakened the sleeping giant."[2]

Other industry watchers, however, noted that the show rated 133 out of 135 programs and was canceled due to "bad ratings, nothing more."[3]

ABRAHAM LINCOLN as a comic figure has inspired a few genuine laughs, and more than a little discomfort, and occasional outrage. In any case, these depictions have nearly always had more to say about the times in which these films and television productions were made than they did about Lincoln and his own era.

Many artists have found unusual inspiration in Lincoln's timeless image, and so the Lincoln of movies and television has repeatedly found himself in situations that have little relation to the facts of his own life and experience. He has wandered, toga-clad, among the Land of Unborn Children. He has done battle on a distant planet, side by side with those futuristic heroes Captain Kirk and Mr. Spock. Lincoln's life story has inspired countless numbers of writers, actors, and filmmakers. But the idea of Lincoln, the essence of the man, has also proven to be a bottomless well for creative thinkers.

The 1940 production of *The Blue Bird,* based on Maurice Maeterlinck's 1908 play, is about two selfish children, Mytyl (Shirley Temple) and Tyltyl (Johnny Russell), who are sent on a quest to find the Blue Bird of Happiness. Guided by Light (Helen Ericson), a cross between an angel and a fairy, they search for the Blue Bird in the Land of Luxury and in the past (visiting their dead grandparents who only come to life when someone is thinking of them). When those places don't deliver, Light guides them to the future—the Land of Unborn Children.

In this odd place, consisting mostly of Grecian columns that don't hold anything up, multitudes of children, barefoot and in togas, while away the time, waiting to be born. Some are already at work on the great inventions they will bring to the earth. One is working on ether, another on an electric light bulb. Some are anxious to be born, and others can't bear the thought of living out what they already know will be short or sad lives. Mytyl and Tyltyl even meet their new little sister, who says that she is coming along soon, but won't be there for long. Tyltyl says, "It hardly seems worthwhile coming at all." The little sister replies, "It would seem so, but we can't pick and choose."

As Mytyl and Tyltyl wander about, looking at all the unborn children with fascination, they suddenly stop, having caught sight of someone very special. Alfred Newman's musical score gives us a clue as to who we're about to meet before we actually see him. The strains of "Lincoln's Theme" from John Ford's masterpiece *Young Mr. Lincoln* comes up on the soundtrack, and sure enough, we are then introduced to a a tall, dark-haired boy (Gene Reynolds) with a prominent nose and a sad expression. He tells Mytyl and Tyltyl that he dreads being born. "You see, up here we're all free, but we aren't born that way, are we?"

"Aren't we?" Tyltyl asks.

"Some are, perhaps. But others are born into slavery, greed and cruelty. That's what I'm going to fight."

Mytyl says, "Then I would think you'd want to be born."

He replies, "They'll destroy me."

He's right, of course. "The Death Trap," an episode of the Irwin Allen science fiction program *The Time Tunnel* (1966–67), begins with assassins plotting to do just that.

The Time Tunnel was about an experiment in time travel that goes wrong when the government decides to stop funding the project. Dr. Tony Newman (James Darren) prematurely begins an experiment and ends up getting lost in time, winding up in 1912, unluckily enough, on the deck of the Titanic. Another scientist, Dr. Doug Phillips (Robert Colbert), is sent to rescue him, but ends up getting lost with him. Unable to retrieve the two scientists, the crew back at the base can only manage to transfer them from one era to another, week after week. These are inordinately ill-timed moves tht place the two scientists in the Alamo the day before the massacre, on Krakatoa just as the volcanic eruption starts, at Custer's Last Stand, and other uncomfortable and dangerous spots.

In this case they materialize in February 1861, right in the midst of a plot to kill Lincoln (Ford Rainey) when he passes through Baltimore on his way to Washington for his inauguration. Oddly, the plot isn't hatched by Southern sympathizers but by a Northern anti-slavery group that hopes Lincoln's death will force the North to invade the South, thus starting the war that they believe will end the institution of slavery once and for all. In midplot, Allan Pinkerton (R. G. Armstrong) and his men attack the barn and kill a couple of the plotters. Doug is captured by Pinkerton and arrested, but Tony escapes with the two surviving conspirators, Matthew (Tom Skerritt) and Jeremiah (Scott Marlowe). He tries to talk them into giving up their plot, especially when he meets their young, impressionable brother, David (Christopher Harris).

When the train arrives, Lincoln seems irritated by Pinkerton's fears of assassination saying, "I'm tired of rumor and hearsay." Since Doug is being held in the depot, Lincoln asks to talk with him. He's very interested in Doug's claim to know what the future holds, a nod to those who think that Lincoln harbored a belief in the supernatural. Insisting that he doesn't believe that the country will go to war, Lincoln asks Doug if the Union will still be standing in a decade. Doug tells him that it will; even more than one hundred years later it will be strong. Lincoln smiles. "Neither of us will live long enough to test your prophecy, but it pleases me."

Turning to Pinkerton, Lincoln says he's ready to go. "Perhaps you've heard I'm a patient man. It's a myth." Then he returns to his railroad car to write his inaugural speech. The assassination attempt, it hardly needs stating, goes awry, with a bomb that travels hither and yon but never seems to be in the right place at the right time. When our two scientists confront the two assassins, they are able to convert one to their point of view, but have to beat up on the other one. Finally they throw the bomb away where it explodes—and doesn't seem to cause any concern around town when it does so.

Lincoln's train leaves the station safely, heading off to Washington and glory. Doug and Tony are rather less lucky—they dematerialize back into the time tunnel and are set down in 1836 just outside the Alamo.

Rainey's Lincoln is rather stern and edgy, impatient to get out from under Pinkerton's protective gaze and onto the important work of his presidency. Thick and powerful where Lincoln was wiry and gaunt, Rainey otherwise makes a very convincing Lincoln, convincing enough to return to the role at least two more times in the television miniseries *The Captains and the Kings* (1976) and the Sunn Classics feature *Guardian of the Wilderness* (1977). He entered Lincoln territory again in 1976, playing Abe and Mary's brother-in-law, Ninian Edwards, in the PBS Television production *The Last of Mrs. Lincoln*, starring Julie Harris as Mary Todd Lincoln.

In the *Time Tunnel* episode, Lincoln has no idea that he is in the midst of a science fiction story, but in "The Savage Curtain," a 1969 episode of *Star Trek*, Lincoln is otherworldy and knows it.

As the Starship *Enterprise* is tooling along across the universe, seeking out new civilizations and going where no man has gone before, Captain James T. Kirk (William Shatner) is nonplussed to see what looks like the Lincoln Memorial looming just outside, in deep space. It turns out it is really Abe Lincoln (Lee Bergere)—stovepipe hat and all—seated in a large chair. He sends warmest greetings to everyone on the *Enterprise* and asks to come aboard.

Kirk knows that Abe isn't the real thing, but he orders all of his officers to put on their dress uniforms to greet the president, whom he beams aboard with all honors. They play ceremonial music (not "Hail to the Chief," which perhaps is no longer required in the distant future). Lincoln is puzzled by the concept of taped music. He says perhaps Mr. Spock (Leonard Nimoy) can explain it to him later.

Kirk doesn't know if it's the real Lincoln but says, "His kindness, his gentleness, his sense of humor is so right." Lincoln calls Lieutenant Uhura (Nichell Nichols), the only black officer, a "charming Negress," but she takes no offense, telling him that they have learned not to fear words. Kirk adds, "We've learned to delight in what we are." Lincoln knows things about the planet he came from, but doesn't know why he knows.

Things become a bit clearer when Kirk, Spock, and Lincoln descend to the planet. There they learn that the beings who live there—who look like big rocks with light bulbs in their heads—want to stage a battle. The Earth concept of good and evil is strange to these beings. Spock reasons that maybe they just want to determine which is stronger. To that end, the beings have conjured up Kirk's ideal of goodness—Lincoln—and Spock's ideal, Surak (Barry Atwater), the founder of Spock's Vulcan race and "Father of all we now hold true."

Ghengis Khan and other infamous interplanetary bad guys will fight on the side of evil. When a tangle comes, the good guys turn them back—termporarily. Abe says proudly, "How delightful at my age to discover I can still wrestle."

The alien light bulb rock now realizes that the human species requires a cause to fight for. So he determines to give them one—he'll blow up the *Enterprise* in four hours if Kirk and company don't win the battle.

Surak tries to negotiate peace but is captured and killed. Abe says gravely to Kirk, "James, the war is forced upon us. History repeats itself." As they plan their defense, the president asks, "Do you drink whiskey, James? You have certain qualities of another general I admire."

Not knowing that Surak is already dead, Abe suggests a plan for sneaking into the camp to rescue him. He suggests that they do what the enemy wants. "But not the way that they want it," Abe says. "We fight on their level—with trickery, brutality, finality. We match their evil. I know, James, I was reputed to be a gentle man. But I was

Commander in Chief during the four bloodiest years of our country's history. I gave orders that sent 100,000 men to their deaths at the hands of their brothers. There's no honorable way to kill. No gentle way to destroy. There's nothing good in war except its ending."

Spock and Kirk attack from the front with spears and rocks while Abe sneaks around behind. Only when Abe gets to Surak does he realize he has been tricked. He appears before Kirk and Spock and manages to say, "James, stay back," before dropping dead, a spear in his back.

Spock and Kirk fight and defeat the evil ones. The light bulb rock admits that he can find no difference between the methods of good and evil. However, he releases them as promised. They are beamed back aboard the *Enterprise*. Both men are awed by having had a connection to their childhood heroes. "I feel that I actually met Lincoln," Kirk says.

Spock replies, "Perhaps, since they were created from our thoughts, how could they be different than we thought they would be?"

NOTES

1. *New York Times*, May 28, 1917, p. 11.
2. *Los Angeles Times*, November 7, 1998, pp. F1, F14.
3. Ibid.

Chapter Five
"Splendid Control and Poetic Clarity"
The Lincoln of the Theater

MOST PEOPLE undoubtedly believe that Abraham Lincoln's major connection to the American stage consists primarily of a play that he attended but of which he saw neither the first act nor the last. The play was Tom Taylor's 1858 comedy *Our American Cousin,* starring the renowned actress Laura Keene.

But, in a sense, there were two performances in progress that night at Ford's Theater in 1865. By his presence as a spectator at one, Lincoln became the star of the other. That performance, which began in laughter and ended in blood and death, cast Lincoln as the central character in a tragic drama that was born of political and patriotic passion, but which was played out with flamboyant theatricality by an actor before an audience.

John Wilkes Booth was that actor, son of the famous Junius Brutus Booth and younger brother to Edwin Booth, considered to be the greatest actor of his time. John Wilkes Booth had also carved out a name for himself in the theater, but his dreams and obsessions demanded a larger arena. Legend has it that someone recognized Booth in a bar the night of the assasination and said with contempt,

"You aren't half the actor your father or brother are." Booth is said to have replied, "When I leave the stage, I'll be the most famous man in America."

Booth planned the assassination as though mounting a production. Indeed, Lloyd Lewis, in his book *Myths After Lincoln*, refers to the gathering of the conspirators as "the assembling of his cast," and calls Booth the "star" of the plot.[1] Booth gave deadly stage directions to David Paine, George Atzerodt, and Lewis Powell, then worked out his own timing, his exit, his curtain speech. *Our American Cousin* had toured the country ceaselessly for several years, and most actors were familiar with its quaint humor. Booth knew where the play's biggest laugh came and timed the firing of his derringer to coincide with the roar of delight from the audience.

After firing a single bullet into Lincoln's head, Booth did not move back into the crowded theater where he might easily have been able to blend in with the pandemonium. Instead, he leapt from the presidential box onto the stage, where he would brandish a dagger and shout, "Sic semper Tyrannis!" before running offstage and out a side exit. The only thing that marred his performance—always a danger when an actor goes onstage under-rehearsed—was that he caught his foot in the red, white, and blue bunting that lined the box and landed with a thud, breaking his leg. He recovered quickly, the mark of a real trouper, and managed to deliver his big line with some authority, but he must have cursed himself for having to limp away with neither grandness nor grace. As he promised the man in the bar, he would soon be the most famous actor in America. But Booth blew his exit, and this was one performance he could never repeat or improve.

Abraham Lincoln was killed in a theater on April 14, 1865. But his character and his good name had already been assassinated onstage many times before that. Throughout the years of the Civil War, Southern producers and playwrights had made savage fun of Lincoln. These productions mocked his appearance as well as his politics and, predictably, took special delight in tweaking him on his views toward blacks in general and the institution of slavery in particular. The first of these, Ahab Lincoln: A Tragedy of the Potomac, was a dramatic poem in blank verse by Stephen Franks Miller, a newspaperman from Milledgeville, Georgia. "Ahab" is a ridiculous and ineffectual president whose stupidity is weighed against the wisdom of Confederate president Jefferson Davis, General Beauregard, and others.

King Linkum the First, a satirical opera, followed in 1863. Crude and insulting, it could have succeeded only as propaganda, since it offers little that can be mistaken for entertainment. Richard Harwell wrote, "[It is] a satire of Lincoln that could be excused only by the most rabid partisan. It possesses, however, a continuing interest (having once been written) as a reflection of the more extreme propaganda that invaded the life of the South during the war years. Of no merit as drama, it is interesting as exposition of the balderdash that could pass as drama in the mid-nineteenth century in a section largely cut off from the theater."[2]

King Linkum the First was written by New Yorker-turned-Southerner John Hill Hewitt (1801–90), the son of James Hewitt (1770–1828), an important figure in early American music. Educated at West Point, Hewitt elected not to go into the army upon graduation but to join his father as a theatrical producer and exhibitor.

Hewitt didn't make much of an impact on the world of drama; in fact, he became best known in his lifetime as a composer of popular songs, including "Rock Me to Sleep, Mother," "All Quiet Along the Potomac Tonight," "When Upon the Field of Glory, an Answer to When This Cruel War Is Over," and "You Are Going to the Wars, Willie Boy!" He became a newspaper editor and writer for publications ranging from The Republican of Greenville, South Carolina, to The Baltimore Saturday Visitor. While in Baltimore, he entered a poetry contest. One of Hewitt's competitors in this contest was Edgar Allan Poe and—possibly because Poe had already won the publication's prize for prose (for "MS Found in a Bottle")—Hewitt won the poetry contest. Poe was furious and carried a grudge against

Hewitt for the rest of his life. Richard Harwell wrote, "The latter, in his declining years soured by his own unsuccess and the early apotheosis of the author of "The Raven," nevertheless came wryly to accept the award as his chief claim to fame. [Hewitt] went on to write forty or more dramatic pieces, most of which were never published or performed. Some were performed while he served as co-manager (with Alfred Waldron) of the Concert Hall in Augusta."

King Linkum was first performed at the Concert Hall on February 23, 1863, and repeated on February 25. The Augusta papers of the day did not review theatrical productions, so we have no indication how enthusiastically either performance was greeted. From an ad on February 22, 1863, however, we can gather that the program was crowded with entertainments of all varieties: "Undiminished attraction of the Thespian Family, or Queen Sisters and Palmetto Band! The grand tragico-comico operatic drama of King Linkum the First. Dance by Misses Fannie and Julia. Music by Palmetto Band. To Conclude with As You Like It. Admission - parquette $1.00, Gallery .50 cents. Children and servants half price."

The playbill for the second performance offers this lineup of the characters and gives a flavor of the production's tone.

KING LINKUM THE FIRST—And the last of his die-nasty, a long drawn tyrant, uneasy in conscience [sic], and addicted to rail-splitting.

GEN. FUSS AND FEATHERS—A discarded "old soldier," the hero of many battles and the original planner of the great "on to Richmond" movement, addicted to taking the oath.

STEWARD—The King's Prime Minister, often primed, who considers "the pen mightier than the sword," afraid of the Democrats and addicted to niggers.

GEN. BOTTLER—A bottle imp, good at speculation, and addicted to hanging rebels.

BOBBY LINKUM—A Prince of much promise, having never settled his tailor's bill, the spoiled pet of his mamma, and addicted to frolicking.

BLACK ORDERLY—A military conscript, rather pugilistic, and addicted to swelling.

BLACK GHOST—A messenger from the spirit-land, in kicking the bucket he turned a little pail, addicted to singing grave songs.

GHOST OF CREDIT—In hot pursuit of specie, having been turned into a myth by being smothered in green-backs, addicted to torturing the conscience of the King.

THE GRAND ARMY OF THE UNION—Addicted to running.

QUEEN LINKUM—An indulgent mother and a fiery wife, addicted to self will.

When we first meet "King Linkum," he is singing mournfully:

Ah ha! - Oh ho! - the lion growls
England is up - Victoria scowls;
A pretty fix we've gotten into,
I'll cast the dice and, maybe, win too.
Mass Meetings - speeches - indignation,
John Russell's speech - great agitation.
Confound you, Steward, why advise
To capture such a ticklish prize
As Slidell, Mason and the rest,
when shelter'd 'neath the British crest?
I think in war we're quite proficient,
for one Bull Run is quite sufficient.
Alas! all over I am a king,
One of the sovereign peoples' making -
Enough I've had of lofty sitting
Oh, for the days of fence-rail splitting!

The play is also filled with invective about slavery, chiding the North for wanting to free the slaves without considering that the slaves will then consider themselves the equal of whites. A black orderly blithely admits beating Linkum's son Bob and sings derisively:

Look har, white folks, my dander's ris,
I'se jist as good as you—I is.
You've made de nigger free; now, say,
If I am free - I want fair play.

And a black ghost confronts Linkum in his chamber, berating him for forcing blacks to give up the security (!) of slavery without offering them anything better. Indeed, the ghost insists, the president's promises mean nothing.

Yer got no conscience, Marster King?
Why it no gall yer wid its sting?
Wha' for yer free de nigger? - say -
Was it to let him die away?
Or beg for bread - or freeze to death,
Or perish jist for want ob breath?
Go long! you tell us we your brodder,
Dat all men should lub one anodder;
Yer take us from our happy home,
An' promise better days to come,
A belly full - no work to do,
But eat and drink de whole day through.
White man! go long - once fool dis nigger,
He'll stick to you jist like a jigger.
Wake up King Abe, de hoe-cake's turning.
You're fiddlin' while all Rome is burning.

The point of view from another Lincoln-related play from 1863 can be guessed at from its title: *The Royal Ape*. Apparently this satire was too negative even for many Southerners. A review in *The Index*, a London weekly published by Confederate interests stated: "*The Royal Ape* is a dramatic poem of which the theme is the Federal defeat at the first battle of Manassas and the consequent confusion and dismay in Washington. There are here and there some vigorous passages, but what might have been smart satire is marred by inexcusable personality. It is to be regretted that even in an avowed fiction a Southern writer should attempt to cast the slightest slur upon the domestic life of Mr. Lincoln . . . If Mr. Lincoln were personally immoral—which he is not—it would still be indecorous to drag his private life into a public controversy."[3]

After Lincoln's death there would be no more mean-spirited theatrical ventures. He was deified almost immediately—not only in the North but through much of the South—and new plays, poems, and stories about him were reverential in the extreme with titles such as *The Play of Destiny* (1867), *A National Drama from the Beautiful World* (1872), *The Qualities of Washington, Lincoln and Humanity* (1916), and *The Masque of the Titans of Freedom* (1918).

Over the years, the many theatrical versions of the life of Lincoln have covered virtually every aspect of his story. There have been plays about his legendary acts of mercy (*Abraham Lincoln's Pardon*); his salad days as a lawyer in Springfield (*Abraham Lincoln's First Case, Lawyer Lincoln,* and *The Lawyer of Springfield*); amusing or inspirational stories of his childhood (*The New Salem Days, A Child of the Frontier, When Lincoln Went Flat Boating from Rockport, Indiana,* and *Prologue to Glory: A Play in Eight Scenes Based on the New Salem Years of Abraham Lincoln*). There were plays about his romance with Ann Rutledge (*The Soul of Ann Rutledge, The Spirit of Ann Rutledge, The Heart of Lincoln,* and *The Woman Lincoln Loved*); and about his relationship with his wife, Mary Todd Lincoln, (*Mary, the Wife of Abraham Lincoln, Love is Eternal: A Play in Three Acts, Mary the Wife, One Love Had Mary,* and *Mrs. Lincoln*). The Lincoln-Douglas debates—a kind of traveling show in real life—became even more theatrical in plays like *The Rivalry* and *Lincoln and Douglas: Years of Decision.* And Lincoln's tragic death at Ford's Theater became the central event in such works as *The Last of*

Lincoln, The Last Days of Lincoln, Madame Surratt, and John Wilkes Booth, or The National Tragedy.

Some of these theatrical works originated in unexpected places. Abraham Lincoln, by Hermann Luedke, debuted in Meineingen, Germany, on November 11, 1928. A New York Times reviewer encapsulated the play like this: "[Abraham Lincoln] represents Lincoln as a rustic lawyer who on his wife's insistence runs in vain for the United States Senate. Later Lincoln is depicted as a good-natured President who yields easily to pressure and is entirely in the hands of his surroundings. He shows firmness on one point only, the abolition of slavery. The dramatist, however, makes him a sympathetic figure. The piece was staged by Director Loehr, whose mise en scene rather than the drama itself was greeted as a noteworthy success."[4]

Sometimes the productions came in unexpected styles, such as President Lincoln: Opera in Four Acts and Nine Scenes (1976) by Sam Raphling. In this work, Lincoln's part is performed by a bass-baritone, who booms out the Gettysburg Address in song. Other characters include Mary, Tad and Willie Lincoln, Edwin Stanton, Frederick Douglass, William Seward, Harriet Beecher Stowe, and Sojourner Truth. The settings range from Mrs. Lincoln's room in the White House to a plantation in the South to President Lincoln's Cabinet room in the White House.

The show begins with preparations for a presidential ball. In the midst of this, they learn that Fort Sumter has been fired upon. The opera then hits the usual high spots in Lincoln's life and ends as he and Mary are leaving for the theater.

Of the hundreds of plays that tell stories about some aspect of Lincoln's life, two are truly important and truly great: Robert E. Sherwood's Abe Lincoln in Illinois (1938) and John Drinkwater's Abraham Lincoln (1919).

Drinkwater was probably not the most obvious playwright to bring this quintessential American story to life. Born in 1882 at Leytonstone, Essex, England, and educated at Oxford High School,

Drinkwater served as an insurance clerk for twelve years, during which time he developed a reputation as a poet and a critic. In 1913 he became manager-producer of the Pilgrim Players, which developed into the Birmingham Repertory Theater. *Abraham Lincoln* was his most successful play, and he followed it with many more plays on historical themes: *Mary Stuart* (1921), *Oliver Cromwell* (1921), *Robert E. Lee* (1923), *Robert Burns* (1925), *Bird-in-Hand* (1928), and *Midsummer Eve* (1932). His critical works include *William Morris* (1912), *Swinburne* (1913), *Oliver Cromwell: A Character Study* (1927), and *Charles James Fox* (1928). His *Collected Poems* was published in 1923 and *Collected Plays* in 1925. John Drinkwater died in 1937.

Drinkwater explained that he approached the subject of Abraham Lincoln "not [as] the historian but [as] the dramatist. While I have, I hope, done nothing to traverse history, I have freely telescoped its events, and imposed invention upon its movement, in such ways as I needed to shape the dramatic significance of my subject."[4]

The play begins with the line, "Abraham. It's a good name for a man to bear, anyway." It is the spring of 1860 in Lincoln's Springfield home. He meets with a delegation from the Republican Party that invites him to be their nominee for president. The play ends with a single shot at Ford's Theater, followed by Edwin Stanton's solemn declaration, "Now he belongs to the ages." In between is a simple, rather straightforward account of some of the crucial moments in Lincoln's life, from the beginning of the war, to his troubles with his generals, to his pardon of a sentry sentenced to death, to Lee's surrender at Appomattox.

But the effect that Drinkwater created was anything but simple and straightforward. His Lincoln is already encased in myth, serious and deliberate, with little trace of the man's jocular wit. Drinkwater's Lincoln is aware of the myth, and this foreknowledge of history, this realization of his own doom and destiny, weighs heavily upon him. He is also possessed of a barely concealed anger. Two women come to visit Mary Todd Lincoln at the White House. One, Mrs. Blow, is a hawk. When she learns of a victory in which the South lost twenty-seven hundred men and the North eight hundred, she says, "How splendid!"

Lincoln replies with some disbelief, "Thirty-five hundred."

Mrs. Blow says brightly, "Oh, but you mustn't talk like that, Mr. President. There were only eight hundred that mattered."

Mrs. Otherly has just lost a son and begs Lincoln to bring an end to the war, an idea that Mrs. Blow scoffs at. Her husband is making a good living because of the war. As the women leave, Lincoln refuses the hand of Mrs. Blow and says:

> Good afternoon, madam. And I'd like to offer you a word of
> advice. That poor mother told me what she thought. I don't agree
> with her, but I honour her. She's wrong, but she is noble. You've told
> me what you think. I don't agree with you, and I'm ashamed of you
> and your like. You, who have sacrificed nothing, babble about destroy-
> ing the South while other people conquer it. I accepted this war with
> a sick heart, and I've a heart that's near to breaking every day. I
> accepted it in the name of humanity, and just and merciful dealing,
> and the hope of love and charity on earth. And you come to me, talk-
> ing of revenge and destruction, and malice, and enduring hate. These
> gentle people are mistaken, but they are mistaken cleanly, and in a
> great name. It is you that dishonour the cause for which we stand—it
> is you who would make it a mean and little thing. Good afternoon.

Flustered, Mrs. Blow leaves. Lincoln calls for the maid, Susan.

> "Susan, if that lady comes here again she may meet with an acci-
> dent."

If Drinkwater's Lincoln is a bit more hot-tempered than most, his Mary Todd is not quite the insane harridan that so often appears in plays and films. She is, at least, more self aware than most Marys. On the night in which he accepts the nomination, Mary tells a friend:

> I'm likely to go into history now with a great man. For I know better than any how great he is. I'm plain looking and I've a sharp tongue, and I've a mind that doesn't always go in his easy, high way. And that's what history will see, and it will laugh a little, and say, 'Poor Abraham.' That's all right, but it's not all. I've always known when he should go forward, and when he should hold back. I've watched, and watched and what I've learnt America will profit by . . . My work's going farther than Illinois—it's going farther than any of us can tell. I made things easy for him to think and think when we were poor, and now his thinking has brought him to this.

Abraham Lincoln was originally produced by the Birmingham Repertory Theater and was, to nearly everyone's surprise, an enormous hit with both critics and the public. St. John Irving wrote in the *North American Review*, "*Abraham Lincoln* was performed in London at an obscure and ugly theater in a distant suburb by an unknown management with a cast which did not contain the name of a single player of reputation. There was not an actor in the cast with sufficient popularity to draw sixpence in the theater. The scenic effects were so slight as to be negligible. There was no orchestra . . . and yet the play was an enormous success."

That first production ran for 466 performances. The title role was played by Irish actor William J. Rea who was, according to Arnold Bennett, "merely great. The audience cried, and I should have cried myself, but for my iron resolve not to stain a well-earned reputation for callousness." After that first performance, Bennett ticked off all the reasons the play could not be a success: "It has no love interest. It is a political play. Its theme is the threatened separation of the Southern States from the Northern States. Nobody ever heard of a play with such an absurd theme making permanent success. No author before John Drinkwater ever had the effrontery to impose such a theme on a London public."[6]

"John Drinkwater was not a dramatist of genius," wrote theater historian Ernest Short, "but he was poet enough to reach the heart of the matter. He knew that this meant cutting out non-essentials in any given recension of history. He was also actor enough to know what players needed if they were to lay down the broad lines of a character and an epoch. Lastly, he was philosopher enough to realize the need for some such device as a Chorus, which would lift his play above mere realism. In a modern chronicle play little more is needed than an illusion of the period. Over-elaboration befogs an audience. Robert Sherwood attempted considerably more than Drinkwater when he wrote his *Abe Lincoln in Illinois* and had it produced by a brother dramatist, Elmer Rice. Robert Sherwood was more interested in his doubting and indecisive politician and the simple machinery of a popular chronicle play would not have carried an elaborate characterization."[7]

On December 15, 1919, *Abraham Lincoln* opened in New York at the Cort Theater. The British cast was not imported to the States since their affected American accents would not be as convincing in America as in Great Britain. Lincoln was portrayed by Frank McGlynn, a little-known actor until then. McGlynn's success in the role would, quite literally, change his life. He had already portrayed Lincoln at least once on film, in the1915 Edison production *The Life of Abraham Lincoln*. But the acclaim that greeted his performance in Drinkwater's play would cement him in the public eye as the very personification of the Great Emancipator. (See chapter 6.)

Critic Alexander Woolcott, a man known for his iconoclastic views and caustic wit, was completely won over by McGlynn's performance. He wrote in the *New York Times*:

When news of this play's triumph in England reached these shores about a year ago and word went out that it would be exhibited here this season, there was great speculation as to who would embody Lincoln in the American production. The guesses ran all the way from Lionel Barrymore to lesser actors whose suitability was suggested by nothing more than their physical resemblance to the emancipator. Then came the New York premiere in December and the instant success won in the title role by Frank McGlynn, a success so complete that few playgoers could conceive a different Lincoln and none ask a better. Whereupon, because McGlynn, for all his five and twenty years upon the stage, was virtually unknown to the New York public, every one marveled. Yet the very fact that McGlynn was (or rather had been) an obscure actor was one of the [qualities] contributing to his peculiar fitness for the role. The very fact that for nine hundred and ninety nine out of every thousand playgoers he is an actor without a past works not against but in favor of, the conviction he carries as Lincoln.

. . . That there should have been found for Mr. Drinkwater's play a native actor who resembled Lincoln, who could play him with eloquence and understanding, and who would trail into the production no clouds of former glories—well that was merely one of the miracles that have attended this play's progress from its inception. An astonishing thing, if you will, but, after all, not more astonishing than the fact that American audiences are now, and for years will be, sitting enraptured at a Lincoln play written by an insurance clerk from Birmingham, England.[8]

McGlynn brought the role back to New York in 1929, playing with great success at the Forrest Theater. Critics believed that it captured the mood of the earlier production and the *New York Times* praised Drinkwater's "splendid control and poetic clarity."[9]

An interesting story accompanied the play's 1940 revival in London. With all its prior acclaim, *Abraham Lincoln* was failing miserably at the Westminster Theater and was about to close. But one day the king and queen dropped in to see it—the Westminster was right across the street from Buckingham Palace. Their royal presence in the audience, and their subsequent praise for the play, revived its box office chances. After their visit, receipts doubled, and the show continued to run for several months.[10]

Sadly, Drinkwater's *Abraham Lincoln* has seldom been revived in the years since. It was filmed in 1930, starring Frank McGlynn, but no prints of this production seem to have survived. In 1952 *Abraham Lincoln* was adapted for television by David Shaw. It starred Robert Pastene as Lincoln, Judith Evelyn as Mary Todd Lincoln, and a young James Dean as William Scott, the sentry who is pardoned by Lincoln. Shortened considerably—quite understandably, Shaw excised the Greek chorus that introduces each scene in blank verse—this television production gives us only a flavor of the power and poetry of the original play. But until someone mounts a full-scale theatrical revival, it's all we have.

NOTES

1. Lloyd Lewis, *Myths After Lincoln* (The Press of the Readers Club, 1929), p. 173.

2. Richard Harwell, introduction to the 1947 reprint (Emory University Publications Sources & Reprints Series IV).

3. *The Index*, September 24, 1863.

4. *New York Times*, November 13, 1928.

5. John Drinkwater, introduction to the first edition of the play (Houghton Mifflin, 1919).

6. Arnold Bennett, introduction to the published edition of the play (Houghton Mifflin, 1919).

7. Ernest Short, *Sixty Years of Theater* (Eyre & Spottiswoode, 1951), p. 180.

8. *New York Times*, March 14, 1920.

9. *New York Times*, October 22, 1929.

10. *New York Times*, May 5, 1940.

Chapter Six
"An Ideal Counterpart of Lincoln in All Particulars"
The Great Lincoln Impersonators

ABRAHAM LINCOLN has been an inspirational figure to Americans and people all over the world for considerably more than a century. For many, that inspiration creates interest in who Lincoln was and what he did. But for some, that interest deepens into something else, something bordering on obsession. There are, at this writing, more than fifty men across the United States who have made it their avocation to impersonate Abraham Lincoln. Many of them belong to the Association of Lincoln Presenters and give presentations as the Great Emancipator at schools, churches, clubs, Civil War reenactments—anywhere a living Abe Lincoln might be appropriate and welcome.

There have even been women Lincoln impersonators. From the press materials for D. W. Griffith's *Abraham Lincoln* (1930) comes this rather eye-opening story about their search for an actor to play Lincoln in the film:

> The remarkable thing is that two women believed they approached Lincoln's character so closely as to compete with professional impersonators.

One of these women was Lucille La Verne, the celebrated American actress who recently startled London by appearing as 'Shylock' in a Shakespearian revival and who even actually accepted another role in [Abraham Lincoln]. The other was Sophia A. Hume of Los Angeles, who took the trouble and expense of being photographed in an exact duplicate of Lincoln's presidential costume, not even omitting the umbrella, beard and small mole on the right cheek.

Both women expressed the keen desire to be given screen and voice tests before any decision was made. Miss Hume's characterization, according to Griffith, was one of the fifteen best submitted.

There may be more Lincoln impersonators today than at any time in the past, but as we have seen, that doesn't mean the idea is a new one. Men and women have come under Lincoln's spell since the president himself walked the earth. And more than a few men *and* women have become so caught up in the image and ideals of Lincoln that they begin to take on his characteristics.

Of the hundreds of actors who have portrayed Lincoln on stage, screen, and television, a few turned the role into a career, a part they lived both onstage and off. George Billings played Lincoln in at least four films, most notably the Rockett brothers' epic *The Dramatic Life of Abraham Lincoln* (1924), but got so immersed in the role that he took to acting and dressing like Lincoln even in his private life. It was said that he wouldn't go out to eat or to a movie—not even to a business meeting—unless he wore the stovepipe hat and shawl and, we can assume, Abe's melancholy air.

Benjamin Chapin played the role in a play he and his sister wrote, then not only portrayed Lincoln, but also Lincoln's father and grandfather in the series of ten films known alternately as *The Lincoln Cycle* and *Son of Democracy*, released sporadically from 1914 to 1918. Chapin, who looked strikingly like Lincoln even without makeup, once said, "This is my lifework. Ever since I was able to think and read about Abraham Lincoln, a vision of him has led me on, to spread the beauty of his adventurous life and by the sheer romance of his rise from poverty to President, inspire the youth of America."[1]

One of the most prolific Lincolns was Frank McGlynn Sr., an actor who not only made an enormous hit in John Drinkwater's 1919 play *Abraham Lincoln*, but went on to play the Rail-splitter in at least thirteen films—perhaps more. It was McGlynn's Lincoln who bounced Shirley Temple on his knee in *The Littlest Rebel* (1935) and whose assassination set in motion *The Prisoner of Shark Island* (1936), the story of Dr. Mudd who was imprisoned for treating the wounds of John Wilkes Booth. Like Chapin and Billings, McGlynn began to immerse himself in Lincoln's character even when there wasn't a picture in the works. He dressed as Lincoln and spoke in a deliberate, Lincolnesque drawl. It is said that the great writer and wit George S. Kaufman once saw McGlynn walking down the street, his sad face etched with the pain of the Civil War, a shawl around his shoulders, and a tall hat atop his head. Kaufman turned to his companion and said, "That fellow will never be happy until he's assassinated."

Of course, not all the actors who have portrayed Lincoln in films over the past century have gone so overboard in their enthusiasm. But each found something unique and compelling in the role. And each was, to a lesser or greater degree, changed by their brush with the great man. Here are brief profiles of some of the major Lincoln interpreters, those actors who, either through an accidental resemblance or a deep-seated belief in Lincoln's ideals, again and again pasted on the beard and the mole, donned the stovepipe hat, and appeared before the cameras to free the slaves, pardon the condemned sentries, or once again attend a production of *Our American Cousin*.

RALPH INCE

The audience at New York's Vitagraph Theater at Broadway and Forty-fourth Street got a rare treat on Lincoln's birthday in 1914.

Ralph Ince in and out of makeup as Lincoln. Ince played the president over a dozen times, despite the fact that he resembled Lincoln barely, if at all.
Courtesy of Bison Archives/Marc Wanamaker

They had just watched the latest Vitagraph production—and a most appropriate one, given the date—*The Man Who Knew Lincoln*, based on the popular book *He Knew Lincoln* by Ida Tarbell. The picture ended with "a pathetic reference to the martyred President."[2] The audience had found the film moving in the extreme, and while they were still wiping the tears from their eyes, the stage lights came up and the curtains parted. The set was an artist's studio where a frustrated painter was having trouble capturing the spirit of Lincoln in a portrait. Finally, unable to complete the picture to his satisfaction, he fell asleep and dreamed.

A reporter wrote, "The substance of this dream is shown when the curtain of his studio window is drawn and there was seen standing in strong silhouette against a distant view of the White House dome the bowed figure of Lincoln. As the lights came up the figure turned and faced the audience and delivered the famous Gettysburg Address. The audience was visibly impressed; the dropping of a pin might have been audible. After delivering the address, which was spoken with great feeling, the form turned, the lights dimmed and the curtain was closed over that pathetic stooping figure."[3]

The actor who delivered the Gettysburg Address was the same one who appeared in the movie that had just finished—Ralph Ince, the most famous and prolific Lincoln of the movies of his generation.

Ralph Ince, born in 1887, was the son of a popular stage comedian, John E. Ince, and brother of the pioneering producer and director Thomas Ince. He followed the family vocation at an early age and became something of a child star on the stage. Ralph's moving picture career began when he joined the Vitagraph Company in 1906, beginning a profitable association that would last for several years. "I was the first Ince to go into pictures," he later said. "I went out to Vitagraph and acted in one-reel pictures. I always liked to write, so I spent all my leisure time pounding out scenarios. I wanted to direct, but for a long time there was no opportunity given me. I heard that I could make a picture on my own and sell it. One Sunday I went over to New Jersey with a cameraman, collected a friend who had a car, and with his wife and my wife, produced a 500-foot comedy. I made the picture in a day." He was paid $300 for the picture, he said, "and I felt like a millionaire."[4]

The speed with which he worked made Ralph Ince an incredibly prolific artist even for a time when nearly all movies were made with the speed of lightning. It's claimed that he had acted in 500 moving pictures by 1914, and had directed at least 150 of them. One trade paper wrote of him, "He has staged more big feature pictures for the Vitagraph than all of their other directors combined. His ability for getting together a picture may be surmised by considering that when he had a large coasting schooner at his disposal, he conceived, within an hour, the story of 'His Last Fight,' placing practically all of the scenes in the picture aboard the schooner."[5]

The busy actor played many kinds of parts, from saints to hoodlums, but when he was cast as Abraham Lincoln—*The Reprieve: An Episode in the Life of Abraham Lincoln* (1908) was probably his first such film—he became thoroughly identified with the role. The odd aspect of this is that, of all actors who have portrayed the president on the screen, Ralph Ince probably bears the least personal resemblance. Columnist Louella Parsons brought this fact up to him in 1922: "You do not look like Lincoln. Why have you specialized in Lincoln roles?"

Ralph Ince replied, "I suppose because I mastered the makeup in the first picture and convinced everyone I could look like him. It was [film pioneer] J. Stuart Blackton who first gave me that part, and it has clung to me ever since, frequently interfering with my directorial duties. Another reason may be my interest in the man. I have read every book available."[6] Which, of course, isn't a particularly enlightening answer.

Ince's duties as Lincoln were varied. In his first stab at the role, *The Reprieve*, he granted a last minute pardon to a sentry who has been caught sleeping on duty and was sentenced to the firing squad. The condemned man writes to his wife, who hurries off to Lincoln where "she succeeds in getting a reprieve in a thrilling manner."[7] Ince pardoned other lucky sentries in *Under One Flag* (1911), *One Flag at Last* (1911), *The Seventh Son* (1912), and *The Highest Law* (1921); he inspired—not once, but twice—Julia Ward Howe to write what would become his theme song in *Battle Hymn of the Republic* (1911) and *Battle Hymn of the Republic* (1917); he delivered a certain brief speech a couple of times in *Gettysburg* (1912) and *Lincoln's Gettysburg Address* (1912); he served as a country lawyer in Springfield in *The Land of Opportunity* (1920); and in *The Song Bird of the North* (1913), he presided over the marriage of singer and patriot Elida Rumsey (played by Ince's sister-in-law Anita Stewart) and her heroic fiancé in "the only marriage solemnized at the capitol."[8]

Perhaps most touching, Ralph Ince's Abe mooned over lovely, doomed Ann Rutledge (played by Ince's sister-in-law Anita Stewart) in *Lincoln the Lover* (1914). This film begins toward the end of Lincoln's presidency. He is seated by the fireplace, staring into the flames, lost in thought about his great love. The film flashes back to his days as a postmaster in New Salem when he delivered a letter to Ann from her faithless fiancé who broke off their engagement. He then recalls his courtship of Ann, his proposal of marriage, and finally her illness and death. At this sad moment, he awakens and the film ends with a Lincoln still heartbroken over the loss he sustained many years earlier. When *Lincoln the Lover* was in the planning stages, a trade magazine item promised that "this Vitagraph production will show Lincoln in a new light and show a phase of his nature never before exploited."[9] And perhaps it did.

"Mr. Ince's impersonation of Abraham Lincoln is startling in its reality," wrote one observer. "Because of his height—he is considerably over six feet tall—the Vitagraph naturally cast him for the Martyred president when the character of Lincoln was required in a picture several years ago. Ralph's ability as an artist, in conjunction with his extraordinary efficiency in making up for the stage, permitted him to produce a representation of Lincoln sufficiently important to make Ralph famous throughout the world. Within the past two years the study of Lincoln, his personality and characteristics, has become Ralph's foremost hobby. Now, old friends of Lincoln unite in declaring that Ralph Ince is as near an ideal counterpart of Lincoln in all particulars as it is possible for one human being to impersonate another."[10]

Ralph Ince never played Lincoln again after *The Highest Law* in 1921. He remained active as an actor, but gradually his starring roles turned into supporting parts and his directing credits became ever more scarce, particularly after talkies replaced silent films. He moved to Great Britain in 1934 where he began acting and directing with a new vigor. Unfortunately, this shot in the arm for his career turned out to be short-lived. Ralph Ince was killed in an automobile accident in England in 1937.

Francis Ford, elder
brother of famed
director John Ford,
suggests what Lincoln
would have looked like
as a professional boxer.
This stern Lincoln is
from *On Secret Service*
(1912).
*Courtesy of the Academy of
Motion Picture Arts and
Sciences*

FRANCIS FORD

The career of Francis Ford had more drama and plot twists than
any of the thrilling serials he directed in the teens. Once one of the
industry's top leading men and most gifted and important directors,
he served as mentor to his younger brother, John Ford, who went on
to become one of the cinema's greatest artists. But by the end of the
twenties, both Francis Ford's directing career and his movie stardom
were over. He continued to work in films until his death in 1953 but
mainly in bit parts and supporting roles. Francis showed up frequently in brother John's classic films, nearly always as a comic
drunkard. Indeed, Francis is perhaps known best today for these
roles in John Ford's *Stagecoach* (1939), *Drums Along the Mohawk*
(1939), *My Darling Clementine* (1946), and *The Quiet Man* (1952),
and for his part as one of the accused men in William A. Wellman's
somber antilynching drama *The Ox-Bow Incident* (1943).

But in the teens, Francis Ford was as big as they came. His serials like *Lucille Love—the Girl of Mystery* (1914) were wildly popular with audiences, and as an actor, he ranked among the top stars of the day.

John Ford told Peter Bogdanovich that Francis was one of his greatest influences: "He was a great cameraman—there's nothing they're doing today—all those things that are supposed to be so new—that he hadn't done; he was really a good artist, a wonderful musician, a hell of a good actor, a good director—Johnny of all trades—and *master* of all."[11]

But, like Ralph Ince, Francis Ford seems an odd choice to portray Abraham Lincoln. He was powerfully built with a strong, broad face and a boxer's nose. In making up, he elected for some reason to streak his hair and beard with grey, a flourish that somehow makes him look less like Lincoln than he otherwise might have. In a review of *The Heart of Lincoln* (1915), in which Abe manages to pardon *both* officers—Northern and Southern—who are in love with pretty Betty (played by Ford's wife and frequent costar Grace Cunard), a *Variety* critic wrote, "The man playing Lincoln had his own idea about the ex-President, but he is safe, for anyone who sees the picture never saw the original."[12] It must be said, however, that as crude and melodramatic as the film may have been, and as inadequate as Ford may have been, *The Heart of Lincoln*, a three-reeler, was rereleased in 1922 to some success.

Ford's Lincoln was a fairly minor presence in the cloak-and-dagger thriller *On Secret Service* (1912), but he stood at center stage in *When Lincoln Paid* (1913)—in which he pardons another soldier—and in *The Sorrows of Lincoln* (1913), another melancholy meditation on his lost love, Ann Rutledge.

Though Francis Ford never played Lincoln again after the mid-teens, he frequently appeared in Lincoln-related films, sometimes interacting with the Great Emancipator himself. He played Confederate president Jefferson Davis in *The Heart of Maryland* (1927), in which Charles Edward Bull played Lincoln. Ford was also a

Lieutenant in *Uncle Tom's Cabin* (1927), and an aide to General Phil Sheridan in D. W. Griffith's *Abraham Lincoln* (1930) with Walter Huston.

But most memorably of all, Ford played Sam Boone, a drunken juror who serves on one of Abe's trials in John Ford's *Young Mr. Lincoln* (1939). During jury selection, when Sam is called forth for questioning, he walks up to the bench and declares, "Guilty."

Lincoln (Henry Fonda) asks, "You drink liquor, Sam?"

"Yep."

"Cuss?"

He nods happily.

"Go to church regular?"

Sam shakes his head no.

"Enjoy hangins'?"

A shy smile and another nod in the affirmative.

"Got a job?"

No.

"Just like to loaf, huh?"

Sam nods again.

"Ever tell a lie?"

Yes.

"Well," Abe says, "you're just the kind of honest man we want on this jury."

The scene is sweetly comic and and expertly played, but it is a shame that even the most knowledgable film buffs today are far more familiar with this Francis Ford than with the director, writer, and leading man that he had been just a few years earlier. In fact, he played grizzled old coots for so long that it comes as something of a shock to realize that he was only seventy years old when he died in 1953. He wasn't one of the greatest Lincolns, but as an early mover and shaker in a fledgling motion picture industry, Francis Ford deserves to be placed in the highest echelon.

An artist's rendition of Benjamin Chapin as Lincoln as it appeared in the February 1, 1913, issue of *The Moving Picture World*. At this time, Chapin had not yet appeared on film as Lincoln but had made a career of playing the Great Emancipator on both vaudeville and legitimate theater stages.
Courtesy of Bison Archives/Marc Wanamaker

BENJAMIN CHAPIN

Benjamin Chapin may not have played Lincoln onscreen more than any other actor, but he certainly played more Lincolns than anyone. In his ambitious ten-part epic, *Son of Democracy* (released from 1914 through 1918), Chapin played the president as well as his father, Tom Lincoln, and his grandfather, Abraham Lincoln. His resemblance to those ancestors may have been minimal, but as a "true, living Lincoln," Chapin was nearly without peer. Many Lincoln impersonators have impressed the critics, but Chapin racked up some positive reviews from people who really knew what they were talking about.

During a stage performance in 1909 of Chapin's four-act play *Abraham Lincoln in the White House*, General O. O. Howard, a friend of Lincoln's, rose after the play and addressed the audience at Chapin's invitation. "I knew and loved Lincoln as my friend and commander," Howard said. "I saw Mr. Chapin's wonderful portrayal several years ago and was greatly pleased and deeply impressed by it. At that time I only had one criticism: the voice seemed to me different—to lack something of the Lincoln vigor and power. But Mr. Chapin's voice has developed with the years and tonight even the voice seems like that of my own Lincoln."[13]

On another occasion, General Frederick D. Grant, the son of former president Ulysses S. Grant, attended one of Chapin's performances. Stepping backstage to meet the actor, Grant said, "I have one criticism to make and that is your portrayal is not long enough."[14]

And no less a spectator than Mark Twain was dragged against his will to see Chapin's performance. Twain protested that he wasn't interested in seeing "some young 'buck' with fake costume and makeup" ruining "his own mental picture of Lincoln." But when the performance was over, Twain asked to be led backstage where he enthusiastically shook Chapin's hand. "I am very glad to meet you, Mr. President," he said. "You haven't changed much in all these years. You know, I think I know Lincoln better than before. I feel as though I spent an evening with him at the White House. Your Lincoln is a miracle."[15]

Benjamin Chapin had been obsessed with Lincoln since childhood. Born in Bristolville, Ohio, on August 9, 1874, he claimed to have had little formal education, basically teaching himself, as Lincoln did, by reading the Bible, Shakespeare, and of course, the writings of Lincoln himself. Chapin was already lecturing on the subject of the Great Emancipator before he was eighteen years old. By 1902 he was touring in vaudeville with a one-man show he called *Lincoln.* Four years later, he and his sister Lucille Ann Chapin, expanded it into a four-act play that toured under various titles: *Abraham Lincoln in the White House, Lincoln,* and *Honest Abe.* By this time, he was known all over the country as the most realistic and convincing Abraham Lincoln ever to set foot on the stage.

"As a matter of fact," Chapin once said, "I do not resemble him any more than hundreds of other men do. I am tall, but I am two inches below his height of six feet four. My frame is not as large as his. My hands are quite unlike his. My face is not like his except in general contour. Of course, if I had been a short fat man with a round face, it wouldn't have been possible. But I wasn't, and with the aid of makeup, I have been able to achieve a very good likeness. When I began I used a false beard, but as time went on, and I devoted myself entirely to the Lincoln work, I grew a beard of my own."[16]

In 1913 W. Stephen Bush wrote an editorial for *The Moving Picture World* suggesting that the time was right for a full-scale motion picture biography of a great historical figure. His choice was Abraham Lincoln. "The great difficulty in securing an accurate impersonation of Lincoln is obvious," Bush wrote. "There are, to begin with, certain physical characteristics. There is the question of facial expression, the task of reproducing the homely, rugged features, the eyes at once so sad, so open and so strong. The peculiarities of his walk, his postures while talking, or standing, or sitting in a chair, are fairly familiar to millions of our countrymen, who have given much time to a loving study of the subject."

With all these marks against bringing Lincoln to the screen, Bush suggested that there was only one person in the theater capable of the job: "What if there is in this country now living and now in his physical and artistic prime, a man whom Nature and Study have helped to give a most life-like representation of Lincoln? The evidence that Benjamin Chapin, the man referred to, may justly be called a true living copy of Lincoln is conclusive and irresistible. His claims to verisimilitude in portrayal, stood the severest test possible—the critical observation of men who knew and loved Lincoln and who would have been sure to resent even slight imperfections."[17]

There is no evidence to suggest that Chapin was inspired by Bush's editorial—although he must certainly have been flattered by it. But the fact remains that within months of its appearance in print, Chapin was hard at work bringing his remarkable portrait of Lincoln to the screen. It was not his plan to tell a brief story about Lincoln in a one-reel drama, such as those starring Ralph Ince or

Francis Ford; Chapin planned a massive and ambitious series of films that he originally called *The Cycle of Lincoln Plays*. The number of films in that cycle, and their length, fluctuated for a while as plans changed and ambitions grew. But the cycle eventually ran to ten episodes of two reels each. The first was produced in 1914, and the final one in 1918. By that time, Chapin had come to call the series *Son of Democracy*.

Chapin told a reporter, "Ever since the first motion picture was shown on a sheet I have felt that this was the way I could best bring my patron saint before the millions." Lincoln's life, he felt, "was a great adventure. Just think. Born in a hut in the woods, uneducated, ugly, awkward, unknown, he rose to the highest position in all the world. No melodrama could dare to take such liberties with human possibilities. No Diamond Dick or paper novel could equal Lincoln's romance. Horatio Alger's plays are tame compared to Lincoln's life. Therefore we couldn't help make the pictures entertaining. If they seem to educate as well we are happy."[18]

The Lincoln Cycle was released in 1917 and consisted of four films: *The Call to Arms* (about Lincoln's anguish over having to call up an army of volunteers), *My Mother (The Spirit Man)*, *My Father (The Physical Man)*, and *Myself (The Lincoln Man)*. *My Mother* and *My Father* survive today at the Library of Congress; the other two seem to be gone.

A year later, all ten episodes were released under the title *Son of Democracy*. This consisted of the four parts of *The Lincoln Cycle* plus *Native State* (also released as *Old Abe*), *Under the Stars* (also released as *Native State*), *Down the River*, *Tender Memories*, *A President's Answer*, and *The Slave Auction*, of which there is no synopsis available.

Another film, *Lincoln's Thanksgiving Story*, was never part of *Son of Democracy*, even though it has the same cast and crew and was produced at about the same time. No prints of the film are known to exist and little or nothing is known about its plot; only a tattered, virtually unwatchable fragment existed until recently at the UCLA

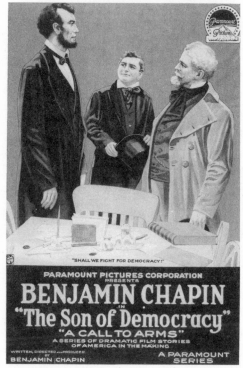

Film and Television Archive. But the last few surviving feet of what seems to be the last print of this film show that it takes place on a flatboat on the river and features scenes of a little black boy hiding in a barrel. *Down the River*, also apparently lost, is said to be about young Abe's trip down the river to try and reunite a little slave boy with his family. These clues suggest that these are simply two titles for the same film. One of the last title cards that it's possible to decipher reads, "How Abe struggles to keep his promise, but is unable to do it until, 31 years later, he freed them by the Emancipation Proclamation, is shown in one of Mr. Chapin's later pictures."

The Lincoln Cycle was never intended as a straight biography of Lincoln, from cradle to grave. Instead, Chapin set about using important moments in Lincoln's life as stepping off points for stories about his ancestry and childhood. The first chapter, *Old Abe* (later released as *Native State*) begins near the start of the Civil War. Senator Edwin Stanton has signed an order that would seize the property of "well-known" Southern sympathizers in Washington, D. C. A title card introduces the president: "President Lincoln, who determines to save the property of those Southerners who he believes can still be induced to support the union."

Lincoln looks over the list and is particularly concerned by the presence of one name. He says to Stanton, "Why, the first man on this list is the grandson of Daniel Boone! Please take his name off the list."

Stanton replies, "Too late. He is one of the worst. The orders are given."

We are then taken to "the Home of Edward Daniel Boone, veteran of the War of 1812," where an officer is saying to Boone's elderly wife, "Madame, as a Southern sympathizer, your property has been confiscated by the government."

"But my husband is blind," she replies.

Blind and mad as a hornet. Boone shouts, "May heaven send down vengeance upon Lincoln."

As it happens, the subject of his curse, along with son Tad

(dressed in a Union uniform), are out for a carriage ride and pass the Boone residence. Lincoln signals for the driver to stop and he approaches the elderly Boone. He explains, without introducing himself, that their grandfathers were friends together back in the wilderness of Kentucky. Lincoln then tells Boone a story of heroism in which the elder Abraham Lincoln's children get lost in the woods and are protected by Fawn, an Indian woman "who likes Whites." They are set upon by evil Indians who want to kill the children, but a last minute battle saves the day. Oddly, Daniel Boone doesn't figure very prominently in either the plot or the battle. Nevertheless when we get back to the present, Abe is telling Boone, "And our grandfathers were friends ever after."

Meanwhile, Lincoln has sent a note to Stanton, ordering that he stop seizing property. Boone's home is restored to him. The Lincoln-cursing old man says to Abe, "Sir, although I am blind I know that I'm in the presence of a great man. I wish our President were a man like you. I was cursing him as you came up."

Lincoln presses a document into his hand. "I have good news. This paper restores your property."

As Lincoln leaves, not having identified himself, Old Boone says, "God bless one of Nature's Noblemen, whatever his other name may be."

Nearly all of the episodes in *The Lincoln Cycle* similarly mixed past and present, and none of them was particularly concerned about the stringencies of history. In *Under the Stars*, as Kentucky is deciding whether to stay neutral or to join the Confederacy, Lincoln tells a story of how his grandfather was killed by Indians while "hewing a path toward civilization."

In *My Mother*, Lincoln recalls the influence of Nancy Hanks on his life, particulary how she urged him to stop fighting and taught him to end conflicts wisely and peacefully. In the film's most touching scenes, Nancy and Abe read to each other, and she talks about how proud she is that he has taught himself so well "with only charcoal and a shovel" to serve as pencil and paper.

When she is afflicted by "the milk sick," Abe is sent out to get wood. A neighborhood bully keeps knocking the wood from his hands, until Abe can't stand it anymore and beats him up. Nancy calls for Abe from her deathbed.

"My boy, you've been fighting again. Promise me to win your battles by love and service—not by fighting."

Abe says, "I won't fight again—I promise."

Nancy has just enough strength for one final prayer before she dies, "Oh God, make him honest, gentle and kind."

Although *The Lincoln Cycle* was not a serial in the *Perils of Pauline* sense of the term—each of its ten episodes was a self-contained story—there were details of plot and character that accumulated from one entry to the next. In *Tender Memories*, the president is criticized on all sides by office seekers who crowd the hallway outside his office in the White House. "He lacks courage," one says. Another adds, "He lacks everything." Lincoln arrives and invites them all in. "Well, then you'd better tell me the way to go." Of course, the mob can't agree on a course of action, since they all have their own points of view, so Abe tells them that his own course is "as straight as a turnpike road—UNION."

He goes to the front to visit the troops. As they walk through a snowy wood, he and Tad have a snowball fight (Tad, by the way, is never identified in any of the films. Chapin obviously assumed that every viewer had a keen enough grasp on the history of the country to know who he was—how times have changed.) A battle rages at the front and Abe steps right onto the battlefield. He helps to secure a cross with a handkerchief for a soldier who has just gone to "winter quarters."

This gesture makes Abe recall his mother's death when he, too, put up a rude cross. Because there was no minister in the area, Nancy never had a proper funeral, so Abe wrote to Pastor Elkins, a friend of Nancy's, and asked him to come pray over his mother's grave.

In the meantime, the boy Abe is still having trouble with the bully, Huck Carter, which makes it doubly hard to keep his promise to Nancy that he would never fight again. When Pastor Elkins arrives for the funeral, he finds Abe and Huck fighting; Abe accidentally punches Huck in the stomach.

"Your actions are a disgrace," Elkins says. "I was deceived by your letter."

Later, however, Elkins finds Abe lying across his mother's grave, crying, "Forgive me mother—I couldn't help it." Elkins meets Abe at his home and says, "I came to hold that service, and I will."

As the funeral goes on, Abe weeps beneath a tree. In a flawless double exposure, his mother appears and his head remains in her lap. Then she fades away again. A title tells us, "That service was in 1818. One hundred years later, in 1918—" there is a picture of the grave as it was at the time the film was made. Nancy Hanks's place is now marked with a large granite headstone. The film ends with a title, "Men are only boys grown tall. Hearts don't change much after all."

This plot bears directly on that of *The President's Answer*. The son of Reverend Elkins has chosen to fight for the South. He is arrested as a spy and sentenced to death. Mr. and Mrs. Elkins come to Washington to plead for their son's life. There in his office, Lincoln shows them the copy of John Bunyan's *Pilgrim's Progress* that Elkins had given Nancy many years earlier. It was one of her treasured keepsakes and one of Abe's favorite books. Abe reminds the reverend of the time when Elkins preached at Nancy's funeral—and when he almost gave up on Abe because of the boy's tendency to fight.

While Lincoln considers what to do about their son, an officer tries to convince him to support the death sentence: "Mr. President, this case is being used as an example of discipline. If you overrule this verdict, you encourage prisoners to mutiny."

Abe is deep in thought as the Elkinses leave weeping. Then he hands a note to an aide, saying, "I think you can overtake them." The note reads: "I suspend sentence of David Elkins Jr. until further orders from me and parole him in custody of his parents. A. Lincoln." Before the aide leaves the room, Abe says, "And tell Elkins his kind deeds are like chickens—they come home to roost."

The chapters of *The Lincoln Cycle* were met with critical acclaim everywhere they played. A critic for *The New York Times* wrote, "Patrons of the Strand [Theater] should be condemned to seeing trashy modern photoplays all the rest of their days if they do not flock to see *The Lincoln Cycle* on exhibition there this week. Here is a group of pictures based on the life of one of the great characters of all history, reproduced with dignity and a painstaking attempt at verisimilitude."[19]

The films were also hugely popular with the public; nearly everyone who saw them marveled at Chapin's almost total personification of the man himself. "Chapin's Lincoln is almost uncanny to behold," wrote one reviewer. "And yet, he does not picture the President with sobs alone. He has given to him all of the general humor that belongs to him in his own life. That sadly whimsical smile plays about Chapin's features as it did on Lincoln's face. The long, gaunt body, the beautiful, ugly features stand out in life from the pages of history. And young America and old America can behold its hero once more."[20]

Sadly, Benjamin Chapin had no time to enjoy the success of his dream project. On June 2, 1918, he died of tuberculosis at the Loomis Sanitarium in Liberty, New York. One obituary claimed that his "illness assumed its serious phase on Lincoln's birthday, when he ceased all activities and was sent to the sanitarium where he died. [*Son of Democracy*] required five years of unremitting study and toil to complete, and though he frequently suffered severely from the malady that was slowly sapping his vitality, he never ceased his labors until the final story was picturized and released on the anniversary of Lincoln's birthday."[21]

In his last months, Chapin received an honorary Doctorate of Literature from the Lincoln Memorial University at Harrowgate, Tennessee. He also took enormous pride in a request from O. H.

Frank McGlynn Sr. as
Lincoln in the mid-
thirties.
Courtesy of the author

Oldroyd of Washington, D. C. Oldroyd owned the house Lincoln died in, across from Ford's Theater and maintained a large collection of material related to Lincoln. After seeing *The Lincoln Cycle* in its Washington engagement, Oldroyd asked Chapin for a portrait to add to the Oldroyd Lincoln Memorial Collection. An item in *The Moving Picture World* stated, "Mr. Chapin felt so pleased with the request that he immediately arranged for a special sitting at his studio, and the portrait has been sent to Mr. Oldroyd by special messenger with a note explaining, 'the Lincoln Man's' gratification at being able to find a place in the Oldroyd Lincoln collection."[22]

FRANK MCGLYNN SR.

It is open to debate whether Frank McGlynn Sr. was the best or most effective Lincoln on film, but he was almost certainly the most prolific. He played the role repeatedly between 1915, when he starred in the Edison film *The Life of Abraham Lincoln*, and 1939, when his Lincoln met Juarez and Empress Carlotta in *The Mad*

Frank McGlynn Sr. as Lincoln joins in a song around the campfire
in this very early sound experiment, *Abraham Lincoln* (1924),
a DeForest Phonofilm.
Courtesy of the Academy of Motion Picture Arts and Sciences

Empress. And in the middle of it all, he made an enormous impact
on Broadway audiences with his powerful, yet understated, performance in the title role of John Drinkwater's 1919 play *Abraham
Lincoln.*

Frank McGlynn Sr. was born in San Francisco in 1867. His first
ambition was the law, but since, as he said, he was only interested
in studying law and not practicing it, he soon realized that it would
be difficult to make a living. McGlynn had early thoughts of being
an actor, and after giving the law only two years, he found roles in
local productions, such as George Lederer's comic opera *The Gold
Bug* and Charles Frohman's *Under the Red Robe.* He then spent
three years in stock companies playing the Proctor, then the Keith
theatrical circuits. He found playing stock to be enormous fun and
highly educational; he was able to play roles of every description
from villains to lovers—everything, he said, "but juveniles."

McGlynn joined the Edison company in 1909, working as both

an actor and director, but left in 1913 to follow the Giants and the Red Sox on their four month long 'round-the-world tour. He and pioneer cameraman Victor Miller filmed all the games and invented entertaining bits of business to insert in the resulting movies. McGlynn himself played a rabid "baseball bug" who could frequently be seen going completely berserk for his favorite team. John McGraw, "the little Napoleon of baseball," and his staff called the actor "Happy" McGlynn, a name that is a little unsettling to movie watchers who are only familiar with McGlynn's serenely dignified character roles and Lincoln portrayals of the thirties.

McGlynn returned to the Edison Company in 1914, and before long, he found himself in Lincoln makeup for the first—but far from the last—time. He portrayed the president in a two-reel biography, *The Life of Lincoln*. The film, which is lost today, was generally admired in 1915, but the consensus was that it tried to shove far too much of Lincoln's life into far too little footage.

However, good or bad, McGlynn must have found something compelling about the role. Soon Abraham Lincoln would cease being simply a part that McGlynn played; it would be a true avocation—perhaps even an obsession.

When John Drinkwater's surprise hit *Abraham Lincoln* was imported from England to the Broadway stage, McGlynn won the title role. It is easy to imagine how this theatrical run gave birth to McGlynn's enthusiasm for Lincoln. The play was incredibly successful, and so was McGlynn's performance. Despite the fact that he had already been acting steadily for well over two decades, he was treated like a newcomer, an overnight success. To critic Alexander Woolcott, McGlynn's very unfamiliarity was the key to his success in the role:

When you sit down before Mr. Drinkwater's tragedy at the Cort [Theater], your first impression of the Lincoln who stalks into the neat, dustless Springfield parlor takes form in words such as these: 'What a close resemblance! What a fortunate choice! How like he is!' Then as the play advances and its curious spell takes hold of you, you no longer think how like McGlynn is to Lincoln. You forget McGlynn entirely and feel rather that this is Lincoln. By the great fifth scene, you have the complete illusion that you are eavesdropping on history. You forget the theater and feel that time has turned backward to let you peep through the window into a farmhouse near Appomattox and see Meade bring in the news, Lincoln give his final injunction to Grant, and Lee offer up his sword in surrender.

Mr. McGlynn's task is all the easier because you do not remember him in other roles. No ghosts of other characterizations throng the Cort stage to distract your attention and dispel the illusion. And whereas the illusion of life is not everything in the theater—is, indeed, not much at all when compared with the faculty for firing the imagination or kindling the emotion—it is quintessential and priceless in such an enterprise as a historical play written around a towering, familiar, canonized, epic figure in our national life.[23]

In 1924 McGlynn became what was almost certainly the first Lincoln in a sound film. Little is known about the exact nature of this all-talking *Abraham Lincoln*, except that it was directed by J. Searle Dawley for the DeForest Phonofilm Company. A few existing stills show Lincoln sitting by a campfire with several Union soldiers who appear to be singing—naturally enough for a sound picture. Another still shows actress Una Merkel, who would play Ann Rutledge six years later in D. W. Griffith's *Abraham Lincoln* starring Walter Huston

By coincidence, the same year that Griffith's film was released, McGlynn appeared in a two-reel adaption of the Drinkwater play that first put him on the map. *Abraham Lincoln* (1930) was released by P. C. Pictures.

From here on out, McGlynn never starred as Lincoln again, with one exception. Rather, his Lincolns appeared at pivotal moments in the plot or simply to get things rolling. At the beginning of Cecil B.

DeMille's *The Plainsman* (1936), Lincoln discusses his plans for settling the West now that the Civil War is over. Speculators in the room who want to traffic in weapons and other contraband, and who see the West as a wide-open market, know they're going to be stymied by Lincoln's scrupulous sense of honor and integrity. Luckily for them, Mrs. Lincoln interrupts the talk with the portentous statement, "Dear, we're going to be late for the theater" (accompanied on the soundtrack with an ominous booming of deep brass). In no time, the speculators are free to profiteer to their hearts' content.

That same year, McGlynn's Lincoln appears in a more comfortable role in *The Littlest Rebel* (1936)—that of the Great Pardoner. Shirley Temple plays Virgie, a little Southern girl whose father (John Boles) has been captured in a Union uniform and sentenced to hang. She and her caretaker Uncle Billy (Bill "Bojangles" Robinson) go to see Lincoln to try to get a pardon for her father. Lincoln invites them both in to his office, peels an apple, and shares it with Virgie as she tells her story. She starts to cry when telling him about her mother's death, and Lincoln pulls her onto his knee and assures her that her father will be spared.

McGlynn isn't always a completely satisfying Lincoln. His voice is too cultured, and he employs an odd tilt to his head that makes him seem whimsical instead of melancholy. But he is quite effective in *The Littlest Rebel*; it's one of his most understated performances. McGlynn plays with Shirley Temple with an easy charm and talks to her with the grave interest of a man who knows how to interact with children. The head tilt is still there, but McGlynn's Lincoln has a wry attitude that serves the scene well and complements Shirley Temple's performance beautifully.

McGlynn's contribution to *Hearts in Bondage* (1936), the story of the ironclad boats the *Monitor* and the *Merrimac*, directed by actor Lew Ayres, is minimal. But there is a lovely scene at the end when the two leads (Mae Clarke and James Dunn) encounter Lincoln walking alone on the banks of the Potomac. The final image of

Wouldn't you pardon a condemned man if she asked you to? Frank
McGlynn Sr. as Lincoln and Shirley Temple as
The Littlest Rebel (1935).
Courtesy of 20th Century-Fox

Lincoln strolling away, deep in thought, perfectly captures the
inherent sadness and loneliness of the man; in moments like these,
McGlynn really does capture Lincoln's essence.

Perhaps best of all is his world-weary performance in the opening scenes of John Ford's *Prisoner of Shark Island* (1936). The film is
the story of Dr. Samuel Mudd (Warner Baxter), the physician who
was unlucky enough to be the man John Wilkes Booth came to see
to set his broken leg. Mudd, not knowing who Booth was or what he
had just done, helped the injured man and sent him on his way. He
was subsequently arrested and convicted of being a part of the conspiracy to assassinate Lincoln; he was sentenced to life on Devil's
Island for his "crimes" and only pardoned after an act of heroism.

Lincoln, of course, figures only in the beginning of the film. The
war has just ended, and a jubilant crowd gathers outside the White
House, hoping to hear some victorious words from the president.

Frank McGlynn Sr. as Lincoln in *Hearts in Bondage* (1936).
Courtesy of Republic Pictures

With a tired smile, he calls for forgiveness and charity toward the South. Then, claiming it as "contraband of war," he asks the band to play one of his favorite tunes: "Dixie."

The next scene is at a scrupulously recreated Ford's Theater. John Ford stages the assassination with delicacy: we hear a shot and, from behind, see Lincoln's hand drop to the side of his chair. Then Ford moves in for a deifying closeup of the president's peaceful face as the screen is covered in a texture that makes the image look like a painted portrait.

Of McGlynn's brief appearance in *Prisoner of Shark Island*, *Variety*'s "Abel." wrote, "Frank McGlynn Sr. in his Abraham Lincoln impersonation is, as ever, realistic in dignified portrayal and uncanny resemblance to the martyred liberator."[24]

There is kindness, weariness, pain, and relief in McGlynn's brief performance; it is so powerful and effective that it becomes even more puzzling how he could so often miss the mark in other films. His cameos aren't nearly so evocative in *Western Gold* (1937), *Wells*

A Lincoln portrait. Frank McGlynn Sr., one of the most prolific of all Lincoln impersonators in the movies. Here, he is made up for his role in Lew Ayres's *Hearts in Bondage* (1936).
Courtesy of Republic Pictures

James Dunn and Mae Clark are just about to meet Abe Lincoln (Frank McGlynn Sr.) strolling along the banks of the Potomac in *Hearts in Bondage* (1936).
Courtesy of Republic Pictures

Fargo (1937), or *The Lone Ranger*, a fifteen-part serial from 1937 that was turned into the feature film *Hi-Yo Silver!* in 1941.

But McGlynn had one more shot at Lincoln up his sleeve. A two-reel Warner Brothers Technicolor production, *Lincoln in the White House* (1939), was one of a series of historical and patriotic short subjects that the studio produced in the late thirties and early forties. The first of these was an Academy Award winner called *Sons of Liberty* (1939), starring Claude Rains. Other subjects included Buffalo Bill Cody, Clara Barton, Patrick Henry, Andrew Jackson, and Francis Scott Key.

Lincoln in the White House is a whirlwind recounting of events during Lincoln's presidency, from the beginning of the Civil War up to his delivery of the Gettysburg Address. Here McGlynn's Lincoln has a warm relationship with his young son Tad (played by former *Our Gang* member Dickie Moore) and a rather contentious one with Mary. Near the beginning of the film she calls him "good for nothing," and later when he and Tad are wrestling and having fun, she scolds them to stop. Lincoln says to her, rather sadly, "Don't deny me a little laughter."

The film ties Tad into two significant events, for reasons that have more to do with dramatic symmetry than historical fidelity. First, when Mrs. Scott comes to beg for the life of her son William—the sentry who falls asleep in film after film after film— Stanton urges Lincoln not to pardon him. But when the president catches sight of Tad, in the Union uniform he loves to wear, sleeping just outside Lincoln's office door, his heart melts; he can no more have someone else's son shot for this than he could shoot his own son.

Just before Lincoln leaves for Gettysburg, Tad suddenly becomes very ill. The doctors fear for his life and Mary begs Abe not to leave them. However, duty calls and he leaves, although bent with worry. On the train to Gettysburg, in legendary fashion, he writes out his little speech on the back of an envelope. He'll give the speech, but his heart isn't in it because of his concern for Tad.

Luckily, a telegram from Mary is delivered to him on the platform at the Gettysburg National Cemetery. It reads, "Tad much improved." And so it is with a happy heart that Lincoln can stand up and declare, "Four score and seven years ago . . . "

Though *Lincoln in the White House* had paint-by-numbers Lincoln, without much drama or vigor, *Variety*'s critic "Abel." thought quite highly of McGlynn and the film:

> Frank McGlynn Sr., a past master in Lincolniana, deftly interprets the human Lincoln. . . . even though beset by civil strife and cabinet bickering. Lincoln's humanitarianism, with his treatment of a Union private's court martial fate, and his request for "Dixie" from a blue-coat band, is to the scripting credit of Charles L. Tedford as well as William McGann's punchy direction.
>
> The sock climax, of course, is McGlynn's masterful reading of the immortal Gettysburg address. If visual education ever assumes the wide proportions its advocates have been urging, this excerpt alone is surefire for every classroom. It's an inspired lesson in elocution and proper public address, plus the literary value of one of the gems in American historic literature.
>
> A corking cast, canny pacing, and ultra production recreates a cross-section of Lincolniana that's surefire in American film theatres and certain to command respect and attention before any English-speaking audience. The blase Music Hall audience salvoed this film like it was the 4th of July. It's a natural, of course, now amidst the world strife between democratic and demagogic advocates, but at all times it is sound entertainment and forthright Americanism."[25]

RAYMOND MASSEY

In an episode of *The Dick Van Dyke Show*, Rob (Dick Van Dyke) and Laura (Mary Tyler Moore) receive a bewildering inheritance from Rob's eccentric grandfather. Among the seemingly useless items is a photograph of a man holding a baby. Only when they

One of the screen's most famous Lincolns, here Raymond
Massey plays the father of the man who killed Lincoln. He is
Junius Brutus Booth in *Prince of Players* (1955).
Courtesy of 20th Century-Fox

remove the frame do they discover (*a*) that it's a genuine Mathew
Brady photograph and (*b*) that there's another figure in the picture—
a tall, gaunt man with a beard and a stovepipe hat. Rob is almost
speechless. "Honey, do you know who this is?" he asks in awe. "It's
the *real* Raymond Massey!"

If Frank McGlynn was the all-purpose movie Lincoln of the thirties, Raymond Massey was the actor's Lincoln, the one whose brilliant performance in Sherwood's *Abe Lincoln in Illinois*—on stage,
screen, *and* television—set the standard for interpreting Lincoln's
complex character. Massey was, in a sense, born to play Lincoln; he
came with a ready-made Lincoln face and figure. More important,
he understood the character both of the president and the awkward
rail-splitter.

Although Raymond Massey's Lincoln spoke with a convincing
and evocative midwestern drawl, the actor himself was born in
Toronto in 1896. He went to England as a teenager and was educated at Oxford, making his stage debut in London. By 1929 he was

appearing in films and soon showed up in some genuine classics: *The Old Dark House* (1932), *The Scarlet Pimpernel* (1935), *The Prisoner of Zenda* (1937), and *Drums* (1938). But it was his brilliant, deceptively simple performance as Lincoln in Robert E. Sherwood's play that gave Massey a permanent place in the public's affection.

Massey played Lincoln in a wide variety of settings. The very first time he played Lincoln—or, at least, a *kind* of Lincoln—was during the troubled production of *The Hurricane* (1937), a John Ford disaster film starring Dorothy Lamour and Jon Hall. As the production stretched out to four and a half months, with no end in sight, Ford concocted a gag for studio boss Samuel Goldwyn. Ford knew that Robert E. Sherwood was even then completing his play about Lincoln, which was to star Massey on Broadway, so he filmed Massey, shirtless, wearing only a sarong and a stovepipe hat. Massey struggled out of the surf, staggered toward the camera, and intoned:

> "Four score and seven years ago, we started *Hurricane*.
> For God almighty's sake, Sam, let me go home!"

Unfortunately, Goldwyn had already decided to do massive reshooting on the picture, scrapping an enormous amount of work that had been done. Wearily, Ford decided that he had better not show his little joke to Goldwyn after all.

Massey, of course, went on to enormous acclaim for his portrayal of Lincoln in Sherwood's play and in the subsequent film based upon it. But the next time he played Lincoln, it was on the new medium of television. On the November 19, 1949, episode of *Perry Como's Chesterfield Supper Club*, the anniversary of the Gettysburg Address was celebrated with a brief sketch. Perry Como talks with his "daughter" about the importance of the address, and she dreams that she meets Lincoln, who explains how the speech came about and then recites it for her. The segment was, according to *Variety*, "well done."[26]

The following year, Massey was on TV again, doing what one

trade paper called "a serious bit" on the *Ken Murray Show* of February 8, 1950. In 1956, only a year after he had played Junius Brutus Booth, the father of John Wilkes Booth, in *The Prince of Players* (1955), Massey was cast as Lincoln once again in what would be one of the most ambitious television productions of the year: *The Day Lincoln Was Shot* (February 11, 1956). Based on Jim Bishop's book, which dissected the events of April 14, 1865, the television production—broadcast in color—was a somber, rather slow, but altogether fascinating portrait of Lincoln's last day. In addition to Massey's Lincoln, the cast included Lillian Gish—who had watched Joseph Henabery's Lincoln die in D. W. Griffith's *The Birth of a Nation* in 1915—as Mary Todd Lincoln and a young Jack Lemmon as John Wilkes Booth. Charles Laughton served as host and narrator, seated behind a podium, reading from a script, and looking more than faintly uncomfortable.

The program began with a touch of surrealism: Lincoln, in his nightshirt, walks down a strange curtained hallway. The moaning sounds of grief fill the soundtrack. He enters a room and sees a coffin surrounded by weeping people, and guarded by a soldier. With dread, Lincoln asks, "Who is dead in the White House?" The soldier answers, "The president. He was killed by an assassin." With the sound of a woman's screams, the credits begin.

The Day Lincoln Was Shot is scrupulously attentive to historical detail, using actual dialogue, when known, and cutting from character to character to give the viewer a sense of how events all over Washington were leading toward that fateful moment in Ford's Theater.

But no matter how historically accurate writers Terry and Denis Sanders and Jean Holloway tried to be, they were still compelled to decide how each of the characters would be presented. Lillian Gish's Mary is not a harridan like Ruth Gordon's in *Abe Lincoln in Illinois*, nor a tortured victim of migraines like Mary Tyler Moore's in *Gore Vidal's Lincoln*. Instead, she is sweet-natured and kind, genuinely distressed when Lincoln tells her about his disturbing dream of death, and truly heartbroken at his deathbed: "Why didn't they kill me instead of my precious husband?"

Mary's relationship to Abe is purely loving, which possibly has more truth to it than some of the more negative portrayals of Mary in film. At least it allows for that sweet, apparently true moment in the Ford's Theater box. Abe takes Mary's hand, and she wonders what others will think if they see the First Couple acting like young people in love. Abe replies, "They won't think a thing about it."

Jack Lemmon's John Wilkes Booth is, like most Booths in film, an arrogant dandy. Lemmon stresses his actorish conceit by making sure that Booth never passes a mirror without taking a pleased look at himself. (In one early shot, he also sees a microphone in the mirror, but that's live television.) This Booth is tortured by what he considers his destiny—and by the fact that his hated enemy will never know who struck him or why: "It galls me," Booth says during one of his solitary rants, "to think that you will die by my hand and not know why I did it. How can you be unaware of me?"

Booth is at Ford's Theater in the afternoon watching a rehearsal of *Our American Cousin*. When the director is trying to get an actor to hold after a big laugh line—"you sockdologizing old man trap!"—Booth has an idea. He realizes that the laugh will cover his shot; he plans the assassination as though it were a theatrical presentation—which, of course, it was. As he is leaving a bar across the street from Ford's Theater, a drunken man says to Booth, "You'll never be the actor your father was." Booth replies, smiling, "When I leave the stage, I'll be the most famous man in America."

Raymond Massey's Lincoln in *The Day Lincoln Was Shot* is neither as compelling nor as meaningful as his Lincoln of *Abe Lincoln in Illinois*, but that has more to do with the differences in script and direction than in any decline in Massey's powers. *The Day Lincoln Was Shot* aspires to be as close as possible to a documentary, whereas *Abe Lincoln in Illinois* is a work of poetry. That poetry is more likely than fact to capture the hearts of both audience and performer isn't surprising.

Junius Brutus Booth (Raymond Massey) passes his crown—and his
career—to his son Edwin (Richard Burton) in *Prince of Players*
(1955). Edwin would go on to become the most famous actor of his
generation. His brother, John Wilkes Booth, would also find lasting
fame on the stage of Ford's Theater.
Courtesy of 20th Century-Fox

But even with this major production, Raymond Massey was not
quite clear of Lincoln. In 1957 he toured the country with Norman
Corwin's play *The Rivalry*, the story of the Lincoln-Douglas debates.
Massey's costars were Martin Gabel as Stephen A. Douglas and
Agnes Moorehead as Douglas's wife. None of them was happy with
the production. Massey considered the script, "a flat documentary
without development and progression. Corwin [who was also direct-
ing] had a reverence for the authentic text of the debates, which
blinded him to the fact that most of the thirty hours which the two
candidates spent discussing the rights of man were just politics and,
as such, a bore in the theater." *The Rivalry* was later produced on
television as a *Hallmark Hall of Fame* production starring Arthur Hill
as Lincoln, Charles Durning as Douglas, and Hope Lange as Adele
Douglas.

Raymond Massey as a
pre-White House
Lincoln in *How the
West Was Won* (1962).
*Courtesy of Metro-
Goldwyn-Mayer*

On April 1, 1961, Massey wore the stovepipe hat again in "Not in Vain," a half hour episode of the *American Heritage* series. "Not in Vain" is the story behind the Gettysburg Address, which, according to teleplay writer Richard Goldhurst, is not something that Lincoln wanted to do. He is convinced to deliver the speech only after an impassioned plea of a mother whose son died in the battle there. Consequently, Lincoln decides to write the address with a more humanistic slant. Not exactly a plot ripped from the pages of history.

"Raymond Massey," wrote a *Variety* critic, "playing Lincoln for the umpteenth time, brought an appropriate solemnity and simplicity to the role and recited the Gettysburg Address without making it a cliche. Others in the cast played competently, but the whole stanza was burdened by self-consciousness as it reenacted the history of a great event."[27]

Raymond Massey's final screen appearance as Abraham Lincoln was in the Cinerama epic *How the West Was Won* (1963). It is a cameo in a brief sequence that introduces the film's middle section on the Civil War. Coming as it does after Massey has portrayed Lincoln in every theatrical medium for nearly thirty years, this poignant moment serves as a kind of benediction. Massey's Lincoln says

Raymond Massey in his brief cameo as Lincoln in the Cinerama epic
How the West Was Won (1962). Ironically, the music that accompanies
this scene is adapted from Alfred Newman's score for John Ford's *Young
Mr. Lincoln* (1939), the film that had once gone head-to-head at the box
office with Massey's *Abe Lincoln in Illinois* (1940).
Courtesy of Metro-Goldwyn-Mayer

nothing in the scene and does little—he is pure image, the perfect
fusion of actor and character.

"All actors who have played Mr. Lincoln have found it a gluti-
nous role," Massey wrote, "liable to stick to a player offstage. Some
actors have revelled in this. I have always maintained that my efforts
as an actor belong exclusively to the theater, and do not carry over
into my private life."[28]

In this respect Massey was not like Benjamin Chapin, Frank
McGlynn, or George Billings, his illustrious predecessors who fell
so completely under Abe Lincoln's powerful sway. Nevertheless, he
symbolized the spirit of the Great Emancipator for audiences of his
own era, as those prior actors did for theirs. Through them we gain
access to Lincoln himself; they are the spirit made flesh, and if some

of them took in more of that spirit than their own personalities could withstand, that merely testifies to the enormous power and strength that survives still of the man whom they all impersonated.

NOTES

1. *The Moving Picture World,* July 10, 1915, p. 290.
2. *The Moving Picture World,* February 28, 1914, p. 1102.
3. Ibid.
4. Interview with Louella Parsons, *New York Telegraph,* January 29, 1922.
5. *The Moving Picture World,* July 11, 1914, p. 285.
6. Interview with Louella Parsons, *New York Telegraph,* January 29, 1922.
7. *The Moving Picture World,* June 28, 1913, p. 1388.
8. *The Moving Picture World,* August 20, 1908, p. 145.
9. *The Moving Picture World,* January 3, 1914, p. 56.
10. *The Moving Picture World,* July 11, 1914, p. 285.
11. Peter Bogdanovich, *John Ford* (University of California Press, 1968), p. 40.
12. *Variety,* March 5, 1915.
13. *The Moving Picture World,* February 1, 1913, p. 443.
14. *The Moving Picture World,* August 7, 1915, p. 1022.
15. Ibid.
16. *New York Sun,* May 25, 1917.
17. *The Moving Picture World,* February 1, 1913, p. 443.
18. *The Moving Picture World,* July 10, 1915, p. 290.
19. *New York Times,* May 28, 1917, p. 11.
20. *The Moving Picture World,* August 7, 1915, p. 1022.
21. *The Moving Picture World,* June 22, 1918, p. 699.
22. *The Moving Picture World,* September 15, 1917, p. 1675.
23. *New York Times,* March 14, 1920.
24. *Variety,* February 19, 1936.
25. *Variety,* January 18, 1939.
26. *Variety,* November 23, 1949.
27. *Variety,* April 5, 1961.
28. Raymond Massey, *A Hundred Different Lives* (Little, Brown and Company, 1979), p. 246.

Chapter Seven
Griffith's Lincoln
The Birth of a Nation and Abraham Lincoln

TO MANY, the high and low points in D. W. Griffith's career can be marked by two films that cover roughly the same period in history: his groundbreaking epic, *The Birth of a Nation* (1915), and his first sound film, *Abraham Lincoln* (1930). *The Birth of a Nation* is one of the greatest, most influential—and most controversial— movies ever made, a breathtaking saga of the Civil War. *Abraham Lincoln* was Griffith's first sound film—he made only two—and though the film has its admirers, it succeeds as neither biography (too trite) nor drama (too stilted and unimaginative).

The Birth of a Nation was composed both of massive and masterfully directed battle scenes, and keenly observed moments of intimate humanity. The film also detailed the founding and growth of the Ku Klux Klan in the years of Reconstruction after the war, and Griffith's glorification of the Klan—and vilification of most of his black characters—has made *The Birth of a Nation* as reviled as it is admired.

For the rest of his life, Griffith remained puzzled about the

Lincoln (Joseph Henabery) has a tense moment with Austin Stoneman (Ralph Lewis), a "Master of Congress" who wants to "put the White South under the heels of the Black South." *Birth of a Nation* (1915). *Courtesy of Bison Archives/Marc Wanamaker*

negative reaction to *The Birth of a Nation*; the film inspired riots, boycotts, and angry editorials from those who believed that the film misused history to stage a savage attack on modern-day blacks. The son of a former Confederate colonel, David Wark Griffith was born in 1875 in a Kentucky that was still permeated with the ideas, beliefs, and prejudices that had caused the war in the first place. In an autobiographical article, Griffith recalled one of his earliest childhood memories: an "old Negro, once [a] slave" who now worked for Colonel Griffith, gave one of young David's brothers a close-cropped haircut. "When father saw this he pretended to be enraged; he went into the house, donned his old uniform, buckled on his sword and pistols, and had the Negro summoned.

"Then, drawing his sword, he went through the technical cuts and thrusts and slashes, threatening the darkey all the time with being cut into mincemeat.

"The old Uncle was scared pale, and I took it seriously myself until a wink and a smile from my father enlightened me."[1] That

Griffith, decades after the fact, still found only amusement in the old man's genuine terror is the real point of this ghastly story; it is not, therefore, surprising that he continued to believe that his portrayal of blacks in *The Birth of a Nation* was fair, and even sympathetic. He genuinely felt that he was telling the truth about the Civil War, based on the stories told to him by his father and other veterans to whom the war was still a fresh, often angry, memory. Apparently, he just as genuinely believed that he had treated the racial themes in *The Birth of a Nation* with impartiality, carefully balancing his portrayal of evil blacks (such as Walter Long's would-be rapist Gus) with good, faithful "Negroes" who happily served their white masters.

This unfortunate—though inescapable—element of *The Birth of a Nation*, however, should not blind us to its incredible power as a motion picture experience, or to its landmark status as the film that literally changed the course of movie making forever. Directed with power and imagination, it contains scenes of such stunning authenticity that it has often been compared to the Civil War photographs of Mathew Brady. Whatever the biases of its director, *The Birth of a Nation* remains among the most accurate and convincing portraits of the Civil War ever put on film.

For such a rabid Southerner, Griffith had enormous respect for Abraham Lincoln, who, he believed, had a plan for peacefully reuniting the North and South without the bitterness and cruelty that defined the actual Reconstruction. Lincoln was to figure in *The Birth of a Nation* in several scenes, including his signing of the Emancipation Proclamation and—like most movie Lincolns—his pardoning of a condemned man. He was also assassinated in a meticulously recreated Ford's Theater—albeit one that was open to the sun for purposes of lighting.

Griffith had no luck finding the right Lincoln for his film until a struggling actor, Joseph Henabery, asked for an audition. He said to Frank Woods, Griffith's head of production, "Mr. Woods, I've seen some people going around here in Lincoln make-up. . . . I think I

Lincoln (Joseph Henabery) signs the Emancipation Proclamation in Griffith's *The Birth of a Nation* (1915). Note the boards under his feet, placed there to raise his knees and give the medium-sized actor the illusion of height.
Courtesy of Bison Archives/Marc Wanamaker

can put on a better make-up than any I've seen here. . . . "[2] When Woods agreed to let Henabery meet Griffith, the actor set to work designing his makeup. Because he bore virtually no resemblance to Lincoln, he had to use a false nose, a fake beard and a wig. Though Henabery was not one of the cinema's great Lincoln look-alikes, the result impressed Griffith.

Griffith was even more impressed by Henabery's knowledge. In his first scene, Henabery sat down in a chair. "By this time," he told film historian Kevin Brownlow, "I was full of the Lincoln story. I had read many books about him, and I knew his physical characteristics, his habits and everything else. And I sat in the chair on my tailbone, sort of hunchbacked. Griffith looked at me with a frown.

"'Don't sit like that,' he said."

Henabery explained that he had studied Lincoln's physical characteristics and started quoting chapter and verse, supporting his view that this was the way Lincoln sat in a chair. Griffith was impressed and asked for two boards to put under Henabery's feet to draw his knees higher and create an illusion of greater height. Henabery then mentioned that Lincoln wore glasses when reading and, to the director's delight, had a pair of old-fashioned spectacles in his pocket. "Use them," Griffith said.

Henabery recalled, "So when the paper was put down I made it part of my business to fish around for my glasses, to take my time putting them on, and then to sign the paper. Well, now [Griffith's] happy. He realizes that I have studied the character, and that I know something about the period. When it came to the Ford's Theater scenes, he'd tell me what he was going to do in the long shots, and I'd tell him what I'd read that Lincoln would be doing."[3]

Henabery went on, by his own estimation, to play thirteen bit parts in *The Birth of a Nation*, including a member of a gang of renegade blacks being chased by white vigilantes, as well as one of the vigilantes. "I was ... chasing myself through the whole sequence."

Joseph Henabery's Lincoln in *The Birth of a Nation* captures some of the spirit of the man, even though the actor's resemblance leaves something to be desired. Unfortunately, Griffith, like so many of his peers during that era, had such esteem for Lincoln that the portrayal is more waxwork than human. Griffith meticulously recreated scenes based on period drawings, paintings, and photographs, but in the Lincoln scenes at least, those scenes rarely take on lives of their own. They remain tableaux—strikingly composed and incredibly authentic tableaux, but tableaux nonetheless.

Fifteen years later, Griffith returned to the character of Abraham Lincoln, having decided to make, as his first sound feature, a full-scale biography of the Great Emancipator. Unfortunately, his continued awe for the subject rendered this full-length Lincoln even more of a mannequin than the Lincoln of *The Birth of a Nation*.

Griffith originally wanted Carl Sandburg to write the script for *Abraham Lincoln,* but the offer was withdrawn when Sandburg wanted $30,000 for the job. Griffith then turned to poet Stephen Vincent Benet, who apparently came in with a friendlier bid.

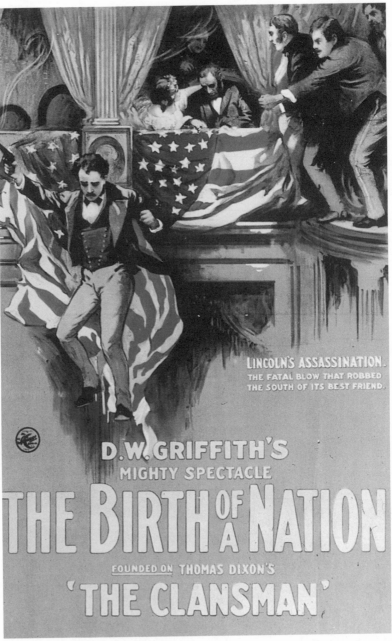

LINCOLN'S ASSASSINATION.
THE FATAL BLOW THAT ROBBED
THE SOUTH OF ITS BEST FRIEND.

D.W. GRIFFITH'S
MIGHTY SPECTACLE

THE BIRTH OF A NATION

FOUNDED ON THOMAS DIXON'S

'THE CLANSMAN'

John Wilkes Booth (Raoul Walsh, soon to be a major Hollywood director) leaps from the presidential box at Ford's Theater after shooting Lincoln (Joseph Henabery) in this poster from *The Birth of a Nation* (1915).
Courtesy of Bison Archives/Marc Wanamaker

His career was nearly over, but D. W. Griffith's was still the name above the title for "The Wonder Picture of the Century," *Abraham Lincoln* (1930).
Courtesy of United Artists

For the first time since the Rockett brothers' *The Dramatic Life of Abraham Lincoln* in 1924, a feature film would cover the whole of Lincoln's life, from his birth in a storm-buffeted cabin through the moment in 1865 when he began to belong to the ages. And, as with the earlier film, the story turned out to be far too large and complex for a single movie.

Griffith auditioned scores of actors—and two actresses—for the role of Lincoln. He carefully considered several of the men who either had already played or would soon play Lincoln in movies: George Billings, Charles Middleton, Frank McGlynn, and many others, but eventually Griffith chose Walter Huston, a well-known stage actor who was still a relative newcomer to the movies. Huston's craggy features certainly filled the bill, and his later, better films showed that he was a master at lighthearted roles with dark underpinnings. However, that old demon reverence reared its ugly head once again. Despite Huston's best efforts, his Lincoln has little dimension and little life.

The film also suffers from a rather serious piece of miscasting in the role of Ann Rutledge. The lovely Una Merkel was a fine comedienne and had a rewarding career as a second lead and a character actress. Her funny little voice made her particularly endearing in most films, but she completely missed the boat in attempting to portray the love of Lincoln's life. Hers is only one of the performances that are found wanting in this film, a fault that must be laid on Griffith rather than on the actors themselves.

Abraham Lincoln does have moments of great imagination, fluidity, and power, but they are virtually always visual in nature—scenes without dialogue. In these moments, Griffith's genius as a filmmaker is still quite evident; he even used sound in creative ways that were still not common in those early days of the talkies. But when it came to dialogue, *Abraham Lincoln* creaked to a halt.

The greatest fault of the film, however, lies in its episodic nature. In their respect for the subject, Griffith and Benet could not find a dramatic core to serve as the basis for an exciting and involving

Lincoln (Walter Huston) has just signed the Emancipation
Proclamation in *Abraham Lincoln* (1930).
Courtesy of United Artists

drama. Lincoln is born, grows up, meets and loses Ann Rutledge,
meets and marries Mary Todd, goes to the White House, presides
over the Civil War, and dies in a theater seat. There are no surpris-
es, and, worse there is no illumination. Griffith was content to bring
alive the pages of history, but he felt so constrained by the facts—or
what he believed to be the facts—that he couldn't quite manage to
make Lincoln live. Consequently, it is difficult for the audience to
feel very sad when Lincoln dies.

The film was greeted enthusiastically by the critics, who
believed that *Abraham Lincoln* showed Griffith again in true form
after several years of disappointing films. *Variety* called it "an out-
standing classic of sound pictures" and "a startlingly superlative
accomplishment; one rejuvenating a greatest Griffith. In characterization and detail perfection it is such as to be almost unbelievable.
In continuity and scenes it projects as one smooth roll of literally
throbbing pulsation, pathos, laughter, with never a moment's inter-
lude for audience let-down."[4]

Harrison's Reports agreed, calling *Abraham Lincoln*, "Excellent!" and, oddly enough, praising the "episodic fashion in which there are shown Lincoln as the boy, the man and then the President; his humor, his ambitions, his love affairs, his ideals and also his peculiarities."[5]

More recently, film historian Anthony Slide has wondered "why contemporary critics were so impressed by this dull, episodic, overlong production. The assassination has none of the sparkle or emotion of the same scene in *The Birth of a Nation*. Indeed, it cannot even compare favorably to John Ford's reconstruction of the event for his 1936 production *The Prisoner of Shark Island*."[6]

Soon after its theatrical release, *Abraham Lincoln* was reedited into four educational programs of varying lengths, ranging from a full-length, ten-reel version to one running about eleven minutes. In this context, the film probably worked much better. Far more interesting and exciting than the average educational film, in the classroom, the linear, episodic nature of *Abraham Lincoln* might actually have been an advantage. As drama, the film today seems little more than a failed experiment enlivened by a few wonderful sequences and weighed down with dozens of dull ones. But as a clear and unembroidered recounting of the life of Abraham Lincoln, the film is most effective, if never particularly memorable.

NOTES

1. D. W. Griffith, "My Early Life" from *Focus on D. W. Griffith*, edited by Harry M. Geduld (Prentice-Hall, 1971), pp. 13–14.

2. Kevin Brownlow, *The Parade's Gone By* (Knopf, 1968), p. 47.

3. Ibid.

4. *Variety*, August 27, 1930.

5. *Harrison's Reports*, September 6, 1930.

6. Edward Wagenecht and Anthony Slide, *The Films of D. W. Griffith* (Crown, 1975), p. 252.

Chapter Eight
Dueling Lincolns
Abe Lincoln in Illinois and Young Mr. Lincoln

THE THIRTIES started off with a major Lincoln film—D. W. Griffith's *Abraham Lincoln* (1930)—and so it must have seemed appropriate to finish the decade with not one but two Lincoln movies: *Abe Lincoln in Illinois* and *Young Mr. Lincoln*. John Ford's *Young Mr. Lincoln* was filmed and released first—and it was the bigger box office success—but *Abe Lincoln in Illinois* had been in the works longer. It was based on the Pulitzer Prize winning play by Robert E. Sherwood, which had enjoyed enormous success on Broadway since its debut in October 1938. Raymond Massey, who starred in both play and film to great acclaim, remembered that Sherwood had mentioned working on the play at least six years earlier. "Long after the play opened," Massey wrote, "Bob told me that it had been the most difficult project he had ever attempted. He felt he had engaged in a collaboration, a task he had always avoided, and that Lincoln himself had written some of the play."[1]

Sherwood's Abraham Lincoln, like John Drinkwater's before him, was a Lincoln of the poet rather than the historian. Over those

Lobby card for *Abe Lincoln in Illinois* (1940).
Courtesy of RKO Pictures

six years, Sherwood meticulously researched Lincoln's life, studying biographies by Ida Tarbell, Carl Sandburg, and Albert Bushnell Hart, as well as the memoirs of those who had known Lincoln: John Nicolay, William Herndon, and others. Having gathered as much factual information as he could, the writer then began to shape his own portrait of Lincoln, feeling free to alter history whenever he felt it suited a greater dramatic purpose. "The playwright's chief stock in trade is feelings, not facts," Sherwood wrote. "When he writes of a subject out of history, or out of today's news, he cannot be a scholarly recorder or a good reporter; he is, at best, an interpreter."[2]

Carl Sandburg wholeheartedly approved Sherwood's approach. "It may be that sometime we shall have a Lincoln drama employing entirely speeches and situations authenticated by documents and evidence," Sandburg wrote, "but whether it will be a drama that people will go to see and value as drama is another question.

"Having seen Sherwood's play, and having noticed how the audience itself participated, I believe it carries some shine of the American dream, that it delivers great themes of human wit, behavior and freedom, with Lincoln as mouthpiece and instrument."[3]

Lincoln (Raymond Massey, far right) is reluctant to accept
his political destiny in *Abe Lincoln in Illinois* (1940).
Courtesy of RKO Pictures

Abe Lincoln in Illinois captures a young Lincoln on the verge of
greatness, beginning with his days in New Salem where he passionately pursues his education, and falls desperately in love with Ann
Rutledge. It details his stormy relationship with Mary Todd—and
his extreme reluctance to marry her—and ends as he is leaving
Springfield for Washington, D. C., the presidency, and destiny.

The love of Sherwood's Lincoln for Ann Rutledge has none
of the ambivalence of, say, James Agee's Lincoln from the 1952
Omnibus production. He loves her outright and can't in his deepest
imagination think that she would return his affection. When he tells
Ann that he has loved her for a long time and "it's only natural I
should have a great regard for you," she replies that his words make
her look at him in a new way, "because now you're like some other
person that I'm meeting for the first time."

ABE: I'm not expecting you to feel anything for me. I'd never dream
of expecting such a thing.

ANN: I know that, Abe. You'd be willing to give everything you have

Raymond Massey as Lincoln in *Abe Lincoln in Illinois* (1940).
Courtesy of RKO Pictures

and never expect anything in return. Maybe you're different in that way from any man I've ever heard of. And I can tell you this much—now, and truthfully—if I ever do love you, I'll be happy about it—and lucky, to be loving a good, decent man . . . If you just give me time to think about it. . . .

ABE: You mean—if you took time—you might get in your heart something like the feeling I have for you?

ANN: I don't know, Abe. But I do know that you're a man who could fill any one's heart—yes, fill it and warm it and make it glad to be living.

Curiously, Sherwood chose to stage Ann's death offstage, concentrating on Abe's grief afterward instead of creating a tearful deathbed scene. The loss of Ann Rutledge, in Sherwood's eyes, is not the source of Lincoln's sadness (as it is in *Young Mr. Lincoln*) but just one more component. It is also one of the reasons that Abe's relationship with firebrand Mary Todd is so tentative. Sherwood suggests that Abe can never again know true romantic love—that's a part of his dead past—and his next partner will fuel the ambitious side of his nature, not the sentimental side. He resists becoming involved with Mary, even to the point of running away, out into the wilderness, in the hopes that she will just forget about him.

But to Sherwood, Mary is not just a wife; she is Lincoln's destiny. His fear of marrying her reflects his reticence to immerse himself in political life, a career that, he senses, will take him down a dark road. While out in the wilderness, he happens to run across two friends who are moving on to settle in Oregon. Their child is ill and—a preacher not being handy—they ask Abe to pray for him. Reluctantly he begins praying, and as he does, he begins to see the responsibility before him and starts to accept his place in history—and his marriage to Mary.

> ABE: Oh God, the father of all living, I ask you to look with gentle mercy upon this little boy who is here, lying sick in this covered wagon. His people are traveling far, to seek a new home in the wilderness, to do your work, God, to make this earth a good place for your children to live in. They can see clearly where they're going, and they're not afraid to face all the perils that lie along the way. I humbly beg you not to take their child from them. Grant them the freedom of life. Do not condemn him to the imprisonment of death. Do not deny him his birthright. Let him know the sight of great plains and high mountains, of green valleys and wide rivers. For this little boy is an American, and these things belong to him, and he to them. Spare him, that he too may strive for the ideal for which his fathers have labored, so faithfully and for so long. Spare him and give him his fathers' strength—give us all strength. Oh God, to do the work that is before us. I ask you this favor, in the name of your son, Jesus Christ, who died upon the Cross to set men free. Amen.

Sherwood knows and the audience knows—and more important, Lincoln knows—that Abe himself will be compelled to "die on the cross to set men free," and it is in this moment on the plains that he comes to accept his dark future.

According to Raymond Massey, this prayer was the first part of the play Sherwood wrote, the inspiration having come to him while he was in Bonwit Teller's buying perfume for six chorus girls in his current play, *Idiot's Delight.* "Bob took his parcels across Fifth Avenue to a nearby Childs Restaurant and ordered butter cakes. He took a paper napkin from the dispenser and started to write. Never, Bob said, did any speech come more smoothly. By the time he had written the two hundred-odd words, his butter cakes were cold, but the first lines of *Abe Lincoln in Illinois* were on paper."[4]

Abe Lincoln in Illinois opened in Washington, D. C. on the evening of October 3, 1938, and at its first performance, a "large audience liberally sprinkled with distinguished personalities whistled and stamped long after the final scene, and there were curtain calls almost too numerous to count . . . 'Honest Abe' is portrayed with extreme sympathy as a charming, able young man who is rent within by bitterly conflicting emotions, a creature of two warring personalities, driven along the road of destiny against his will by forces beyond his control."[5]

When the play opened in New York, a *Times* critic wrote, "In the chief part Raymond Massey gives a glorious performance—rude and lazily humorous on the surface, but lighted from within. He suffuses the simplicity of Mr. Sherwood's writing with the luminous beauty of inspired acting. Fortunately, the entire performance, under Elmer Rice's illuminating direction, is all of one piece, and *Abe Lincoln in Illinois* is a profoundly moving portrait of our human lore and our spiritual heritage."[6]

No sooner had the play opened than RKO Radio Pictures began planning a motion picture version, despite the fact that John Ford also had a Lincoln film currently in the works. The usual Hollywood way of doing things when adapting a hit Broadway play was to replace the stage star with a more bankable Hollywood star, but Raymond Massey became so quickly identified with Sherwood's Lincoln that he was brought to Hollywood to recreate his role on film. Richard Gaines replaced Massey on Broadway with the agreement that, after filming completed, Massey would rejoin the company for a national tour.

Sherwood's play was adapted for the screen by veteran script writer Grover Jones, and actor-turned-director John Cromwell was chosen to direct. Interiors were filmed in Hollywood, but the beautiful exteriors, standing in for New Salem and Springfield, were shot in Eugene, Oregon. In the inevitable expansion that takes place in all translations from stage to screen, at least two key elements were changed. First, Abe and Ann Rutledge got the tearful deathbed scene they had been denied in the play. The scene works beautifully on film, adding an extra dimension of emotion that helps to more sharply define Abe's later actions. But Raymond Massey was not pleased with the second change. The prayer in the prairie—to Massey, the heart of the play—was excised. "Without it," Massey wrote, "the story had become a documentary, a procession of episodes."[7]

Massey did indeed rejoin the touring company of *Abe Lincoln in Illinois* after filming completed, and he went on to play Lincoln many more times throughout his long and distinguished career on stage, screen, and television. He also often portrayed other characters who had some deep connection with Lincoln—Junius Brutus Booth, the father of Edwin and John Wilkes Booth in *Prince of Players* (1955); and that fiery abolitionist John Brown in *Santa Fe Trail* (1940) and *Seven Angry Men* (1955). In fact, in the stage production of Stephen Vincent Benet's poem *John Brown's Body*, Massey read the parts of both Lincoln *and* John Brown. In 1950 Massey brought his performance in *Abe Lincoln in Illinois* to television in a production that costarred Betty Field as Mary Todd.

As early in the life of television as this was, it wasn't actually the first production of *Abe Lincoln in Illinois* ever televised. Stephen Courtleigh had starred in an adaptation of the play, broadcast over three nights in 1945. Now apparently lost, this production was high-

"Did I ever tell you about the time I butted two fellas' heads together?" Young
lawyer Abe Lincoln (Henry Fonda) solves a case the old-fashioned way—with
the threat of violence—in *Young Mr. Lincoln* (1939).
Courtesy of 20th Century-Fox
Bison Archives/Marc Wanamaker

ly praised for its excellence, but also for the depth of its ambition; it
was a big task for a very primitive medium. A critic for *Variety* singled out the production's strongest element: its star. "Just as the legit
[stage] version of Sherwood's great drama will be forever associated
with the name of Raymond Massey, so television's greatest play to
date must be tied in with the name of the man who grew before your
eyes and insinuated himself into your heart—Stephen Courtleigh."[8]

In the years since, *Abe Lincoln in Illinois* has been revived
countless times. Both Hal Holbrook and Sam Waterston had great
success with the role on Broadway, and Jason Robards Jr. performed
it in a stagebound—but attractive—production for television in
1964. Robert Sherwood's deceptively simple and poetic treatment of
Lincoln's life makes the play an enduringly moving and inspiring
experience. The full beauty of its language and emotion didn't quite

translate to the only motion picture production (to date), but there are still stage productions to come and new actors to find the determined and melancholy heart of Abraham Lincoln through the perceptive and sympathetic words of Robert E. Sherwood.

BY THE TIME Raymond Massey's screen performance of *Abe Lincoln in Illinois* came to movie theaters around the country, another treatment of Lincoln's life had already been in release for several weeks. John Ford's *Young Mr. Lincoln* was, by and large, a fictional version of Lincoln's early days as a lawyer. It briefly but poignantly covered his doomed romance with Ann Rutledge, sketched in the early phases of his rivalry—professionally and privately—with Stephen A. Douglas, and introduced him to the young woman with whom he wants "to dance in the worst way," Mary Todd.

The plot of *Young Mr. Lincoln* centers around a trial in which two brothers are accused of murder. Screenwriter Lamar Trotti, formerly an Atlanta newspaperman, admitted that he drew most of the elements of the trial, not from Lincoln's past, but from a murder trial Trotti himself had once covered.

Nevertheless, although *Young Mr. Lincoln* had little to do with the hard facts of Lincoln's life, it is a beautiful and powerfully mythic portrait of the Lincoln spirit, told with a sense of poetic Americana by the cinema's greatest poet, John Ford. Young Abe's tender scene with Ann Rutledge is the loveliest depiction of their romance in any film, even though virtually nothing romantic is said. With the aid of Alfred Newman's evocative musical score, Ford and Fonda keep Ann's spirit alive throughout the film, although she is only mentioned one more time, when Abe is talking to the wife of one of the accused men. "I knew a girl a lot like you. Her name was Ann. She died." But every time Abe gazes at a river or retreats into his own thoughts, Ann's theme comes up on the soundtrack, and we know, without otherwise being told, of whom he is thinking.

Henry Fonda gives a remarkable, understated performance as Abe: shy and friendly, with a dry wit and a brute strength that he only occasionally sees fit to exhibit. ("Did I ever tell you," he says to two stubborn litigants, "about the time I butted two fellas' heads together?") At the party where he meets Mary Todd (Marjorie Weaver), Abe is far more comfortable trading quips with a group of men than in interacting with the women—particularly the beautiful and poised Mary. She has to coerce him to dance with her, and after he has satisfied her that he really does dance "in the worst way," she invites him out to the veranda to talk. But even there, with the moonlight shimmering on the river, his thoughts go to Ann, leaving Mary seated by herself, a bit puzzled by his odd behavior, but intrigued nonetheless.

A town festival gives us a glimpse of various sides of Lincoln's nature. He cheats in a tug of war by hitching his team's end of the rope to a horse and wagon that pulls the other team into the mud. Judging a pie contest, he simply can't come to a decision, taking a bite out of one piece, then another, then the first, and so on as the scene fades. It is also during the festivities that we see the legendary rail-splitter in action; this is one contest in which Abe doesn't have to cheat—after all, who could split rails better than Abe Lincoln?

John Ford also wanted to include a moment of prescience. He told Peter Bogdanovich, "I had a lovely scene in which Lincoln rode into town on a mule, passed by a theater and stopped to see what was playing, and it was the Booth family doing *Hamlet*; we had a typical old-fashioned poster up. Here was a poor shabby country lawyer wishing he had enough money to go see *Hamlet* when a very handsome young boy with dark hair—you knew he was a member of the Booth family—fresh, snobbish kid, all beautifully dressed—just walked out to the edge of the plank walk and looked at Lincoln. He looked at this funny, incongruous man in a tall hat riding a mule, and you knew there was some connection there. They cut it out—too bad."[9]

In his role as defense lawyer, Abe emphasizes his country ways,

Abe Lincoln (Henry Fonda) holds back a lynch mob in
Young Mr. Lincoln (1939).
Courtesy of 20th Century-Fox
Bison Archives/Marc Wanamaker

frequently cracking jokes and asking seemingly insignificant questions, lulling his puffed-up opponent (Donald Meek) into believing
that he is too dim-witted to worry about. But Abe is in charge of the
truth (like all movie Lincolns, he simply knows it; he doesn't have to
learn it) and easily wins the case at the very last minute, letting the
real killer bask smugly until, with a snap, Lincoln closes his trap.

After the trial, Douglas congratulates him and assures Abe that
he will never underestimate him again. Mary Todd is also favorably
impressed, realizing for the first time that the power in their bur-
geoning relationship has shifted from her to him. Finally, bidding
farewell to the family he has made whole by freeing the two men,
Abe walks away, even though a storm is brewing. A friend asks if he
isn't going back into town. "No," Abe replies, "I think I'll walk for a
spell. Maybe to the top of that hill." And amid crashes of thunder,
he walks into his destiny, the scene dissolving into the Lincoln

memorial as "The Battle Hymn of the Republic" swells up on the soundtrack.

Fonda is perfectly cast as Lincoln, and his performance is flawless. But he did everything he could to avoid taking on the part. After Lamar Trotti read the script to him, he was impressed, but he just couldn't see himself as Lincoln. Trotti convinced him to do a costume test, and when Fonda saw himself onscreen, even he was impressed by how much like Lincoln he looked. But when he heard his own distinctive voice coming from that legendary face, he balked again.

Finally, John Ford called him into his office and dressed him down in language that was both colorful and to the point. Fonda recalled, "He was full of words you don't use in polite society. What happened was that he was trying to shame me into playing Young Lincoln, and that was the point he made. He *wasn't* the Great Emancipator. He *was* a young jacklegged lawyer from Springfield. We don't know at the end of the movie what's going to happen to this guy. That's not it. It's a good movie about a young lawyer in 1830. Anyway, Ford shamed me into it, I agreed, and I did the film."[10]

Henry Fonda, unlike Raymond Massey, Frank McGlynn, Benjamin Chapin, Ralph Ince, or many others, did not play Abraham Lincoln more than once. Yet this single performance so perfectly caught the essence of young Abe—perhaps not of Lincoln the man, but of Lincoln the myth—that he must always be considered one of the screen's greatest Lincolns. And *Young Mr. Lincoln* must be considered among the greatest of Lincoln films.

NOTES

1. Raymond Massey, *A Hundred Different Lives* (Little, Brown and Company, 1979), p. 218.
2. Robert E. Sherwood, "The Substance of *Abe Lincoln in Illinois*" in the published edition of the play (Charles Scribner's Sons, 1939), p. 189.

3. Carl Sandburg, foreword to the published edition of the play, (Charles Scribner's Sons, 1939), p. xi–xii.

4. Raymond Massey, *A Hundred Different Lives* (Little, Brown and Company, 1979), p. 231.

5. *New York Times,* October 4, 1938.

6. *New York Times,* October 23, 1938.

7. Raymond Massey, *A Hundred Different Lives* (Little, Brown and Company, 1979), p. 253.

8. *Variety,* May 30, 1945.

9. Peter Bogdanovich, *John Ford* (University of California Press, 1968).

10. Henry Fonda and Howard Teichmann, *Fonda: My Life* (New American Library, 1981), p. 127.

Abraham Lincoln
Filmography

The name of the actor who portrayed Lincoln in each film, when known, is enclosed in brackets.

Uncle Tom's Cabin (July 1903) Edison
The Blue and the Grey or *The Days of '61* (1908) Edison. Directed by Edwin S. Porter
The Reprieve: An Episode in the Life of Abraham Lincoln (1908) Vitagraph [Ralph Ince]
Scenes from the Battlefield of Gettysburg, the Waterloo of the Confederacy (1908) Lubin
Life of Abraham Lincoln (1908) Essannay [Logan Paul]
The Assassination of Abraham Lincoln, also known as *The Assassination of President Lincoln* (1909) The Penn Motion Picture Company
Stirring Days in Old Virginia, also known as *Stormy Days in Old Virginia* (1909) Selig Polyscope. Directed by Otis Turner
Abraham Lincoln's Clemency, also known as *Lincoln's Clemency* and *The Clemency of Abraham Lincoln* (1910) Pathe Freres [Leopold Wharton]. Directed by Theodore Wharton. Based on the poem "The Sleeping Sentinel" by Francis De Haes Janiver.
The Old Man and Jim (1911) Champion. Based on the poem by James Whitcomb Riley.
The Fortunes of War (1911) Independent Moving Pictures Corp.
A Romance of the 60s (November 18, 1911) Lubin
Lieutenant Grey of the Confederacy (1911) Selig Polyscope

Under One Flag (1911) Vitagraph [Ralph Ince]

One Flag at Last (1911) Vitagraph [Ralph Ince]

Grant and Lincoln (September 4, 1911) Champion

Battle Hymn of the Republic (1911) Vitagraph [Ralph Ince]. Based on the poem by Julia Ward Howe.

Gettysburg (1912) Vitagraph [Ralph Ince]

His Father's Bugle (1912) Selig Polyscope

The Seventh Son (1912) Vitagraph [Ralph Ince]. Scenario by Hal Reed.
     CAST: Tefft Johnson (Stanton), Mary Maurice (Widow).

The Fall of Black Hawk (1912) [H. G. Lonsdale]

Lincoln's Gettysburg Address (1912) [Ralph Ince]. Directed by J. Stuart Blackton and James Young. Based on an idea by James Young.
     CAST: Clara Kimball Young, James Young.

On Secret Service (1912) Kay-Bee, New York Motion Picture Company [Francis Ford]. Released by Mutual Film Corp.

When Lincoln Paid (1913) Kay-Bee, New York Motion Picture Company [Francis Ford]. Released by Mutual Film Corp.

Lincoln for the Defense (1913) Pilot

When Lincoln was President (1913) Pilot

The Song Bird of the North (1913) Vitagraph [Ralph Ince]
     CAST: Anita Stewart.

The Battle of Gettysburg (1913) New York Motion Picture Company. [Willard Mack]. Mutual Film Corporation. Five reels. Director: Thomas H. Ince. Lab Work Supervisor: Alfred Brandt. The *American Film Institute Catalog: Feature Films 1911–1920* suggests that Charles Giblyn may have been the film's codirector. The scenarist may have been C. Gardner Sullivan or the team of Charles Brown, Thomas Ince, and Richard Spencer.
     CAST: The *American Film Institute Catalog: Feature Films 1911–1920* suggests that the following actors may have appeared in this film: Burton King, Joe King, Gertrude Claire, Shorty Hamilton, Mr. Hadley, and Mr. Edlar. Another source names the following cast members: Charles K. French, Enid Bennett, Herschel Mayall, Walter Edwards, Frank Borzage, J. Barney Sherry, Anna Little, George Fisher, J. Frank Burke, and Enid Markey.

From Railsplitter to President (1913) Gold Seal.

The Toll of War (1913) 101 Bison.
     CAST: William Clifford, Ethel Grandon.

Sorrows of Lincoln (1913) Nestor [Francis Ford]

Francis Ford is a particularly dour Lincoln in *When Lincoln Paid* (1913). Ford played the president in several films, some of which he also directed. Years later, he played the role of a comic drunken juror in *Young Mr. Lincoln* (1939), directed by his younger brother John Ford.
Courtesy of the Academy of Motion Picture Arts and Sciences

Willard Mack as Lincon in
Thomas Ince's lost epic,
The Battle of Gettysburg
(1913).
*Courtesy of Bison
Archives/Marc Wanamaker*

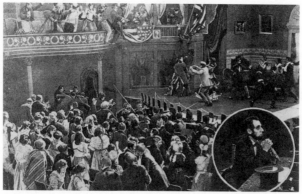

A view of the assassination from D. W. Griffith's *The
Birth of a Nation* (1915), including an inset closeup of
Joseph Henabery's Lincoln in a prayerful pose. The
Ford's Theater set was built outdoors and lit by
sunlight, a common practice of the era.
Courtesy of the author

Lincoln the Lover (1914) Vitagaph [Ralph Ince]. Directed by Ralph Ince. Written
by Ralph Ince and Catherine Van Dyke.
CAST: Anita Stewart (Ann Rutledge), E. K. Lincoln, Logan Paul, Johnny
Hines.
The Sleeping Sentinel (1914) Lubin [George Stelle]. Based on the poem by
Francis De Haes Janiver.
The Man Who Knew Lincoln (1914) Vitagraph [Ralph Ince]. Based on the book
He Knew Lincoln by Ida Tarbell.
Lincoln's Thanksgiving Story (1914) [Benjamin Chapin]
The Birth of A Nation (February 8, 1915) David W. Griffith Corp. [Joseph
Henabery]. Presented, produced, and directed by D. W. Griffith. Assistant
Directors: Thomas E. O'Brien, George Andre Beranger, Monte Blue,
William Christy Cabanne, Elmer Clifton, Donald Crisp, Howard Gaye,
Fred Hamer, Erich von Stroheim, Herbert Sutch, Tom Wilson, Baron von
Winther. Scenario by D. W. Griffith and Frank E. Woods. Camera: G. W.
Bitzer. Assistant Camera: Karl Brown. Costumes: Goldstein Co., Los
Angeles. Master Carpenter: Frank "Huck" Wortman. Special Effects:
"Fireworks" Wilson. Musical Accompaniment: Joseph Carl Breil. Based
upon the novel *The Clansman: An Historical Romance of the Ku Klux Klan*
by Thomas Dixon (New York, 1905) and his play of the same name (New
York, January 8, 1906).

CAST: Henry Walthall (Colonel Ben Cameron), Miriam Cooper (Margaret Cameron), Mae Marsh (Flora Cameron), Josephine Crowell (Mrs. Cameron), Spottiswoode Aitken (Dr. Cameron), J. A. Beringer (Wade Cameron), Maxfield Stanley (Duke Cameron), Jennie Lee (Mammy), Ralph Lewis (Hon. Austin Stoneman), Lillian Gish (Elsie Stoneman), Elmer Clifton (Phil Stoneman), Robert Harron (Tod Stoneman), Wallace Reid (Jeff), Mary Alden (Lydia Brown), George Siegmann (Silas Lynch), Walter Long (Gus), Raoul Walsh (John Wilkes Booth), Donald Crisp (General U. S. Grant), Howard Gaye (General Robert E. Lee), Sam de Grasse (Charles Sumner), William Devaull (Nelse), William Freeman (Jake), Thomas Wilson (Stoneman's servant), Violet Wilkey (Flora Cameron as a child), Alberta Lee (Mary Todd Lincoln), William Freeman (hospital sentry), Olga Grey (Laura Keene), Eugene Pallette (Union soldier), Elmo Lincoln (White-Arm Joe, among other roles), Mme. Sul-te-Wan, Erich von Stroheim, Gibson Gowland, John Ford, Fred Burns, Allan Sears.

The Heart of Lincoln (1915, reissued 1922) Gold Seal [Francis Ford]. Released by Universal Film Manufacturing Company. Produced and directed by Francis Ford.

CAST: Grace Cunard (Betty), Ella Hall, William Quinn, Elmer Morrow, Lew Short.

The Battle Cry of Peace (1915) Vitagraph [William J. Ferguson]. Produced and directed by J. Stuart Blackton and Wilfrid North. Written by J. Stuart Blackton. Based on the book *Defenseless America* by Hudson Maxim. Cinematography: Arthur T. Quinn and Leonard Smith. Musical Accompaniment: S. L. Rothapel. Musical Accompaniment Editors: S. M. Berg and Ivan Rudisill.

CAST: Charles Richman (John Harrison), L. Rogers Lytton (Mr. Emanon), James Morrison (Charley Harrison), Mary Maurice (Mrs. Harrison), Louise Beaudet (Mrs. Vandergriff), Harold Hubert (Mr. John Vandergriff), Jack Crawford (Poet Scout), Charles Kent (the Master), Julia Swayne Gordon (Magdalen), Evart Overton (Vandergriff's son), Belle Bruce (Alice Harrison), Norma Talmadge (Virginia Vandergriff), Lucille Hammill (Dorothy Vandergriff), George Stevens (Butler), Thais Lawton (Columbia), Lionel Braham (the War Monster), Joseph Kilgour (George Washington), Paul Scardon (General Grant), Hudson Maxim (Himself), Tefft Johnson, Blanche Earle, Alice Joyce.

The Life of Abraham Lincoln (1915) Edison [Frank McGlynn, Sr.]. Directed by Langdon West. Written by James Oppenheim.

Samuel D. Drane as Lincoln in a tableau that opens the Civil War epic *The Crisis* (1916), based on the novel by Winston Churchill. *Courtesy of the Academy of Motion Picture Arts and Sciences*

Lincoln's Gettysburg Address (1915) National Association of the Deaf.
    CAST: Dr. Thomas Francis Fox.

The Magistrate's Story (1915) Edison. Released by General Film Corp.
    CAST: Gertrude Mccoy, Richard Tucker, Pat O'Malley, William West.

The Crisis (December 24, 1916) Selig Polyscope Co.; A Super Film [Sam D. Drane]. Supervised by William N. Selig. Directed by Colin Campbell. Assistant Director: Leo Pierson. Written by Colin Campbell. Based on the novel by Winston Churchill (1901). Cinematography: G. Mckenzie. Musical Arranger: Michel Mowschine. Art Director: Gabriel Pollock. Filmed with the cooperation of the Mississippi, Missouri, and Tennessee National Guards.
    CAST: Marshall Neilan (Clarence Colfax), Eugenie Besserer (Mrs. Brice), Matt B. Snyder (Colonel Comyn Carvel), Tom Santschi (Stephen Brice), Bessie Eyton (Virginia Carvel), George Fawcett (Judge Silas Whipple), Cecil Holland (General W. T. Sherman), Will Machin (Lige Brent), Leo Pierson (Jack Brinsmade), Frank Weed (Eliphalet Hopper), George Snyder, Alfred E. Green, Frank Green.

Battle Hymn of the Republic (1917) Vitagraph [Ralph Ince]. Broadway Star Feature. Directed by Lawrence Trimble. Written by Bera Breuil. Based on the poem by Julia Ward Howe.
    CAST: Julia Swayne Gordon (Julia Ward Howe), Mary Maurice.

Her Country's Call (1917) [Benjamin Chapin] Presented by Samuel S.

Hutchinson. Directed by Lloyd Ingraham. Written by Benjamin Chapin and Charles T. Dazey.
CAST: Mary Miles Minter (Jess Slocum), George Periolat (Jim Slocum), Allan Forrest (Captain Earle), Neville Henry A. Barrows (Colonel Tremaine), Margaret Shelby (Marie Tremaine), Ashton Dearholt (John Reynolds), Nellie Widen (Miss Neville), Spottiswoode Aitken (Dr. Downie).

The Battle of Gettysburg (1917) Hiller and Wilk

Son of Democracy (1918) [Benjamin Chapin] Also known as *The Lincoln Cycle* (see below), *The Life of Abraham Lincoln*, and *The Cycle of Photodramas Based on the Life of Abraham Lincoln*. Select Safety Film Service, Providence, RI, Charter Features Corp., Benjamin Chapin, President. Supervised, produced, directed, and written by Benjamin Chapin. (Some sources credit John M. Stahl as director, but the films themselves credit Chapin.) Camera: J. Roy Hunt, Walter Blakely, Harry A. Fishbeck, and Freyer [first name unknown].
CAST: Benjamin Chapin (Abraham Lincoln, his father Tom Lincoln, and his grandfather Abraham Lincoln), Charlie Jackson (Abraham Lincoln as a boy), Madeline Clare (Nancy Hanks Lincoln), John Stafford (Carter).
Son of Democracy consisted of ten separate episodes:
Native State (also released as *Old Abe*), *Under the Stars*, *My Mother (The Spirit Man)*, *My Father (The Physical Man)*, *Myself (The Lincoln Man)*, *Down the River*, *Tender Memories*, *A President's Answer*, *The Call to Arms*, *The Slave Auction*
Note: *The Lincoln Cycle* was released in 1917 and consisted of four of these ten episodes: *My Mother*, *My Father*, *Myself*, and *The Call to Arms*.

The Birth of a Race (December 1, 1918) (Original Title: *Lincoln's Dream*) Birth of a Race Photoplay Corp. Frohman Amusement Corp. Supervised and directed by John W. Noble. Assistant Directors: Charles Horan, Arthur Vaughan, Ralph Dean. Scenario: George F. Wheeler, Rudolph De Cordova, John W. Noble, and Anthony P. Kelly. Titles: Tom Bret. Cinematography: Herbert O. Carleton. Technique: W. Bruce Bradley. Art Titles: Ferdinand Pinney Earle. Musical Accompaniment: Joseph Carl Breil.
CAST: Louis Dean (the Kaiser), Harry Dumont (Crown Prince), Carter B. Harkness (Adam), Doris Doscher (Eve), Charles Graham (Noah), Ben Hendricks (Fritz Schmidt), Alice Gale (Frau Schmidt), John Reinhardt (Oscar Schmidt), Gertrude Braun (Louisa Schmidt), Stephen Reinhardt (Pat O'Brien), Mary K. Carr (Mrs. O'Brien), Jane Grey (Jane O'Brien), Edward Elkas (Herr Von H.), Anna Lehr, Philip Van Loan, George Le

Guere, Warren Chandler, Anita Cortez, Edward Boring, Dick Lee, David Wall, Belle Seacombe.

Victory and Peace (GB, 1918)

Children of Democracy (1918)

My Own United States (April 7, 1918) Frohman Amusement Corp. Metro Pictures Corp. [Gerald Day]. Presented by William L. Sherrill. Directed by John W. Noble. Written by Anthony Paul Kelly. Based on the story "The Man Without a Country" by Edward Everett Hale (*Atlantic Magazine*, Dec., 1863). Cinematography: Herbert O. Carlton. Art Director: W. Bruce Bradley.

CAST: Arnold Daly (Lieutenant Philip Nolan), Charles E. Graham (Colonel Aaron Burr), Duncan McRae (General Alexander Hamilton), Sidney Bracey (Captain Rene Gautier), P. R. Scammon (President Thomas Jefferson), Thomas Donnelly (General George Churchill), John Levering (Justice Colonel George Morgan), Edward Dunn (General Wilkinson), Claude Cooper (William Bayard), William V. Miller (Mr. Van Ness), Frederick Truesdell (Mr. Pendleton), F. C. Earle (Andrew Jackson), Jack Hamilton (Lieutanant Gaines), Richard Wangeman (Dr. Hossack), Fred Herzog (Admiral Stephen Decatur), Frank Murray (General U. S. Grant), Jack Burns (the Prosecutor), Anna Lehr (Agnes Churchill), Marie Du Chette (Natalie Somers), Helen Mulholland (Theodosia Burr), Mrs. Allen Walker (Mrs. Nolan), Mary Kennevan Carr (Mrs. Alexander Hamilton), Baby Carr (Baby Hamilton), James A. Furey (John Nolan).

The Test of Loyalty (June, 1918) Credits unavailable. According to the *American Film Institute Catalog of Feature Films, 1911–1920*, the synopsis, deposited with the Library of Congress has deteriorated and only part of the original story is known today.

Madam Who (January 1, 1918) Paralta Plays [Clarence Barr]. Directed by Reginald Barker. Scenario by Monte M. Katterjohn. Adapted by Clyde De Vinna. Story by Harold Macgrath. Camera: Clyde De Vinna. Art Director: Robert A. Brunton.

CAST: Bessie Barriscale (Jeanne Beaufort), Edward Coxen (John Armitage), Howard Hickman (Henry Morgan), Joseph J. Dowling ("Parson" John Kennedy), David M. Hartford (Alan Crandall), Fanny Midgley (Mrs. Howard), Nicholas Cogley (Mose), Eugene Pallette (Lieutenant Conroy), Wallace Worsley (Albert Lockhart), Bert Hadley (General Grant).

The Copperhead (January 25, 1920) Famous Players-Lasky Corp. [Nicolas Schroell]. A Paramount-Artcraft Special. Written and directed by Charles

Maigne. Based on the play *The Copperhead* by Augustus E. Thomas (New York, February 18, 1918) and the novel *The Glory of His Country* by Frederick Landis (New York, 1910).

CAST: Lionel Barrymore (Milt Shanks), William P. Carlton (Lieutenant Tom Hardy), Frank Joyner (Newt Gillespie), Richard Carlyle (Lem Tollard), Arthur Rankin (Joey), Doris Rankin ("Ma" Shanks), Leslie Stowe (Brother Andrew), William David (Tom Hardy), Harry Bartlett (Dr. James), Jack Ridgeway (Theodore Roosevelt), Mayor N. M. Cartmell (Captain Mercer), Carolyn Lee (Grandma Perley), Anne Cornwall (Madeline), Francis Haldorn (Elsie).

The Land of Opportunity (1920) Selznick Pictures [Ralph Ince]. Produced for the Americanization Committee. Produced by Louis J. Selznick. Directed by Ralph Ince.

The Civil War Period (1921) Ford Motor Co. Ford Motion Picture Laboratories. Released by Fitzpatrick and McElroy.

The Highest Law (1921) Selznick Pictures [Ralph Ince]. Directed by Ralph Ince. Based on a story by Lewis Allen Browne.

CAST: Robert Agnew, Margaret Sedden, Aleen Burr, Cecil Crawford.

Lincoln's Gettysburg Address (1922; sound)

In the Days of Buffalo Bill (1922) Universal [Joel Day]. Directed by Ed Laemmle.

CAST: Art Acord, Dorothy Woods, Duke R. Lee.

An eighteen-chapter serial. The chapter titles are *Bonds of Steel, In the Enemies' Hands, The Spy, The Sword of Grant and Lee, The Man of the Ages, Prisoners of the Sioux, Shackles of Fate, The Last Shot, From Tailor to President, Empire Builders, Perils of the Plains, The Hand of Justice, Trails of Peril, The Scarlet Doom, Men of Steel, The Brink of Eternity, A Race to the Finish,* and *Driving the Golden Spike.*

Abraham Lincoln (1923) Urban-Kineto

Wild Bill Hickok (November 18, 1923) Famous Players-Lasky. Paramount Pictures. Presented by Adolph Zukor. Produced by William S. Hart. Directed by Clifford S. Smith. Written by William S. Hart and J. G. Hawks. Cinematography by Arthur Reeves and Dwight Warren.

CAST: William S. Hart (Wild Bill Hickok), Ethel Grey Terry (Calamity Jane), Kathleen O'Connor (Elaine Hamilton), James Farley (Jack McQueen), Jack Gardner (Bat Masterson), Carl Gerard (Clayton Hamilton), William Dyer (Colonel Horatio Higginbotham), Bert Sprotte (Bob Wright), Leo Willis (Joe McCord), Naida Carle (Fancy Kate), Herschel Mayall (Gambler), Fritz (Paint).

An Episode in the Life of Abraham Lincoln (1924)

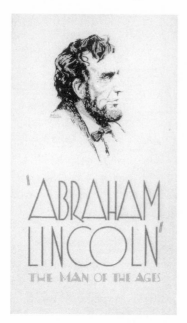

A poster for the Rockett Brothers' production of *The Dramatic Life of Abraham Lincoln* (1924), sometimes called, as it is here, simply *Abraham Lincoln*.
Courtesy of the Academy of Motion Picture Arts and Sciences

Abraham Lincoln, also known as *The Dramatic Life of Abraham Lincoln* (January 21, 1924) Rockett-Lincoln Film Co. [George A. Billings]. Associated First National Pictures. Produced by Al Rockett and Ray Rockett. Directed by Phil Rosen. Written by Frances Marion. Original Music: Joseph Carl Breil. Cinematography: Lyman Broening and Robert Kurrle.

CAST: *Kentucky and Indiana Period:* Fay McKenzie (Sarah Lincoln), Westcott B. Clarke (Thomas Lincoln), Irene Hunt (Nancy Hanks Lincoln), Charles French (Isom Enlow, neighbor), Calvert Carter (Mr. Gallagher, neighbor), Madge Hunt (Mrs. Gallagher), Raymond Lee (Austin Gallagher, boy chum), Ida McKenzie (Sarah Lincoln, ten years old), Danny Hoy (Abraham Lincoln, seven years old).

CAST: *The New Salem Period:* Ruth Clifford (Anne Rutledge), Ed Burns (John McNeil), Pat Hartigan (Jack Armstrong, leader of Clary Grove Gang), Otis Harlan (Denton Offut, employer of Lincoln), Jules Hanft (James Rutledge), Julia Hesse (Mrs. Rutledge), Louise Fazenda (Sally, a country girl), Robert Bolder (a country politician), William Humphrey (Stephan A. Douglas), William McIllwain (Dr. Allen), Fred Kohler (auctioneer at New Orleans slave market), Robert Milasch (Southern planter), George Reehm (another Southern planter).

CAST: *The Springfield Period:* Nell Craig (Mary Todd, afterwards Mrs.

Lincoln), Genevieve Blinn (Mary Todd's sister, Mrs. Ninian Edwards), Mickey Moore (Willie Lincoln), Newton Hall (Tad Lincoln), Francis Powers (Richard J. Oglesby).

CAST: *The Washington Period*: Homer Willits (John Hay, secretary to the president), Jim Blackwell (Tom, a colored servant), Eddie Sutherland (William Scott, Union soldier), Frances Raymond (Scott's mother), Jack Rollings (Union sentry), William McCormick (Corporal of the Guard), Frank Newburg (Bixby, Union soldier), William Moran (John Wilkes Booth), John Steppling (Chairman of the Delegation), Wanda Crazer (a dancer), Walter Rogers (General U. S. Grant), Alfred Allen (General George Meade), James Welch (General Robert E. Lee), Miles McCarthy (Major, afterwards General, Anderson), Earl Schenck (Colonel Rathbone), Dolly McLean (Miss Harris), Cordelia Callahan (Mrs. Surratt), Dallas Hope (Stable Boy), Dick Johnson (Bartender), Jack Wynn (Ned Spangler), Lawrence Grant (Actor at Ford's Theater), Ivy Livingston (Actress at Ford's Theater), Kathleen Chambers (another actress), Henry Rattenbury (Stagehand), W. L. McPheeters (Allan Pinkerton, Chief of the Secret Service).

CAST: *President Lincoln's Cabinet*: Willis Marks (William H. Seward, Secretary of State), Joel Day (Simon Cameron, Secretary of War), Nick Cogley (Edwin M. Stanton, Secretary of War), Charles Smiley (Salmon P. Chase, Secretary of the Treasury), C. A. Smiley (Hugh McCulloch, Secretary of the Treasury), R. G. Dixon (Gideon Welles, Secretary of the Navy), Harry Kelsey (Caleb B. Smith, Secretary of the Interior), Joseph Mills (Montgomery Blair, Postmaster-General), Fred Manly (Edward Bates, Attorney-General), Van Hardenburg (James Speed, Attorney-General), R. J. Duston (William Dennison, Postmaster-General).

Abraham Lincoln (1924; sound) Deforest Phonofilm Co. [Frank McGlynn Sr.]. Directed by J. Searle Dawley. Sound Recording by Lee Deforest.
CAST: Una Merkel.

Barbara Frietchie (September 26, 1924) Regal Pictures. [George A. Billings]. Producers Distributing Corp. Supervised by Thomas H. Ince. Directed by Lambert Hillyer. Written by Lambert Hillyer and Agnes Christine Johnston. Cinematographer: Henry Sharp.
CAST: Florence Vidor (Barbara Frietchie), Edmund Lowe (William Trumbull), Emmett King (Colonel Frietchie), Joseph Bennett (Jack Negly), Charles Delaney (Arthur Frietchie), Louis Fitzroy (Colonel Negly), Gertrude Short (Sue Rogers), Mattie Peters (Mammy Lou), Slim Hamilton (Fred Gelwek), Jim Blackwell (Rufus).

The Iron Horse (August 26, 1924) Fox Film Corp. [Charles Edward Bull]. Presented by William Fox. Produced and directed by John Ford. Scenario: Charles Kenyon. Titles: Charles Darnton. Story: Charles Kenyon and John Russell. Original music: John Lanchbery. Cinematography: George Schneiderman. Additional Photography: Burnett Guffey. Assistant Director: Edward O'Fearna. Musical Score: Erno Rapee.
CAST: George O'Brien (Davy Brandon), Madge Bellamy (Miriam Marsh), Cyril Chadwick (Peter Jesson), Fred Kohler (Deroux), Gladys Hulette (Ruby), James A. Marcus (Judge Haller), J. Farrell Macdonald (Corporal Casey), Jim Welch (Private Schultz), Walter Rodgers (General Dodge), George Waggner (Buffalo Bill), Jack Padjan (Wild Bill Hickok), Charles O'Malley (Major North), Charles Newton (Collis P. Huntington), Colin Chase (Tony), Chief John Big Tree (Cheyenne Chief), Chief White Spear (Sioux Chief), Edward Piel Sr. (Old Chinaman), James Gordon (David Brandon Sr.). Winston Miller (young Davy), Peggy Cartwright (young Miriam), Thomas Durant (Jack Ganzhorn), Stanhope Wheatcroft (John Hay), Frances Teague (Polka Dot), Will Walling (Thomas Marsh), John B. O'Brien (Dinny), Francis Powers (Sergeant Slattery). "And a regiment of United States troops and cavalry; 3,000 railway workmen; 1,000 Chinese laborers; 800 Pawnee, Sioux and Cheyenne Indians; 2,800 horses; 1,300 buffalo; 10,000 Texas steers."
The Last White Man (1924) Sanford Productions. Directed by Frank S. Mattison. CAST: Matty Mattison.
The Heart of Abraham Lincoln (1924) Distributed by Pictorial Clubs.
The Pony Express (September 13, 1925) Famous Players-Lasky. Paramount Pictures. Presented by Jesse L. Lasky and Adolph Zukor. Produced and directed by James Cruze. Screenplay: Walter Woods. Story: Henry James Forman and Walter Woods. Based on the novel *The Pony Express: A Romance* (New York, 1925). Cinematography: Karl Brown. Assistant Director: Harold Schwartz. Music Score Arranged by Hugo Riesenfeld.
CAST: Betty Compson (Molly Jones), Ricardo Cortez (Jack Weston), Ernest Torrence ("Ascension" Jones), Wallace Beery ("Rhode Island" Red), George Bancroft (Jack Slade), Frank Lackteen (Charlie Bent), John Fox Jr. (Billy Cody), William Turner (William Russell), Al Hart (Senator Glen), Charles Gerson (Sam Clemens), Rose Tapley (Aunt), Vondell Darr (Baby), Hank Bell, Ernie Adams, Toby Wing (Child).
The Man Without a Country (February 11, 1925) Fox Film Corp. [George A. Billings]. Produced by William Fox. Directed by Rowland V. Lee. Adapted and written by Robert N. Lee. Based on the story "The Man Without a

Country" by Edward Everett Hale (Boston, 1865). Original music: Erno
Rapee. Cinematography: G. O. Post.
CAST: Edward Hearn (Philip Nolan), Pauline Starke (Anne Bissell), Lucy
Beaumont (Mrs. Nolan), Richard Tucker (Aaron Burr), Earl Metcalfe
(Lieutenant Riddle), Edward Coxen (Lieutenant Harper), Wilfred Lucas
(Major Bissell), Francis Powers (Colonel Morgan), Harvey Clark (Peter),
Will Walling (Captain Shaw), William Conklin (Captain Danforth),
Edward Piel Sr. (Captain Kearney), Albert Hart (President Jefferson),
Emmett King (President Monroe), Pauline Neff (Mrs. Burke), Edward
Martindel, Fred Becker.
"That Royle Girl" (1925) Note: Lincoln himself does not appear in this film,
which takes place in modern times. However, Jean Daisy Royle (Carol
Dempster) is an idealist who likes to visit the Saint-Gaudens statue of
Lincoln in Chicago's Lincoln Park; she communes with Lincoln and tries
to pattern her behavior after his. Famous Players-Lasky. Paramount
Pictures. December 7, 1925. Ten reels. Presented by Adolph Zukor and
Jesse L. Lasky. Director: D. W. Griffith. Screenplay: Paul Schofield.
Photography: Harry Fischbeck and Hal Sintzenich. Art Director: Charles
M. Kirk. Film Editor: James Smith.
CAST: Carol Dempster (Joan Daisy Royle); W. C. Fields (her father);
James Kirkwood (Calvin Clarke, Deputy District Attorney); Harrison Ford
(Fred Ketlar "the King of Jazz"); Marie Chambers (Adele Ketlar); Paul
Everton (George Baretta); George Rigas (his henchman); Florence Auer
(Baretta's "girl"); Ida Waterman (Mrs. Clarke); Alice Laidley (Clarke's
fiancée); Dorothea Love (Lola Neeson); Dore Davidson (Elman); Frank
Allworth (Oliver); Bobby Watson (Hofer).
Hands Up (1926) Famous Players-Lasky [George A. Billings]. Paramount
Pictures. Presented by Jesse L. Lasky and Adolph Zukor. Directed by
Clarence G. Badger. Scenario: Monte Brice and Lloyd Corrigan, Story:
Reginald Morris. Cinematography: H. Kinley Martin.
CAST: Raymond Griffith (Confederate spy), Marian Nixon (the girl he
loves), Virginia Lee Corbin (Alice Woodstock), Charles K. French
(Brigham Young), Noble Johnson (Sitting Bull), Montague Love (Union
general), Mack Swain (Silas Woodstock).
The Heart of Lincoln (1927) Pathe Exchange
Uncle Tom's Cabin (1927) Universal Pictures. Presented by Carl Laemmle.
Supervised by Edward J. Montaigne and Julius Bernheim. Directed by
Harry Pollard. Scenario by Harvey Thew and Harry Pollard. Titles: Walter
Anthony. Photography: Charles Stumar and Jacob Kull. Film Editing:

George A. Billings as a serious
Lincoln in an otherwise hilarious
film, *Hands Up* (1926), starring
Raymond Griffith.
*Courtesy of the Academy of Motion
Picture Arts and Sciences*

Gilmore Walker, Daniel Mandell, and Byron Robinson. Musical Score: Hugo Riesenfeld. Technical Advisor: Colonel George L. Byram.

CAST: James Lowe (Uncle Tom), Virginia Grey (Eva St. Clare), George Siegmann (Simon Legree), Margaritz Fisher (Eliza), Eulalie Jensen (Cassie), Arthur Edmund Carew (George Harris, a slave), Adolph Milar (Haley), Jack Mower (Mr. Shelby), Vivian Oakland (Mrs. Shelby), J. Gordon Russell (Tom Loker), Skipper Zeliff (Edward Harris, a slave owner), Lassie Lou Ahern (Little Harris), Mona Ray (Topsy), Aileen Manning (Miss Ophelia), John Roche (St. Clare), Lucien Littlefield (Lawyer Marks), Gertrude Astor (Mrs. St. Clare), Gertrude Howard (Uncle Tom's wife), Geoffrey Grace (the Doctor), Rolfe Sedan (Adolph), Marie Foster (Mammy in St. Clare house), Francis Ford (Lieutenant), Martha Franklin (Landlady), Nelson McDowell (Phineas Fletcher), Grace Carlisle (Mrs. Fletcher), C. E. Anderson (Johnson), Dick Sutherland (Sambo), Tom Amardares (Quimbo), Bill Dyer (Auctioneer).

The Heart of Maryland (1927) Warner Bros. Pictures [Charles Edward Bull]. Directed by Lloyd Bacon. Scenario: C. Graham Baker. Based on the play *The Heart of Maryland* by David Belasco (1895). Cinematography: Hal Mohr. Assistant Director: Ross Lederman.

CAST: Dolores Costello (Maryland Calvert), Jason Robards (Major Alan Kendrick), Warner P. Richmond (Captain Fulton Thorpe), Helene Costello (Nancy), Carroll Nye (Lloyd Calvert), Erville Alderson (Major General Kendrick), Paul Kruger (Tom Boone), Walter Rodgers (General

Grant), Jim Welch (General Lee), Orpha Alba (Mammy), Myrna Loy (Mulatta), Harry Northrup (General Joe Hooker), Nick Cogley (Eli Stanton), Lew Short (Allan Pinkerton), Leonard Mellon (Young Stewart), Madge Hunt (Mrs. Abraham Lincoln), Charles Force (Colonel Lummon), Francis Ford (Jeff Davis), Ruth Cherrington (Mrs. Gordon), S. D. Wilcox (General Scott).

Lincoln's Gettysburg Address (1927) Vitaphone. Released by Warner Bros. Pictures.
  CAST: Rev. Lincoln Caswell.

Court Martial (1928) Columbia Pictures Corporation [Frank Austin]. Produced by Harry Cohn. Directed by George B. Seitz. Titles: Morton Blumenstock. Story: Elmer Harris. Scenario: Anthony Coldeway. Cinematography: Joseph Walker. Film Editing: Arthur Roberts. Assistant Director: Max Cohn. Art Director: Robert E. Lee.
  CAST: Jack Holt (James Camden), Betty Compson (Belle Stone), Pat Harmon (Bull), Doris Hill (General's Daughter), Frank Lackteen ("Devil" Dawson), George Cowl (General Robert Hackathorne), Zack Williams (Negro).

Lincoln (1929) American Films Foundation, New York, under the direction of L. M. Bailey [George Billings]. RCA Photophone Recording. Editor: Terry Ramsaye.

Two Americans (1929) Paramount Famous Lasky. Written and directed by John Meehan.
  CAST: Walter Huston.

Marching On (1929) Fox. Distributed by Wholesome Film Services. Directed by Marcel Silver. Story and scenario by Ben Holmes.
  CAST: Charles 'Chic' Sales.

Lincoln's Gettysburg Address (1930)

Abraham Lincoln (1930) National Cinema Service

Abraham Lincoln (1930) United Artists [Walter Huston]. Presented by Joseph M. Schenck. Directed by D. W. Griffith. Dialogue and Continuity: Stephen Vincent Benet and Gerrit J. Lloyd. Adaptation: Stephen Vincent Benet. Original Music: Hugo Riesenfeld. Cinematography: Karl Struss. Costume Design: Walter J. Israel. Film Editing: Hal C. Kern and James Smith. Story and Production Advisor: John W. Considine Jr. Art Director: William Cameron Menzies and Park French. Dialogue Director: Henry Stubbs. Sound Recording: Harold Witt. Production Manager: Orville O. Dull. Production Staff: Raymond A. Klune and Herbert Sutch. Costumes: Walter J. Israel.

CAST: Una Merkel (Ann Rutledge), William L. Thorne (Tom Lincoln), Lucille La Verne (Midwife), Helen Freeman (Nancy Hanks Lincoln), Otto Hoffman (Offut), Edgar Dearing (Armstrong), Russell Simpson (Lincoln's employer), Charles Crockett (sheriff), Kay Hammond (Mary Todd Lincoln), Helen Ware (Mrs. Edwards), E. Allyn Warren (Stephen Douglas), Jason Robards Sr. (Herndon), Gordon Thorpe (Tad Lincoln), Ian Keith (John Wilkes Booth), Cameron Prud'Homme (John Hay), James Bradbury Sr. (General Scott), James Eagles (Young Soldier), Fred Warren (General U.S. Grant), Oscar Apfel (Stanton), Frank Campeau (General Sheridan), Hobart Bosworth (General Robert E. Lee), Henry B. Walthall (Colonel Marshall), Hank Bell, Robert Brower, Mary Forbes (woman), Francis Ford (Sheridan's aide), Robert Homans (man), Henry Kolker (New Englander), Ralph Lewis, George Macquarrie, Carl Stockdale, Harry Stubbs.

Note: This feature was also made available in four distinct educational editions: the complete, ten-reel film called *The Entire Life and Career of Abraham Lincoln*; a five-reel version, *The Private and Public Life of Abraham Lincoln*; a three-reel edition, *The Public Life of Abraham Lincoln*; and a one-reel version, *Highlights of Lincoln's Career*, "held to eleven minutes in order to allow time for group discussion immediately after the screening."

Abraham Lincoln (1930) P. C. Pictures [Frank McGlynn Sr.]. Based on the play by John Drinkwater (1919).

Phantom President (1932) Paramount Publix Corp. [Charles Middleton]. Directed by Norman Taurog. Written by Walter Deleon and Harlan Thompson. Based on the novel by George F. Worts. Original music by Richard Rodgers. Cinematography: David Abel. Lyrics: Lorenz Hart. Camera Operator: Ernst Laszlo. Assistant Camera: Arthur Lane. Sound: Eugene Merritt. Still Photographer: Irving Lippman. Song: "The Country Needs a Man."

CAST: George M. Cohan (T. K. Blair/Doc Varney), Claudette Colbert (Felicia Hammond), Jimmy Durante (Curly Cooney), George Barbier (Boss Jim Ronkton), Sidney Toler (Professor Aikenhead), Louise Mackintosh (Senator Sarah Scranton), Jameson Thomas (Jerrido), Julius McVicker (Senator Melrose), Hooper Atchley (announcer), Eleanor Boardman (woman in audience), Paul Hurst (sailor), Alan Mowbray (George Washington), Victor Donald (Jefferson), E. J. Ratcliffe (Teddy Roosevelt).

Abraham Lincoln the Pioneer (1933) Eastman Teaching Films. Released by

Lincoln (Walter Huston) signs the Emancipation
Proclamation in D. W. Griffith's *Abraham Lincoln* (1930).
Courtesy of United Artists

Encyclopedia Brittanica Films. Digest culled from scenes from *The Dramatic Life of Abraham Lincoln* (1924).

Abraham Lincoln the Statesman (1933) Eastman Teaching Films. Released by Encyclopedia Brittanica Films. Digest culled from scenes from *The Dramatic Life of Abraham Lincoln* (1924).

Are We Civilized? (1934) Raspin Productions [Frank McGlynn Sr.]. Produced and directed by Edwin Carewe. Assistant Director: William Reiter. Second Assistant Director: H. Maynard Dickinson. Screenplay: Finis Fox. Story and Dialogue: Harold Sherman. Photography: Leon Shamroy and Al M. Greene. Assistant Camera: Milton Bridenbecker. Special Effects Phtography, Dunning Process: Bud Thackeray. Gaffers: Dudley Campbell, Edward Cox, Jennings McClellan, Ray Jones, and Harry Hodges. Art Director: Harrison Wiley. Film Editor: Dan Miner. Costumes: Rene Viehover. Music Performed by the Manhattan Symphony Orchestra of New York. Special Score: Mussina Wachtel and Matthew Ray. Special Makeup: Blagoe Stephanoff. Grip: Neal Neal. Props: Rene Viehover and Harry Grundstrum. Still Photographer: Shirley Vance Martin.

CAST: William Farnum (Paul Franklin Sr.), Anita Louise (Norma Bockner), Frank McGlynn Sr. (Abraham Lincoln and Felix Bockner), Leroy Mason (Paul Franklin Jr.), Oscar Apfel (Dr. Leonard Gear), Stuart Holmes (Colonel Salter), Alin Cavin (Moses), Conrad Siderman (Buddha), Sidney T. Pink (Confucius), Harry Berkhart (Caesar), Charles Requa

Abraham Lincoln (Charles "Chic" Sale) looks over a list of condemned men presented to him by Secretary of War Edwin Stanton (Oscar Apfel). As he did so often in life—and as he does nearly constantly in the movies—Lincoln decides to pardon them all in *The Perfect Trubute* (1935).
Courtesy of Metro-Goldwyn-Mayer

(Christ), J. C. Fowler (Mohammed), Bert Lindley (Christopher Columbus), Aaron Edwards (George Washington), William Humphrey (Napoleon).

The Perfect Tribute (1935) Metro-Goldwyn-Mayer [Charles 'Chic' Sale]. Directed by Edward Sloman. Written by Ruth Cummings. Based on the story by Mary Raymond Shipman Andrews. Cinematography: Jack Rose.
CAST: Oscar Apfel (Stratton), Walter Brennan (stone cutter), William Henry (soldier), Claude King (Everett), Edward Norris (orderly).

The Littlest Rebel (1935) Twentieth Century-Fox [Frank McGlynn Sr.]. Executive in Charge of Production: Darryl F. Zancuk. Associate Producer: Buddy G. Desylva. Directed by David Butler. Assistant Director: Booth McCracken. Screenplay: Edwin J. Burke and Harry Tugend. Based on the play *The Littlest Colonel* by Edward Peple (New York, November 14, 1911). Original Music: Cyril J. Mockridge. Cinematography: John F. Seitz. Film Editing: Irene Morra. Editoral Assistants: Eleanor Morra and Mary Crumley. Assistant Director: Booth McCracken. Scenery: Thomas K. Little. Costumes: Gwen Wakeling. Sound: S. C. Chapman and Roger Heman. Art Director: William Darling.
CAST: Shirley Temple (Virgie Cary), John Boles (Captain Herbert Cary), Jack Holt (Colonel Morrison), Karen Morley (Mrs. Cary), Bill Robinson (Uncle Billy), Guinn Williams (Sergeant Dudley), Willie Best (James Henry), Bessie Lyle (Mammy), Hannah Washington (Sally Ann).

Ruggles of Red Gap (1935) Note: Lincoln does not appear in this comedy about a

Frank McGlynn Sr. and Shirley Temple between scenes of *The Littlest Rebel* (1935). *Courtesy of 20th Century-Fox*

British butler named Ruggles (Charles Laughton) who is "won" in a card game by a crude but likeable American millionaire. In a climactic scene, Ruggles recites the Gettysburg Address. Paramount Productions, Inc. Presented by Adolph Zukor. Produced by Arthur Hornblow Jr. Executive Producer: Emanuel Cohen. Directed by Leo McCarey. Assistant Director: A. F. Erickson. Screenplay by Walter Deleon and Harlan Thompson. Based on the novel by Harry Leon Wilson (New York, 1915). Adapted by Humphrey Pearson. Contributors to Adaptation: Jack Cunningham and William Slavens McNutt. Contributor to Special Sequence: Arthur Macrae. Contributor to Treatment: Garnett Weston. Cinematography: Alref Gilks. Art Directors: Hans Dreier and Robert Odell. Film Editor: Edward Dmytryk. Costumes: Travis Banton. Sound: Phil G. Wisdom. Press Agent: Robert M. Gillham.

CAST: Charles Laughton (Marmaduke "Bill" Ruggles), Mary Boland (Effie Floud), Charlie Ruggles (Egbert "Sourdough" Floud), Zasu Pitts (Prunella Judson), Roland Young (Earl of Burnstead), Leila Hyams (Nell Kenner), Maude Eburne (Ma Pettingill), Lucien Littlefield (Charles Belknap-Jackson), Leota Lorraine (Mrs. Belknap-Jackson), James Burke (Jeff Tuttle), Dell Henderson (Sam the bartender), Clarence Wilson (Jake Henshaw), Ernie Adams (dishwasher), Augusta Anderson (Mrs. Wallaby), Alice Ardell (Lisette, a French maid), Harry Bernard (Harry, a second bartender), Harry Bowen (photographer), George Burton (Doc Squires), Ricardo Lord Cezon (Baby Judson), Heinie Conklin (waiter at the Grill),

Carrie Daumery (Effie's guest in Paris), Sarah Edwards (Mrs. Myron Carey), Charles Fallon (Max, Paris cafe waiter), Brenda Fowler (Judy Ballard), Willie Fung (Willie, a Chinese servant), Armand Kaliz (clothing salesman), Lee Kohlmar (jailer at Red Gap), Isabel La Mal (Effie's guest in Paris), Edward Le Saint (diner at the Grill), Jack Norton (barfly), Frank O'Connor (station agent), Albert Petit (waiter at Carousel), Victor Potel (Curly, a cowboy), Frank Rice (Hank Adams), Henry Roquemore (Fred, diner at the Grill), Rolfe Sedan (barber), Genaro Spagnoli (Frank the cab driver), Rafael Storm (clothing salesman), Libby Taylor (Libby, a black servant), Jim Welch (man in saloon), William Welsh (Eddie).

The Plainsman (1936) Paramount Pictures, Inc. [Frank McGlynn Sr.]. A C. B. Demille Production. Presented by Adolph Zukor. Executive Producer: William Lebaron. Produced and directed by Cecil B. Demille. Screenplay: Waldemar Young, Harold Lamb, and Lynn Riggs. Material Comp.: Jeannie Macpherson. Based on stories by Courtney Ryley Cooper and the novel *Wild Bill Hickok: The Prince of Pistoleers* by Frank J. Wilstach (Garden City, NY, 1934). Dialogue Supervision: Edwin Maxwell. Original music by George Antheil. Cinematography by Victor Milner and George Robinson. Costume Design: Joe De Young, Dwight Franklin, and Natalie Visart. Film Editor: Anne Bauchens. Art Direction: Roland Anderson and Hans Dreier. Special Camera Effects: Farciot Edouart, Gordon Jennings, and Dewey Wrigley . Set Decorator: A. E. Freudeman. Assistant Director: Richard Harlan. Special Camera Effects: Gordon Jennings. Sound: Harry Lindgren and Louis Mesenkop. Musical Director: Boris Morros. Costumes: Visart, Dwight Franklin, and Joe Deyong. Stunt Doubles: John Eckert, Lloyd Sanders, Al Burk, Slim Hightower, and Jimmy Phillips.

CAST: Gary Cooper (Wild Bill Hickok), Jean Arthur (Calamity Jane), James Ellison (Buffalo Bill Cody), Charles Bickford (John Lattimer), Helen Burgess (Louisa Cody), Porter Hall (Jack McCall), Paul Harvey (Chief Yellow Hand), Victor Varconi (Painted Horse), John Miljan (General George Armstrong Custer), Granville Bates (Van Ellyn), Frank Albertson (Young Trooper), Purnell Pratt (Captain Wood), Fred Kohler (Jake), Pat Moriarity (Sergeant McGinnis), Charles Judels (Tony the barber), Harry M. Woods (Quartermaster Sergeant), Anthony Quinn (Cheyenne Warrior), Francis McDonald (river gambler), George Ernest (an urchin), George Macquarrie (General Merritt), George Hayes (Breezy), Fuzzy Knight (Miner Dave), Lona Andre (southern belle), Arthur Aylesworth (Van Ellyn assistant), Irving Bacon (hysterical trooper), Davison Clark (James Speed), George Cleveland (Van Ellyn assistant), Edgar Dearing (Custer's messenger), Francis Ford (old veteran), Wadsworth Harris (William Dennison), Charles Herzinger (William H. Seward), William Humphrey (Hugh McCulloch), John Hyams (Schuyler Colfax), Sydney Jarvis (Gideon Welles), Edwin Maxwell (Stanton), Leila McIntyre (Mary Todd Lincoln), Charles Stevens (Injun Charlie), Mark Strong (Wells Fargo agent), Harry Stubbs (John F. Usher), Bruce Warren (Captain of the Lizzie Gill), Douglas Wood (Van Ellyn assistant), Hank Worden (Deadwood townsman), Chuck Hamilton, Lane Chandler, Hank Bell, Myron Geiger, Bob Burns, Duke Lee, Jack Walters, Frank Watson, Kenneth Gibson, Ben F. Hendricks, James Baker, Kenny Cooper, Cecil Kellogg, Whitey Severn, Ervey Collins, Frank Cordell, John Eckert, Lloyd Saunders, Al Burk, Slim Hightower, Jimmy Phillips (Troopers), Wilbur Mack, Stanley Andrews, Sherwood Bailey, Edgar Deering, Edwin Maxwell, Bruce Warren, Mark Strong, P. E. (Tiny) Newland, Sidney D'Albrook, Ed Schaefer, Bob Ellsworth, Nelson McDowell, Marty Joyce, Blackjack Ward, Jess Craven, Jane Keckley, Cora Shumway, Everett Brown, Louis Natheaux, Colin Chase, Jack Fife, Bud Fine, Edgar Blue Washington, Chief Thundercloud, Dennis O'Keefe, Gail Sheridan.

The Prisoner of Shark Island (1936) Twentieth Century-Fox [Frank McGlynn Sr.]. Presented by Joseph M. Schenck. Produced by Darryl F. Zanuck. Associate Producer: Nunnally Johnson. Directed by John Ford. Written by Nunnally Johnson. Cinematography: Bert Glennon. Costumes: Gwen Wakeling. Film Editor: Jack Murray. Art Director: William Darling. Sound: W. D. Flick and Roger Heman. Settings: Thomas Little. Assistant Director: Edward O'Fearna. Musical Director: Louis Silvers. Editorial Assistants: Harvey Manger and Thomas Vincent.

CAST: Warner Baxter (Dr. Samuel Alexander Mudd), Gloria Stuart (Mrs. Peggy Mudd), Claude Gillingwater (Colonel Dyer), Arthur S. Byron (Mr. Erickson), O. P. Heggie (Doctor Macintyre), Harry Carey (Commandant), Francis Ford (Corporal O'Toole), John McGuire (Lieutenant Lovett), Francis McDonald (John Wilkes Booth), Douglas Wood (General Ewing), John Carradine (Sergeant Rankin), Joyce Kay (Martha Mudd), Fred Kohler Jr. (Sergeant Cooper), Ernest Whitman (Buck), Paul Fix (David Herold), Frank Shannon (Mr. Holt), Leila McIntyre (Mrs. Abraham Lincoln), Etta McDaniel (Aunt Rosabelle), J. M. Kerrigan (Judge Maiben), Arthur Loft (carpetbagger), Paul McVey (General Hunter), Maurice Murphy (orderly), Frank Baker, Whitney Bourne, Robert Dudley (druggist), Jan Duggan (actress), Dick Elliott (actor), Bud Geary (a sergeant), Robert Homans (a sergeant), Beulah Hall Jones (Blanche), Duke Lee (a sergeant), Wilfred

His name is Mudd. In John Ford's *Prisoner of Shark Island* (1936), Warner Baxter played Dr. Samuel Mudd, the physician sentenced to life in prison for setting the broken leg of John Wilkes Booth. In the film's opening scenes, Lincoln was portrayed by Frank McGlynn Sr.
Courtesy of 20th Century-Fox

Lucas (colonel), Murdock Macquarrie (Spangler), James A. Marcus (blacksmith), Merrill McCormick (commandant's aide), J. P. McGowan (ship's captain), Robert Parrish, Jack Pennick (signalman), Paul Stanton (an orator), Harry Strang (ship's mate), Cyril Thornton (Maurice O'Laughlin), Cecil Weston (Mrs. Surratt), Lloyd Whitlock (Major Rathbone).

Hearts in Bondage (1936) Republic Pictures Corp. [Frank McGlynn Sr.]. Executive Producer: Herman Schlom. Produced by Nat Levine. Supervised by Colbert Clark. Directed by Lew Ayres. Assistant Director: Bob Beche. Written by Olive Cooper and Bernard Schubert. Adapted by Karl Brown. Original story by Wallace Macdonald. Original Music: Hugo Riesenfeld. Cinematography: Jack A. Marta and Ernest Miller. Film Editor: Ralph Dixon. Supervising Film Editors: Joseph H. Lewis and Murray Seldeen. Musical Director: Harry Grey. Technical Advisor: Franklyn Adreon, U.S.M.C. Special Effects: John T. Coyle, Bud Thackeray, Bill Bradford. Sound: John Stransky Jr. Sound Engineer: Terry Kellum.

CAST: James Dunn (Kenneth), Mae Clarke (Constance), David Manners (Raymond), Charlotte Henry (Julie), Henry B. Walthall (Buchanan), Fritz Leiber (Ericsson), George Irving (Commodore Jordan), Irving Pichel (Secretary Welles), J. M. Kerrigan (Paddy), Ben Alexander (Eggleston), Oscar Apfel (Captain Gilman), Clay Clement (Worden), Edward Gargan (McPherson), Russell Hicks (Pillsbury), George Hayes (Ezra), Douglas Wood (Farragut), Bodil Rosing (Mrs. Adams), Erville Alderson (Jefferson Davis), John Hyams (Bushnell), Etta McDaniel (Mammy), Warner P. Richmond (Bucko), Lloyd Ingraham (timekeeper), Hooper Atchley, Maurice Brierre, Smiley Burnette, Lane Chandler, Earl Eby, Pat Flaherty,

Frank McGlynn Sr. in one of his many film portrayals of
Abraham Lincoln. This one is from *Hearts in Bondage*
(1936). The only film directed by actor Lew Ayres, *Hearts
in Bondage* concerns the Civil War battle of the ironclad
boats the *Monitor* and the *Merrimac*.
Courtesy of Republic Pictures

Eugene Jackson, Frankie Marvin, Henry Roquemore, Clinton Rosemond,
Helen Seamon, Arthur Wanzer, Cecil Watson.

John Ericsson—Segraren vid Hampton Roads (Swedish, 1936) [John Ericsson]
American Title: *John Ericsson, the Victor of Hampton Roads.* Directed by
Gustaf Edgren. Written by Gustaf Edgren and Oscar Rydqvist. Original
music: Eric Bengtson. Cinematography: Åke Dahlqvist. Costume Design:
Allan Egnell and Mimmi Törnqvist-Zedell. Film Editing: Edwin
Hammarberg. Assistant Camera: Stig Berns. Production Manager: Stellan
Claësson. Assistant Director: Bertil Edgardh. Still Photographer: Louis
Huch. Makeup Artist: Börje Lundh. Title Designer: Alva Lundin. Sound
Assistant: Nils Lovén. Assistant Art Director: Olle Oldenburg. Unit
Manager: Gösta Ström. Sound: Terence Wendt. Art Director: Arne
Åkermark.

CAST: Victor Sjöström (John Ericsson), Märta Ekström (Amelia Ericsson),
Anders Henrikson (Taylor), Hilda Borgström (Ann Cassidy), Carl
Barcklind (Stephen Mallory), Marianne Aminoff (Mary), Kotti Chave
(James Kerrigan), Edvin Adolphson (Sanders), Ivar Kåge (Harry
Delameter), Olof Winnerstrand (Smith), Richard Lund (Paulding), Erik
Rosén (Davis), Helga Görlin (Jenny Lind), Sigurd Wallén (Karl "Charlie"
Petterson), Nils Jerring (prologue narrator), Jussi Björling (singer), Eric
Abrahamsson (clerk at the Navy Department), Greta Almroth (Amelia's

friend in England), C. A. Andersson (First Mate on *Minnesota*), Bror Berger (unemployed), Sven Björklund (Lieutenant on *Merrimac*), Gösta Bodin (Phineas Taylor Barnum), Carl Deurell (foreman), Bengt Djurberg (Lieutenant on *Monitor*), Hasse Ekman (Second-in-command), August Falck (sailor), George Fant (Lieutenant on *Monitor*), Georg Fernqvist (officer), Emil Fjellström (worker), Knut Frankman (seaman), Gösta Grip (Confederate minister), Wictor Hagman (sailor), Hester Harvey (black girl), Folke Helleberg (officer), John Hilke (Jefferson Davis, President of the Confederation), Torsten Hillberg (judge), Anders Holmgren (train driver), Helge Karlsson (soldier on *Monitor*), Helge Kihlberg (young man at the station), Alf Kjellin (young man on Delamater's office), Axel Lagerberg (member of the Marine Committee), Herman Lantz (young man waiting for the Cunard Ferry), Axel Lindberg (Lincoln's secretary), Richard Lindström (Chairman of the Marine Committee), Walter Lindström (Member of the Marine Committee), Gösta Lycke (Commander on *Minnesota*), Helge Mauritz (singer), Nils Nordstähl (Commander on *Cumberland*), Yngve Nyqvist (General Robert E. Lee), Gabriel Rosén (Confederate Chief of Guards), Robert Ryberg (draft officer), Gunnar Sjöberg (seaman), Ingeborg Strandin (worried mother), Carl Ström (chief guard), James Westheimer (sailor), John Westin (member of Congress), Charles White (Jim, negro), Eric von Gegerfelt (Confederate minister), Oscar Åberg (manager of the Confederate shipyard).

Trailin' West (1936) First National Productions [Robert Barrat]. Warner Bros. Executive Producers: Hal B. Wallis and Jack L. Warner. Produced by Bryan Foy. Directed by Noel Smith. Story and Screenplay: Anthony Coldeway. Original Music: M. K. Jerome and Jack Scholl. Cinematography: Sidney Hickox and Ted D. McCord. Costume Design: Milo Anderson. Film Editor: Frank McGee. Art Director: Hugh Reticker. Dialogue Director: Harry Seymour. Assistant Director: Drew Eberson. Gowns: Milo Anderson. CAST: Dick Foran (Lieutenant Red Colton), Paula Stone (Lucy Blake), William "Wild Bill" Elliott (Jefferson Duane), Addison Richards (Curley Thorne), Joseph Crehan (Colonel Douglas), Frank Prince (Lieutenant Daid), Eddie Shubert (Happy Simpson), Henry Otho (Hawk), Stuart Holmes (Elwin H. Stanton), Milton Kibbee (bandit), Carlyle Moore Jr. (hotel clerk), Edwin Stanley (Pinkerton), Jim Thorpe (Black Eagle), Gene Alsace, Bud Osborne (stagecoach driver), Cliff Saum (Jim), Glenn Strange (Tim), Tom Wilson (livery stable owner), Lee "Lasses" White (card dealer), Sam Rice (bartender), Baldy Belmont (old man).

Cavalry (1937) [Lincoln appears in one scene, but only in silhouette. The actor

who portrays him is not credited] Supreme Pictures Corp. Republic
Pictures Corp. Produced by A. W. Hackel. Directed by Robert N.
Bradbury. Original Story: Robert North Bradbury. Adaptation and
Screenplay: George S. Plymton. Cinematographer: Bert Longnecker. Film
Editor: Roy Claire. Sound Recording: Clifford Ruberg.

CAST: Bob Steele (Captain Ted Thorn), Frances Grant (Betty Lee
Harvey), Karl Hackett (Gavin Rance), Hal Price (Horace Leeds), Earle
Ross (Colonel Lafe Harvey), Edward Cassidy (Bart Haines), William
Welsh (General John Harvey), Budd Buster (Jake, the wagon boss), Horace
B. Carpenter (Carter), William Desmond (Major), Earl Dwire
(henchman), Perry Murdock (henchman Jase), Martin Turner (Mose).

Stand-in (1937) Walter Wanger Productions [Charles Middleton]. United
Artists. Presented by Walter Wanger. Directed by Tay Garnett. Screenplay:
Gene Towne and Graham Baker. Based on the story "Stand-In" by
Clarence Budington Kelland (*Saturday Evening Post*, February 13–March
20, 1937). Director of Photography: Art Baker. Cinematography: Charles
Clarke. Costume Design: Helen Taylor. Film Editing: Otho Lovering and
Dorothy Spencer. Assistant Director: Charles Kerr. Second Assistant
Director: Paul Schwegler. Sound Recording: Paul Neal. Musical Director:
Rox Rommell and Heinz Roemheld. Art Director: Alexander Toluboff.
Associate Art Director: Wade Rubottom. Stand-in for Leslie Howard:
Richard Foster. Stand-in for Joan Blondell: Connie Rae.

CAST: Leslie Howard (Atterbury Dodd), Joan Blondell (Lester Plum),
Humphrey Bogart (Douglas Quintain), Alan Mowbray (Koslofski), Marla
Shelton (Thelma Cheri), C. Henry Gordon (Ivor Nassau), Jack Carson
(Tom Potts), Tully Marshall (Fowler Pennypacker), J. C. Nugent (Junior
Pennypacker), William V. Mong (Cyrus Pennypacker), Pat Flaherty
(bouncer at nightclub), Hal Gleason (bit part), Esther Howard (landlady),
Olin Howlin (hotel manager), Harry Myers (member of bank's board),
Anne O'Neal (Elvira's mother), Charles Williams (boarder), Harry M.
Woods (studio employee), Theodore von Eltz ("Sir Geoffrey" in "Sex and
Satan").

Western Gold (1937) Principal Productions [Frank McGlynn Sr.]. Twentieth
Century-Fox. Produced by Sol Lesser. Directed by Howard Bretherton.
Assistant Director: George Sherman. Written by Forrest Barnes and Earl
Snell. Based on the novel *Helen of the Old House* by Harold Bell Wright
(New York, 1921). Original music by Arthur Lange. Cinematography by
Harry Neumann. Art Director: F. Paul Sylos. Film Editors: Arthur Hilton

and Carl Pierson. Wardrobe: Albert De Anno. Sound Engineer: Corson Jowett.

CAST: Smith Ballew (Bill Gibson), Heather Angel (Jeannie Thatcher), Leroy Mason (Fred Foster), Howard C. Hickman (Thatcher), Ben Alexander (Bart), Bud Osborne (Steve), Otis Harlan (Jake), Victor Potel (Jasper), Wesley Giraud (Bud), Lew Kelly (Ezra), Al Bridge (Holman), Tom London (Clem), Horace Murphy (squatter), Steve Clark (Carl), Harry Semels (barber).

Wells Fargo (1937) Paramount Pictures, Inc. [Frank McGlynn Sr.]. Executive Producer: William Le Baron. Produced and directed by Frank Lloyd. Associate Producer: Howard Estabrook. Staff Director: John Boland. Screenplay: Paul Schofield, Gerald Geraghty, and Frederick J. Jackson. Story: Stuart N. Lake. Additional Dialogue: Eddie Welch and Duke Atteberry. Contributor to Dialogue and Script Construction: Howard Estabrook. Contributor to Literary Research and Original Idea: Seena Owen. Original Music: Victor Young. Cinematographer: Theodor Sparkuhl. Costume Design: Edith Head. Film Editing: Hugh Bennett. Staff Director: John Boland. Sound: John Cope. Art Director: Hans Dreier. Interior Decorator: A. E. Freudeman. Art Director: John B. Goodman. Special Photographic Effects: Gordon Jennings. Sound: Harold Lewis and John Cope. Musical Director: Boris Morros. Assistant Director: William Tummel. Assistant Prop Man: Jack Leys.

CAST: Joel McCrea (Ramsay Mackay), Bob Burns (Hank York), Frances Dee (Justine), Lloyd Nolan (Dal Slade), Henry O'Neill (Henry Wells), Mary Nash (Mrs. Pryor), Ralph Morgan (Mr. Pryor), Johnny Mack Brown (Talbot Carter), Porter Hall (James Oliver), Jack Clark (William Fargo), Clarence Kolb (John Butterfield), Robert Cummings (Dan Trimball, prospector), Granville Bates (Bradford, banker), Harry Davenport (Ingalls, banker), Frank Conroy (Ward, banker), Brandon Tynan (Edwards, newspaper publisher), Peggy Stewart (Alice Mackay), Bernard Siegel (Pawnee), Stanley Fields (Abe, prosecutor), Jane Dewey (Lucy Dorsett Trimball), Henry Brandon, Spencer Charters, Lucien Littlefield.

The Man in the Barn (1937) Note: This is an examination of the story that John Wilkes Booth actually escaped after killing Lincoln and that the man killed in the barn was not Booth. Lincoln does not appear in this short film. Metro-Goldwyn-Mayer. Directed by Jacques Tourneur. Written by Morgan Coxe. Historical Compilations: Charles E. Whittaker. Narrator: Carey Wilson.

The Man Without a Country (1937) Warner Bros. Pictures. Broadway Brevities.

The Vitaphone Corporation [Charles Middleton]. Directed by Crane Wilbur. Screenplay by Forrest Barnes. Based on the story by Edward Everett Hale. Photographed in Technicolor.

Courage of the West (1937) Universal Pictures [Albert Russell]. Produced by Trem Carr. Associate Producer: Paul Malvern. Directed by Joseph H. Lewis. Assistant Director: Glen Cook. Story and Screenplay: Norton S. Parker. Cinematography: Virgil Miller. Film Editing: Charles Craft. Art Director: Charles Clague. Music Director and Arranger: Frank Santuck. Sound Recording: Robert Pritchard and Jesse Bastian.

CAST: Bob Baker (Jack Saunders), Lois January (Beth Andrews), J. Farrell Macdonald (Buck Saunders), Fuzzy Knight (Hank Givens), Carl Stockdale (Rufe Lambert), Harry Woods (Al Wilkins, also known as Jed Newman), Charles French (Secretary Stanton), Thomas Monk (Secretary Seward), Oscar Gahan (George Wilkins), Buddy Cox (Jackie Saunders), Richard Cramer (Murphy), Jack Montgomery (U.S. Marshal), Tom London, Forrest Taylor.

Triumph (1937)

Victoria the Great (GB 1937) [Percy Parsons] Produced and directed by Herbert Wilcox. Written by Miles Malleson and Charles de Grandcourt. Based on the play by Laurence Housman. Original Music: Anthony Collins. Cinematography: William V. Skall (Technicolor sequence, F. A. Young). Production Design: Tom Heslewood and Doris Zinkeisen. Film Editing: Jill Irving. Assistant Matte Artist: Peter Ellenshaw. Technicolor Color Director: Mrs. Natalie Kalmus. Musical Director: Muir Mathieson. Sound: L. E. Overton. Makeup Artist: Guy Pearce. Hairstylist: Patricia Pearce. Assistant Director: Lloyd Richards. Production Manager: Tom White. Supervising Editor: James Elmo Williams. Art Director: Lawrence P. Williams. Black and White with Technicolor Sequence.

CAST: Anna Neagle (Queen Victoria), Anton Walbrook (Prince Albert), Walter Rilla (Prince Ernest), H. B. Warner (Lord Melbourne), Mary Morris (Duchess of Kent), James Dale (Duke of Wellington), Felix Aylmer (Lord Palmerston), Charles Carson (Sir Robert Peel), Gordon McLeod (John Brown), C. V. France (Archbishop of Canterbury), Arthur Young (Rt. Hon. William Gladstone), Grete Wegener (Baroness Lehzen), Paul Leyssac (Baron Stockmar), Derrick De Marney (Younger Disraeli), Hugh Miller (Older Disraeli), Hubert Harben (Lord Conyngham), Joyce Bland (Florence Nightingale), Bert Bendon, Wyndham Goldie (Cecil Rhodes), Henry Hallett (Joseph Chamberlain), Syd Crossley, William Dewhurst (John Bright), Hal Gordon, Frank Birch (Sir Charles Dilke), Miles

Malleson (physician), Robert Atkins, Joan Young (Miss Pitt), Edgar Driver, Tom Heslewood (Sir Francis Grant), G. Moore Marriott, Lewis Casson (Archbishop of Canterbury, Jubilee), Charles Lefeaux, Ivor Barnard (assassin), O. B. Clarence, Arnold Lucy, Clarence Blakiston, Neil McKay, Vi Kaley, Marie Wright, Frank Cellier, Paul Henreid, C. Aubrey Smith.

The Lone Ranger (1937) Republic Pictures [Frank McGlynn Sr.]. Fifteen-part serial. Produced by Sol C. Siegel. Directed by John English and William Witney. Written by Franklin Adreon, Lois Eby, Barry Shipman, George Worthing Yates. Cinematographer: William Nobles. Film Editing: Edward Todd and Helene Turner.

CAST: Lee Powell (Allen King), Herman Brix (Bert Rogers), Chief Thundercloud (Tonto), Stanley Andrews (Captain Smith, alias Jeffries), George Cleveland (George Blanchard), Lynne Roberts (Joan Blanchard), Lane Chandler (Dick Forrest), Hal Taliaferro (Bob Stuart), George Letz (Jim Clark), Billy Bletcher (Lone Ranger voice), Raymond Hatton (Smokey), Dickie Jones (the Boy), Sammy McKim (Sammy, Cannon's grandson), Tom London (Belton), John Merton (Kester, a thug), Charles King (Morley, a thug), Maston Williams (Joe Snead, a thug), William Farnum (Father McKim), Forbes Murray (the real Col. Marcus Jeffries), Reed Howes (Lieutenant Brown), Allan Cavan (Major Brennan), Carl Stockdale (refugee leader at Stockade), Fred Burns (Holt, lead settler at finale), Edmund Cobb (ranger running from behind rock), Tex Cooper (white-bearded refugee), Art Dillard (Morgan thug), Frank Ellis (Morgan thug), Jimmy Hollywood (fort cellblock guard), Jack Ingram (thug restraining Jeffries), Walter James (Joe Cannon), Joe Kirk (Morgan thug with round face), Edna Lawrence (Marina, the servant-girl), George Magrill (fort gate sentry), Millard McGowan (Morgan thug), Bud Osborne (Morgan thug finding loot), Jack Perrin (Morgan, gang leader), Carl Saxe (stockade wall sentry), Francis Sayles (Texan congratulating Smith), Blackie Whiteford (thug-soldier).

The Mad Empress (Mexican, 1939) Warner Bros.—First National [Frank McGlynn Sr.]. Presented, produced, and directed by Miguel Contreras Torres. Assistant Directors: "Doc" Merman, C. Cabello, and M. Delgado. Original Story: Miguel C. Torres. Screenplay and Dialogue: Jean Bart, Jerome Chodorov, and Miguel C. Torres. Cinematography: Arthur Martinelli and Alex Phillips. Film Editing: Carl Pierson. Art Director: Frank Paul Sylos. Music Director: James Bradford, A. Esparza, Oteo and Mario Talavera. Sound Recording: Farrell Redd. Production Managers:

Bartlett Carre, P. Castelainand, J. Centeno. Production Advisor: Lionel Atwill.

CAST: Medea De Novara (Empress Carlotta), Lionel Atwill (Bazaine), Evelyn Brent (Empress Eugenie), Nigel De Brulier (Father Fisher), Earl Gunn (Porfino Diaz), Conrad Nagel (Maximilian), Guy Bates Post (Napoleon III), George Regas (Mariano Escobedo), Jason Robards Sr. (President Benito Juarez), Michael Visaroff (Dr. Samuel Basch), Claudia Dell (Agnes Salm), Gustav von Seyffertitz (Metternick), Rudolph Amendt (Hertzfield), Duncan Renaldo (Colonel Miguel Lopez), Graciela Romero (Madame Bazaine), Julian Rivero (Tomas Megia), Franklin Murrell (Martin Garralaga), Rolf Sedan, Robert Frazier, Rina De Lguoro, Marin Sais, Edgar Norton, Charles Bobbett, Kurt von Fuerberg.

Lincoln in the White House (1939) Warner Bros. Pictures. Vitaphone Corporation [Frank McGlynn Sr.]. Directed by William McGann. Written by Charles L. Tedford. Cinematography: Wilfred M. Cline. Costume Design: Milo Anderson. Film Editing: Everett Dodd. Sound: Oliver S. Garretson. Color Consultant: Natalie Kalmus. Art Director: Charles Novi. Color by Technicolor.

CAST: Dickie Moore (Tad Lincoln), Sybil Harris (Mary Todd Lincoln), John Harron, Raymond Brown, Erville Alderson, Nana Bryant, Earl Dwire, Gordon Hart, Edward Le Saint, Ian Wolfe.

Land of Liberty (1939) Note: This is a history of America told through clips from dozens of films. Lincoln is represented by clips starring both Frank McGlynn Sr. and Walter Huston. Motion Picture Producers and Distributor of America, Inc. Narration written by Jeanie Macpherson and Jess L. Lasky Jr. Editor: Cecil B. Demille. Assistant Editor: Herbert L. Moulton, William H. Pine, Francis S. Harmon, and Arthur H. Debra. Historical Consultant: James T. Shotwell.

Failure at Fifty (1939) Metro-Goldwyn-Mayer. Directed by Will Jason. Written by Howard Dimsdale. Based on the story "He Could Take It" by Arno B. Reincke. Music: Daniele Amfitheatrof. Narrated by Carey Wilson.

Of Human Hearts (1939) Metro-Goldwyn-Mayer Corp. [John Carradine]. Produced by John W. Considine Jr. Directed by Clarence Brown. Assistant Directors: Edward Woehler, Al Shenberg and E. Mason Hopper. Screenplay: Bradbury Foote. Based on the novel *Benefits Forgot* by Honore Morrow (New York, 1917). Contributor to Treatment: Conrad Richter. Music: Herbert Stothart. Cinematography: Clyde De Vinna. Costume Design: Dolly Tree. Film Editing: Frank E. Hull. Art Direction: Cedric Gibbons. Associate Art Directors: Harry Oliver and Edwin B. Willis.

Recording Engineer: Douglas Shearer. Montage Effects: Slavko Vorkapich. Technical Advisor: Charles Whittaker. Makeup: Jack Dawn and Joe Norin. CAST: Walter Huston (Ethan Wilkins), James Stewart (Jason Wilkins), Beulah Bondi (Mary Wilkins), Gene Reynolds (Jason Wilkins as a child), Guy Kibbee (George Ames), Charles Coburn (Dr. Charles Shingle), Ann Rutherford (Annie Hawks), Leatrice Joy Gilbert (Annie Hawks as a child), Charley Grapewin (Jim Meeker), Leona Roberts (Sister Clarke), Gene Lockhart (Quid), Clem Bevans (Elder Massey), Arthur Aylesworth (Rufus Inchpin), Sterling Holloway (Chauncey Ames), Charles Peck (Chauncey Ames as a child), Robert McWade (Dr. Lupus Crumm), Minor Watson (Captain Griggs), Guy Bates (horse buyer), Ward Bond (lout), Esther Dale (Mrs. Cantwell), Stanley Fields (horse owner), Joe Forte (intern), Brenda Fowler (Mrs. Ames), Rosina Galli (Mrs. Ardsley), Frank McGlynn Sr. (lout), John Miljan (Captain Griggs), Roger Moore (attendant), Jack Mulhall (soldier), Anne O'Neal (Mrs. Hawks), William Stack (salesman), Phillip Terry (intern), Morgan Wallace (Dr. Crandall).

Yankee Doodle Goes to Town (1939) Warner Bros. Pictures [Albert Russell]. Produced by John Nesbitt. Directed by Jacques Tourneur. Written by Sommerfield Alvan, Richard Goldstone, Joseph Sherman. Original Music: David Snell. Additional Music: Pyotr Ilyich Tchaikovsky (from Symphony No. 5). Film Editor: Harry Komer.
CAST: John Nesbitt (Narrator), Josiah Tucker.

Young Mr. Lincoln (1939) Working Titles: *The Young Lincoln, A Younger Lincoln, The Life of Young Abraham Lincoln,* and *Lawyer of the West.* Twentieth Century-Fox Film Corp. [Henry Fonda]. A Darryl F. Zanuck Production. Directed by John Ford. Screenplay: Lamar Trotti. Assistant Director: Wingate Smith. Produced by Kenneth MacGowan and Darryl F. Zanuck. Music: Alfred Newman. Cinematography: Bert Glennon and Arthur Miller. Costume Design: Royer. Production Design: Richard Day and Mark-Lee Kirk. Film Editing: Walter Thompson. Stunts: Yakima Canutt. Sound: Eugene Grossman and Roger Heman. Set Decoration: Thomas Little. Sound Effects Editor: Robert Parrish. Academy Award Nomination: Original Story (Lamar Trotti).
CAST: Alice Brady (Abigail Clay), Marjorie Weaver (Mary Todd), Arleen Whelan (Hannah Clay), Eddie Collins (Efe Turner), Pauline Moore (Ann Rutledge), Richard Cromwell (Matt Clay), Donald Meek (John Felder), Dorris Bowdon (Carrie Sue), Eddie Quillan (Adam Clay), Spencer Charters (Judge Bell), Ward Bond (John Palmer Cass), Milburn Stone (Stephen A. Douglas), Cliff Clark (Sheriff Billings), Robert Lowery (juror),

Henry Fonda as *Young Mr. Lincoln* (1939).
Courtesy of 20th Century-Fox Bison Archives/Marc Wanamaker

Charles Tannen (Ninian Edwards), Francis Ford (Frank Ford), Fred Kohler (Scrub White), Arthur Aylesworth (man), Virginia Brissac (woman), Paul E. Burns (loafer), George Chandler (loafer), Judith Dickens (Carrie Sue), Harold Goodwin (man), Charles Halton (Hawthorne), Herbert Heywood (official), Robert Homans (Mr. Clay), Dickie Jones (Adam as a boy), Jack Kelly (young Matt), Kay Linaker (Mrs. Edwards), Louis Mason (court clerk), Edwin Maxwell (John T. Stuart), Sylvia McClure (baby), Ivor McFadden (juror), Dave Morris (loafer), Frank Orth (loafer), Jack Pennick (Buck), Steven Randall (juror), Russell Simpson (Woolridge), Harry Tyler (barber), Dorothy Vaughan (woman), Eddy Waller (father), Delmar Watson (Adam Clay), Clarence Wilson (Dr. Mason).

Abe Lincoln in Illinois (1940) RKO Pictures, Inc. Max Gordon Plays and Pictures Corp. [Raymond Massey]. Produced by Max Gordon. Directed by John Cromwell. Screenplay by Robert E. Sherwood. Adaptation: Grover Jones. Based on the play *Abe Lincoln in Illinois* by Robert E. Sherwood (New York, October 15, 1938). Original Music: Roy Webb. Cinematography: James Wong Howe. Second Camera: Eddie Pyle and James Daly. Assistant Camera: Emmett Berkholtz and Ledge Haddow. Costume Design: Walter Plunkett. Ladies' Wardrobe: Ann Landers. First Wardrobe Man: Tommy Clark. Second Wardrobe Man: Frank Carr. Raymond Massey's Wardrobe: Bert Hall. Film Editing: George Hively. Art Director: Van Nest Polglase. Associate Art Director: Carroll Clark. Sound Recording: Hugh McDowell Jr. Dance Director: David Robel. Set Decorator: Casey Roberts. Assistant Directors: Dewey Starkey, Bill Dorfman, Henry Mancke, and Grayson

Rogers. Montage: Douglas Travers. Special Effects: Vernon L. Walker, H. Hulburd, D. Kohler, W. Kimpton, and K. Koontz. Technical Director: Lillian K. Deighton. Hairstylists: Hazel Rogers and Doris Harris. Makeup: James Barker, Mauri Seiderman, Don Cash, and Norbert Miles. Unit Manager: Harold Lewis. Script Clerk: Corynn Kiehl and Adele Cannon. Electrician: William Monroe. Grips: H. J. Brandon, Stan Chandler, William Record, Earl Gilpin, Eugene Fribourge, E. T. Harris, William Handy, and Jack McCrackin. Props: Charles Matthews and William Hartman. Location Manager: Louis Shapiro. Casting Director: Charles Richards. Soundstage Manager: Dan Kellerber. Still Photographer: Alex Kahle. Publicity: Charles Leonard. Stand-in for Raymond Massey: Stafford Campbell. Academy Award Nominations: Best Actor (Raymond Massey), Cinematography (James Wong Howe).

CAST: Gene Lockhart (Stephen A. Douglas), Ruth Gordon (Mary Todd Lincoln), Mary Howard (Ann Rutledge), Minor Watson (Joshua Speed), Alan Baxter (Billy Herndon), Harvey Stephens (Ninian Edwards), Howard Da Silva (Jack Armstrong), Dorothy Tree (Elizabeth Edwards), Aldrich Bowker (Judge Bowling Green), Maurice Murphy (John McNeil), Louis Jean Heydt (Mentor Graham), Clem Bevans (Ben Mattingly), Harlan Briggs (Denton Offut), Herbert Rudley (Seth Gale), Andy Clyde (Stage Driver), Fay Helm (Mrs. Gale), Roger Imhof (Mr. Crimmin), Edmund Elton (Mr. Rutledge), Florence Roberts (Mrs. Bowling Green), Leona Roberts (Mrs. Rutledge), George Rosener (Dr. Chandler), Trevor Bardette (John Hanks), Syd Saylor (John Johnstone), Elizabeth Risdon (Sarah Lincoln), Charles Middleton (Tom Lincoln), Alec Craig (Trem Cogdall), Peggy Ann Garner (little girl), Napoleon Simpson (Gobey), John Cromwell (John Brown), Edwin Mills (Robert Lincoln), Sonny Bupp (Willie Lincoln), Henry Blair (Tad Lincoln), Erville Alderson (Andrew Jackson), Dorothea Wolbert (woman in store), Jane Corcoran, Kathleen Proctor (women in street), Adda Cleason (maid), Harry Humphries (Daniel Webster). Tom Chatterton, Robert Middlemass, Ed Fielding, Bryant Washburn, William Worthington, Lorin Raker, Ian Wolfe, Guy Usher, George Guhl, Dan Clark, Gus Glassmire, Paul Everton, Del Henderson, Wallis Clark, Paul Guilfoyle, Victor Kilian, Emory Parnell, George Chandler, Selmer Jackson, Robert Elliott, Kathryn Sheldon, Fern Emmett, C. Hayes, Byron Foulger, Dick Elliott, Milt Kibbie, Landers Stevens, Esther Dale, John St. Polis, Florence Rutledge, William Royle.

The Blue Bird (1940) Twentieth Century-Fox Film Corp. [Gene Reynolds]. A Darryl F. Zanuck Production. Associate Producer: Gene Markey. Directed by Walter Lang. Assistant Director: Gene Bryant. Screenplay: Ernest Pascal. Based on the play *L'Oiseau bleu* by Maurice Maeterlinck (Moscow, 1908). Additional Dialogue: Walter Bullock. Cinematography: Arthur Miller Asc. and Ray Rennahan Asc. Technicolor Director: Natalie Kalmus. Art Directors: Richard Day and Wiard B. Ihnen. Film Editor: Robert Bischoff. Set Decorator: Thomas Little. Costumes: Gwen Wakeling. Music: Alfred Newman. Dance Director: Geneva Sawyer. Sound: E. Clayton Ward and Roger Heman. Academy Award Nominations: Color Cinematography (Arthur Miller and Ray Rennahan), Special Effects (Photographic: Fred Sersen, Sound: E. H. Hansen).

CAST: Shirley Temple (Mytyl), Spring Byington (Mummy Tyl), Nigel Bruce (Mr. Luxury), Gale Sondergaard (Tylette), Eddie Collins (Tylo), Sybil Jason (Angela Berlingot), Jessie Ralph (Fairy Berylume), Helen Ericson (Light), Johnny Russell (Tyltyl), Laura Hope Crews (Mrs. Luxury), Russell Hicks (Daddy Tyl), Cecelia Loftus (Granny Tyl), Al Shean (Grandpa Tyl), Leona Roberts (Mrs. Berlingot), Stanley Andrews (Wilhelm), Frank Dawson (caller of roll), Sterling Holloway (Wild Plum), Thurston Hall (Father Time), Edwin Maxwell (Oak), Herbert Evans, Brandon Hurst (footmen), Keith Hitchcock (Major Domo), Tommy Baker and Dorothy Joyce (young lovers), Billy Cook (chemist), Scotty Beckett, Juanita Quigley, Payne Johnson (children), Ann Todd (little sister), Diane Fisher (little girl), Dorothy Dearing (Cypress), Claire Du Brey (nurse), Dewey Robinson (royal forester), Buster Phelps (boy inventor), Alice Armand (Weeping Willow), Eric Wilton (door man), Alec Craig (groom), Otto Hoffman (Crab Apple Tree), Imboden Parrish (Walnut Tree), Eddy Waller (Birch Tree), Edward Earle (Maple Tree), Paul Kruger (Pine Tree), James Blaine (Beech Tree), Harold Goodwin (Hickory Tree), Dick Rich (Elm Tree), Dickie Moore (boy).

Virginia City (1940) Warner Bros. Pictures, Inc. [Victor Kilian]. Jack L. Warner in charge of production. A Warner Bros.-First National Picture. Executive Producer: Hal B. Wallis. Associate Producer: Robert Fellows. Directed by Michael Curtiz. Screenplay: Robert Henry Buckner. Dialogue Director: Jo Graham. Original Music: Max Steiner. Music Director: Leo F. Forbstein. Orchestra Arranger: Hugo Friedhofer. Cinematography: Sol Polito. Production Design: Ted Smith and Robert Haas. Film Editing: George Amy. Stunts: Yakima Canutt. Special Effects: Byron Haskin and Hans F. Koenekamp. Assistant Director: Sherry Shourds. Makeup Artist: Perc Westmore. Sound Recording: Oliver Garrettson and Francis J. Scheid. Unit Manager: Frank Mattison.

CAST: Errol Flynn (Kerry Bradford), Miriam Hopkins (Julia Haynes), Randolph Scott (Vance Irby), Humphrey Bogart (John Murrell), Frank McHugh (Mr. Upjohn), Alan Hale (Olaf Swenson), Guinn "Big Boy" Williams ("Marblehead"), John Litel (Marshal), Douglass Dumbrille (Major Drewery), Moroni Olsen (Cameron), Russell Hicks (Armistead), Dickie Jones (Cobby), Frank Wilcox (Union soldier), Russell Simpson (Gaylord), Charles Middleton (Jefferson Davis), Monte Montague (stage driver), Bud Osborne (stage driver), Lane Chandler (soldier clerk), Trevor Bardette (fanatic), Edward Keane (officer), George Regas (half-breed), Thurston Hall (General Meade), Charles Trowbridge (Seddon), Howard C. Hickman (General Page), Charles Halton (Ralston), Roy Gordon (Major General Taylor), Ward Bond (Sergeant Sam McDaniel), Spencer Charters (bartender), George Guhl (bartender), Eddie Parker (lieutenant), William Hopper (lieutenant), Paul Fix (Murrell's henchman), Walter Miller (sergeant), Reed Howes (sergeant), George Reeves (telegrapher), Wilfred Lucas (toutherner), Brandon Tynan (Trenholm), Tom Dugan (Spieler), Harry Cording (scarecrow).

A Dispatch from Reuters (1940) Note: Lincoln does not appear in this film, which tells the story of the birth of the famous Reuters news agency. However, the story of Lincoln's assassination is a crucial one in the plot—Reuters is able to report the news in England long before any other news agency can confirm the story. Warner Bros. Pictures, Inc. Jack L. Warner in charge of production. A Warner Bros.–First National Picture. Executive Producer: Hal B. Wallis. Associate Producer: Henry Blanke. Directed by William Dieterle. Dialogue Director: Jo Graham. Assistant Director: Jack Sullivan. Screenplay: Milton Krims. Original Story: Wolfgang Wilhelm and Valentine Williams. Original Music: Max Steiner. Cinematography: James Wong Howe. Costume Design: Orry-Kelly. Film Editing: Warren Low. Special Effects: Robert Burks and Byron Haskin. Music Supervisor: Leo F. Forbstein. Orchestra Arranger: Hugo Friedhofer. Art Director: Anton Grot. Sound: C. A. Riggs. Makeup: Perc Westmore. Technical Advisor: Jonah M. Ruddy. Unit Manager: Al Alleborn.

CAST: Edward G. Robinson (Julius Reuter), Edna Best (Ida Magnus), Eddie Albert (Max Wagner), Albert Bassermann (Franz Geller), Gene Lockhart (Bauer), Otto Kruger (Dr. Magnus), Nigel Bruce (Sir Randolph Persham), Montague Love (Delane), James Stephenson (Carew), Walter Kingsford (Napoleon III), David Bruce (Bruce), Dickie Moore (Reuter as a boy), Billy Dawson (Max Wagner as a boy), Richard Nichols (Herbert, age five), Lumsden Hare (chairman), Norman Ainsley (newspaper vendor),

Mary Anderson (girl), Hazel Boyne (companion), Egon Brecher (Reingold), Alec Craig (Geant), Cyril Delevanti (newspaper vendor), Gilbert Emery (Lord Palmerston), Lawrence Grant (member of Parliament), Bobby Hale (newspaper vendor), Ernst Hausman (Heinrich), Holmes Herbert (member of Parliament), Stuart Holmes (attendant), Kenneth Hunter (member of Parliament), Ellis Irving (Parliament speaker), Paul Irving (Benfey), Frank Jaquet (Stein), Edward McWade (scientist), Frederic Mellinger (man), Leonard Mudie (member of Parliament), Pat O'Malley (laborer), Grace Stafford (woman), Robert Warwick (opposition Parliament speaker), Paul Weigel (Gauss), Wolfgang Zilzer (clerk at post office), Theodore von Eltz (actor).

Hi-yo Silver (1940) [Frank McGlynn Sr.] Produced by Sol C. Siegel. Directed by John English and William Witney. Written by Franklin Adreon, Lois Eby, Barry Shipman, and George Worthing Yates. Cinematographer: William Nobles. Film Editing: Edward Todd and Helene Turner.

CAST: Lee Powell (Allen King), Herman Brix (Bert Rogers), Chief Thundercloud (Tonto), Stanley Andrews (Captain Smith, alias Jeffries), George Cleveland (George Blanchard), Lynne Roberts (Joan Blanchard), Lane Chandler (Dick Forrest), Hal Taliaferro (Bob Stuart), George Letz (Jim Clark), Billy Bletcher (Lone Ranger voice), Raymond Hatton (Smokey), Dickie Jones (the boy), Sammy McKim (Sammy, Cannon's grandson), Tom London (Belton), John Merton (Kester, a thug), Charles King (Morley, a thug), Maston Williams (Joe Snead, a thug), William Farnum (Father McKim), Forbes Murray (the real Colonel Marcus Jeffries), Reed Howes (Lieutenant Brown), Allan Cavan (Major Brennan), Carl Stockdale (refugee leader at stockade), Fred Burns (Holt, lead settler at finale), Edmund Cobb (ranger running from behind rock), Tex Cooper (white-bearded refugee), Art Dillard (Morgan thug), Frank Ellis (Morgan thug), Jimmy Hollywood (fort cellblock guard), Jack Ingram (thug restraining Jeffries), Walter James (Joe Cannon), Joe Kirk (Morgan thug with round face), Edna Lawrence (Marina, the servant-girl), George Magrill (fort gate sentry), Millard McGowan (Morgan thug), Bud Osborne (Morgan thug finding loot), Jack Perrin (Morgan, gang leader), Carl Saxe (stockade wall sentry), Francis Sayles (Texan congratulating Smith), Blackie Whiteford (thug–soldier).

Nor Long Remember (1941) Jam Handy Organization

Tennessee Johnson (1942) Original title: *The Man on America's Conscience.* Metro-Goldwyn-Mayer [Ed O'Neill]. Produced by J. Walter Ruben. Directed by William Dieterle. Screenplay by John L. Balderston and Wells

Root. Story by Milton Gunzburg and Alvin Meyers. Musical Score: Herbert Stothart. Cinematography: Harold Rosson, A.S.C. Film Editing: Robert J. Kern. Recording Engineer: Douglas Shearer. Art Director: Cedric Gibbons. Associate: Malcolm Brown. Set Decorations: Edwin B. Willis. Associate: Hugh Hunt. Special Effects: Warren Newcombe. Men's Costumes: Lon Anthony. Makeup created by Jack Dawn. Technical Advisor: Sloan Nibley. CAST: Van Heflin (Andrew Johnson), Ruth Hussey (Eliza McCardle), Lionel Barrymore (Thaddeus Stevens), Marjorie Main (Mrs. Fisher), Regis Toomey (McDaniel), Montague Love (Chief Justice Chase), Porter Hall (the Weasel), Charles Dingle (Senator Jim Waters), J. Edward Bromberg (Coke), Grant Withers (Mordecai Milligan), Alec Craig (Andrews), Morris Ankrum (Jefferson Davis), Sheldon Leonard (Atzerodt), Noah Beery (Sheriff Cass), Lloyd Corrigan (Mr. Secretary), Charles Trowbridge (Lansbury), Harry Worth (John Wilkes Booth), Robert Warwick (Major Crooks), Bernard Zanville (Wirts), Robert Emmett O'Connor (Robinson), Lee Phelps (deputy), Brandon Hurst (senator), Charles Ray (senator), Harlan Briggs (senator), Hugh Sothern (senator), Frederick Burton (senator), Allen Pomeroy (assassin), Duke York (assassin), Roy Barcroft (officer on crutches), Jack Norton (drunk), Russell Simpson (Kirby), Louise Beavers (Addie), Jim Davis (reporter), William Roberts (reporter), Frank Jaquet (reporter), Emmett Vogan (reporter), Pat O'Malley (reporter), William Wright (alderman), William B. Davidson (Vice President Breckenridge), Russell Hicks (Lincoln's emissary), Lynne Carver (Martha), William Farnum (Senator Huyler), Carl Benton Reid (Congressman Hargrove), Patsy Nash (child), Jeff Corey (captain).

Anna and the King of Siam (1946) Produced by Louis D. Lighton. Directed by John Cromwell. Written by Sally Benson and Talbot Jennings. Based on the book by Margaret Landon. Original Music: Bernard Herrmann. Cinematography: Arthur C. Miller, A. S. C. Film Editing: Harmon Jones. Production Design: William S. Darling, Frank E. Hughes, Thomas Little, and Lyle R. Wheeler. Costume Design: Bonnie Cashin. Special Effects: Fred Sersen.

CAST: Irene Dunne (Anna Owens), Rex Harrison (King Mongkut), Linda Darnell (Tuptim), Lee J. Cobb (Kralahome), Gale Sondergaard (Lady Thiang), Mikhail Rasumny (Alak), Dennis Hoey (Sir Edward), Tito Renaldo (Prince), Richard Lyon (Louis Owens), William Edmunds (Moonshee), John Abbott (Phya Phrom), Leonard Strong (interpreter), Mickey Roth (Prince), Connie Leon (Beebe), Chabing (wife of king), Oie Chan (old woman), Si-Lan Chen (dance director), Dorothy Chung

A drunken Andrew Johnson (Van Heflin) takes the oath of
office as vice-president as Abraham Lincoln looks on from the
balcony in *Tennessee Johnson* (1942). Johnson was, until 1998,
the only United States president to face impeachment.
Tennessee Johnson is a sympathetic portrayal of his turbulent
time in office.
Courtesy of Metro-Goldwyn-Mayer

(Amazon guard), Buff Cobb (wife of king), Rico De Montez (guard),
Marjorie Eaton (Miss Macfarlane), Joe Garcia (whipper), Helena Grant
(Mrs. Cortwright), Ted Hecht (judge), Aram Katcher (guard), Sydney
Logan (wife of king), Loretta Luiz (wife of king), Stanley Mann (Mr.
Cortwright), Lillian Molieri (wife of king), Neyle Morrow (Phra Palat),
Marianne Quon (wife of king), Pedro Regas (guide), Addison Richards
(Captain Orton), Julian Rivero (government clerk), Yvonne Rob (Lady Son
Klin), Constantine Romanoff (whipper), Hazel Shon (slave), Diane Van der
Ecker (Princess Fa-Ying), Chet Voravan (Siamese guard), Ben Welden
(third judge), Jean Wong (Amazon guard).
Note: While Lincoln does not appear in this film, he serves as an important
off-camera presence. The King of Siam attempts to pattern himself after
Lincoln and seeks to help his fellow leader win the Civil War by sending
him a herd of elephants. The story has been refilmed three times, with the
character of Lincoln figuring in each movie. *The King and I* (1956), the
Rodgers and Hammerstein musical version, originated on the stage. The
film version starred Yul Brynner and Deborah Kerr and was directed by
Walter Lang. It was filmed in Cinemascope 55. Four decades later, the
musical was transformed into an animated film, also called *The King and I*

(1999). Miranda Richardson provided the speaking voice for Anna while Christiane Noll did all the singing. Martin Vidnovic gave voice to The King of Siam. Also in 1999, a nonmusical version was filmed. Called, simply, *Anna*, it starred Jodie Foster and Chow Yung Fat.

Johnson and Reconstruction (1950) Teaching Film Custodians. An educational short adapted from the Metro-Goldwyn-Mayer feature *Tennessee Johnson* (1942).

Lincoln Speaks at Gettysburg (1950) A.F. Films. Produced by Paul Falkenberg and Lewis Jacobs.

Rock Island Trail (1950) Republic Pictures [Jeff Corey]. Produced by Paul Malvern. Directed by Joseph Kane. Screenplay by James Edward Grant. Based on the novel *A Yankee Dared* by Frank J. Nevins. Original music: R. Dale Butts. Cinematography: Jack A. Marta. Film Editing: Arthur Roberts. Art Director: Frank Arrigo. Assistant to Associate Producer: Harvey Parry. Sound: T. A. Carman and Howard Wilson. Costume Design: Adele Palmer. Set Decoration: John McCarthy Jr. and George Milo. Special Effects: Howard and Theodore Lydecker. Makeup: Bob Mark. Hairstylist: Peggy Gray. Technical Advisor: William E. Hayes, Rock Island Railroad. Photographed in Trucolor.

CAST: Forrest Tucker (Reed Loomis), Adele Mara (Constance Strong), Adrian Booth (Aleeta), Roy Barcroft (Barnes), Bruce Cabot (Kirby Morrow), Dick Elliott (conductor), Sam Flint (mayor), Barbara Fuller (Annabelle), Lorna Gray (Aleeta), John Holland (Major Porter), Olin Howlin (saloon keeper), Jimmy Hunt (Stinky), Kate Drain Lawson (Mrs. McCoy), Emory Parnell (Senator Wells), Valentine Perkins (Annette), Pierre Watkin (Major), Billy Wilkerson (Lakin), Chill Wills (Hogger), Grant Withers (David Strong).

Lincoln in Illinois (1950) State of Illinois, Division of Department Reports [G. William Horsley]. Distributed by Illinois State Film Library. Produced by Kling Studios. Color.

Transcontinental Express (1950)

Lincoln's Gettysburg Address (1951) Sterling Films
CAST: Canada Lee.

Abraham Lincoln (1951) Emerson Film Corp. Released by Encyclopedia Brittanica Films. Collaborator: J.G. Randall.

New Mexico (1951) [Hans Conreid] Produced by Irving Allen and Joseph Justman. Directed by Irving Reis. Written by Max Trell. Original Music: Lucien Moraweck. Cinematography: Jack Greenhalgh and William E.

Snyder. Film Editing: Louis Sackin. Assistant Director: Robert Aldrich. Production Assistant: Robert H. Justman.

CAST: Lew Ayres (Captain Hunt), Jack Briggs (Private Lindley), Donald Buka (Private Van Vechton), Raymond Burr (Private Anderson), Jeff Corey (Coyote), Lloyd Corrigan (Judge Wilcox), Andy Devine (Sergeant Garrity), Bob Duncan (Corporal Mack), Verna Felton (Mrs. Fenway), Walter Greaza (Colonel McComb), John Hoyt (Sergeant Harrison), Robert Hutton (Lieutenant Vermont), Jack Kelly (Private Clifton), Arthur Lowe (Private Finnegan), Ian Macdonald (Private Daniels), Allen Matthews (Private Vale), Marilyn Maxwell (Cherry), Robert Osterloh (Private Parsons), Peter Edward Price (Chia-Kong), William Tannen (Private Cheever), Ralph Volkie (Rider), Ted de Corsia (Acoma, Indian chief).

The Tall Target (1951) [Leslie Kimmel] Produced by Richard Goldstone. Directed by Anthony Mann. Written by Art Cohn, Geoffrey Homes, and George Worthing Yates. Cinematography: Paul C. Vogel. Film Editing: Newell P. Kimlin. Art Director: Cedric Gibbons and Eddie Imazu. Special Effects: A. Arnold Gillespie and Warren Newcombe. Hairstylist: Sydney Guilaroff. Set Decorator: Ralph S. Hurst. Recording Engineer: Douglas Shearer. Makeup Artist: William Tuttle. Set Decorator: Edwin B. Willis.

CAST: Dick Powell (John Kennedy), Paula Raymond (Ginny Beaufort), Adolphe Menjou (Caleb Jeffers), Marshall Thompson (Lance Beaufort), Ruby Dee (Rachel), Richard Rober (Lieutenant Coulter), Will Geer (Homer Crowley), Leif Erickson (stranger), Florence Bates (Mrs. Charlotte Alsop), Barbara Billingsley (young mother), Peter Brocco (Fernandina), Dan Foster (dapper man), Jonathan Hale (passenger), James Harrison (Allan Pinkerton), Paul Harvey, Percy Helton (passenger), Victor Kilian (John K. Gannon), Tom Powers (Simon G. Stroud), Jeff Richards (policeman), Regis Toomey (Tim Reilly), Katherine Warren (Mrs. Gibbons), Will Wright (Thomas I. Ogden).

San Antone (1953) [Richard Hale] Produced by Joseph Kane. Directed by Joseph Kane. Written by Curt Carroll and Steve Fisher. Original Music: R. Dale Butts. Cinematography: Bud Thackery. Costume Design: Adele Palmer. Film Editing: Tony Martinelli.

CAST: Rodolfo Acosta (Chino Figueroa), Andy Brennan (Ike), Argentina Brunetti (Mexican woman), Rod Cameron (Carl Miller), Harry Carey Jr. (Dobe), George Cleveland (Colonel Allerby), Paul Fiero (bandit leader), Martin Garralaga (Mexican), Katy Jurado (Mistania Figueroa), Douglas Kennedy (Captain Garfield), James Lilburn (Jim), Roy Roberts (John

Lobby Card for *The Tall Target* (1951).
Courtesy of Metro-Goldwyn-Mayer

Secret Service man meets suspects in a plot against Lincoln in Anthony Mann's *The Tall Target* (1951). Left to right: Adolphe Menjou, Ruby Dee, Paula Raymond, Marshall Thompson, and Dick Powell.
Courtesy of Metro-Goldwyn-Mayer

Chisum), Bob Steele (Bob), Forrest Tucker (Brian Culver), Arleen Whelan (Julia Allerby).

The Cavalcade of America: "Moonlight Witness" (1954) E. I. du Pont de Nemours. Made by Flying A Productions. Produced by Armand Schaefer. Written and directed by Maurice Geraghty. Film Editor: Anthony Wollner.
CAST: Bruce Bennett, Rhys Williams, Claire du Brey, Walter Reed, Michael Hall.

The Prince of Players (1955) Twentieth Century-Fox [Stanley Hall]. A Cinemascope Production. Executive in Charge of Production: Darryl F. Zanuck. Produced and directed by Philip Dunne. Written by Moss Hart. Based on the book by Eleanor Ruggles. Original Music: Bernard Herrmann. Director of Photography: Charles G. Clarke, A.S.C. Art

Direction: Lyle Wheeler and Mark-Lee Kirk. Set Decorations: Walter M. Scott and Paul S. Fox. Special Photographic Effects: Ray Kellogg. Film Editor: Dorothy Spencer, A.C.E. Wardrobe Direction: Charles Le Maire. Costume Design: Mary Wills. Makeup Artist: Ben Nye. Hair Styling: Helen Turpin. Sound: Alfred Bruzlin and Harry M. Leonard. Assistant Director: Eli Dunn. Special Consultant on Shakespearean Scenes: Eva La Gallienne. Color Consultant: Leonard Doss. Color by Deluxe. Cinemascope Lenses by Bausch and Lomb.

CAST: Richard Burton (Edwin Booth), John Derek (John Wilkes Booth), Raymond Massey (Junius Brutus Booth), Maggie McNamara (Mary Devlin Booth), Charles Bickford (Dave Prescott), George Melford, Sarah Padden (Mary Todd Lincoln), Mae Marsh (witch in *Macbeth*), Richard Deacon (theater manager), Betty Flint (Lady Macbeth in *Macbeth*), Ian Keith (Claudius in *Hamlet*), Eva Legallienne (Gertrude in *Hamlet*), Dayton Lummis (English doctor), Elizabeth Sellars (Asia Booth), Paul Stader (Laertes in *Hamlet*), Percival Vivian (Polonius in *Hamlet*).

The Face of Lincoln (1955) Note: In this film, sculptor/professor Merrill Gage of Ucla sculpts a bust of Lincoln as he tells Lincoln's life story. The sculpture is in a constant state of change as Lincoln ages and his appearance alters.

University of Southern California. Department of Cinema. Released by Cavalcade Pictures. Produced by Wilbur T. Blume. Associate Producer: David W. Johnson. Directed by Edward Freed. Photographed and edited by Richard Harber. Assistant Camera: Akira Asakura. Sound: Daniel Wiegand. Assistant Director: John Clayton. Academy Award: Short Subject (two reel). Academy Award Nomination: Documentary Short Subject.

CAST: Merrell Gage, Professor of Fine Arts.

The Cavalcade of America: "The Palmetto Conspiracy" (1955) E. I. du Pont de Nemours. Made by Jack Denove Productions. Produced by Jack Denove. Written and directed by Charles Bennett. Music Supervisor: Josef Zimanich.

The Battle of Gettysburg (1955) Metro-Goldwyn-Mayer [Frank Ferguson, voice only]. Written and produced by Dore Schary. Directed by Herman Hoffman. Cinematography: George Folsey. Film Editing: Frank Santillo. Advisor and Consultant: J. Walter Coleman. Music adapted and conducted by Adolph Deutsch. Recording Supervisor: Wesley C. Miller. Academy Award Nomination: Documentary Short Subject.

CAST: Leslie Nielsen (Narrator).

Springfield Incident (1955)

The King and I (1956) [see *Anna and the King of Siam* (1946)]

The Booth brothers at odds in *Prince of Players* (1955): John
Wilkes (John Derek, left) and Edwin (Richard Burton) discuss
various approaches to becoming famous on the stage.
Courtesy of 20th Century-Fox

The Abductors (1957) Note: This film is based on the true story of men who
planned to kidnap Lincoln's body from his new tomb in Springfield and
hold it for ransom. Lincoln himself, of course, does not appear in the film.
Twentieth Century-Fox. Regal Films, Inc. Executive Producer: E. J.
Baumgarten. Produced by Ray Wander. Directed by Andrew V. McLaglen.
Story and screenplay by Ray Wander. Original Music: Paul Glass. Music
Director: Ingolf Dahl. Cinematography: Joseph Lashelle. Filmed in
Regalscope. Film Editor: Betty Steinberg. Assistant Director: Howard
Joslin. Sound: James Brock. Art Director: Rudi Feld.
  CAST: Victor McLaglen (Tom Muldoon), George Macready (Langley), Fay
Spain (Sue Ellen), Carl Thayer (Jed), Gavin Muir (Evans), John Morley (F.
Winters), Carlyle Mitchell (Chief Becker), George Cisar (Hansen), Jason
Johnson, Pat Lawless, James Logan, Finton Meyler, Joe Hamilton, Nolan
Leary, Gene Walker, Calvin Booth, Cliff Lyons.
The Story of Mankind (1957) Warner Bros. Pictures [Austin Green]. Produced
and directed by Irwin Allen. Screenplay by Irwin Allen and Charles
Bennett. Based on the novel by Henrik Van Loon. Associate Producer:
George E. Swink. Costumes: Marjorie Best. Director of Photography: Nick
Musucara. Art Direction: Art Loel. Set Decoration: Arthur Krams. Music:
Paul Sawtell. Sound: Stanley Jones. Film Editor: Gene Palmer.
Photographed in Technicolor.
  CAST: Peter Lorre (Nero), Jim Ameche (Alexander Graham Bell), Francis
X. Bushman (Moses), John Carradine (Khufu), Charles Coburn (Hippo-
crates), Ronald Colman (The Spirit of Man), Melville Cooper (Major

Domo), Nick Cravat, Dani Crayne (Helen of Troy), Henry Daniell (Bishop of Beauvais), Anthony Dexter (Columbus), Cedric Hardwicke (High Judge), Dennis Hopper (Napoleon Bonaparte), Hedy Lamarr (Joan of Arc), Chico Marx (Monk), Groucho Marx (Peter Minuit), Harpo Marx (Sir Isaac Newton), Melinda Marx, Virginia Mayo (Cleopatra), Agnes Moorehead (Queen Elizabeth), Cathy O'Donnell (Early Christian Woman), Franklin Pangborn (Marquis de Varennes), Vincent Price (the Devil), Ziva Rodann, Reginald Sheffield (Caesar), Marie Windsor (Marie Antoinette).

Lincoln at Gettysburg (1960) Pathe News

How the West Was Won (1963) Metro-Goldwyn-Mayer [Raymond Massey]. Produced by Bernard Smith. Directed by John Ford ("The Civil War" segment), Henry Hathaway ("The Rivers," "The Plains," and "The Outlaws" segments), George Marshall ("The Railroad" segment), Richard Thorpe (uncredited). Written by James R. Webb (and, uncredited, John Gay). Music: Ken Darby and Alfred Newman. Cinematography: William H. Daniels, Milton R. Krasner, Joseph Lashelle ("The Civil War"), and Charles Lang. Film Editing: Harold F. Kress. Art Direction: George W. Davis, William Ferrari, Addison Hehr. Set Decoration: Henry Grace, Don Greenwood Jr., Jack Mills. Costume Design: Walter Plunkett. Hairstylist: Sydney Guilaroff. Makeup: William Tuttle. Assistant Directors: George Marshall Jr., William McGarry, Robert Saunders, William Shanks, Wingate Smith. Special Effects: A. Arnold Gillespie and Robert R. Hoag. Stunts: John Epper, Loren Janes, Bob Morgan, Boyd "Red" Morgan, Chuck Roberson. Production Supervisor for Cinerama: Thomas Conroy. Music Coordinator: Robert Emmett Dolan. Color Consultant: Charles K. Hagedon. Recording Supervisor: Franklin Milton. Camera Operator, Second Unit: Harold E. Wellman.

CAST: Carroll Baker (Eve Prescott), Lee J. Cobb (Marshal Lou Ramsey), Henry Fonda (Jethro Stuart), Carolyn Jones (Julie Rawlings), Karl Malden (Zebulon Prescott), Gregory Peck (Cleve Van Valen), George Peppard (Zeb Rawlings), Robert Preston (Roger Morgan), Debbie Reynolds (Lillith Prescott), James Stewart (Linus Rawlings), Eli Wallach (Charlie Gant), John Wayne (General William Tecumseh Sherman), Richard Widmark (Mike King), Spencer Tracy (narrator), Brigid Bazlen (Dora Hawkins), Walter Brennan (Colonel Hawkins), David Brian (Lillith's attorney), Andy Devine (Corporal Peterson), Agnes Moorehead (Rebecca Prescott), Harry Morgan (General Ulysses S. Grant), Thelma Ritter (Agatha Clegg), Mickey Shaughnessy (Deputy Stover), Russ Tamblyn (Confederate deserter), Rodolfo Acosta (Gant gang member), Kim Charney (Sam Prescott), Jay C.

Based on a true story, *The Abductors* (1957) concerns a group of
men who plot to kidnap Lincoln's body from its tomb in
Springfield and hold it for ransom. The debut of director
Andrew McGlaglen, *The Abductors* starred his father Victor
McGlaglen (right) and George MacReady (left).
Courtesy of 20th Century-Fox

Flippen (Huggins), Barry Harvey (Angus), Jerry Holmes (railroad clerk),
Claude Johnson (Jeremiah Rawlings), Tudor Owen (Parson Harvey), Jamie
Ross (Bruce), Bryan Russell (Zeke Prescott), Clinton Sundberg (Hylan
Seabury), Lee Van Cleef (Marty), Ken Curtis (Union soldier), John Damler
(lawyer), Ken Dibbs (blacksmith), Ben Black Elk Sr. (Indian chief), Sol
Gorss (henchman), William Henry (staff officer), Roy Jenson (henchman),
Robert Nash (lawyer), Harvey Parry (henchman), Jack Pennick (Corporal
Murphy), Gil Perkins (henchman), Red Perkins (Union soldier), Victor
Romito (henchman), Harry Dean Stanton (henchman), Karl Swenson
(train conductor), Jack Lambert (henchman), Christopher Dark (poker
player), Gene Roth (riverboat poker player), Joe Sawyer (ship's officer),
James Griffith (poker player), Walter Burke (wagon poker player), John
Larch (Grimes), J. Edward McKinley (auctioneer), Mark Allen (Colin),
Craig Duncan (James Marshall), Charlie Briggs (barker), Paul Bryar
(Auctioneer's assistant), Beulah Archuletta (Indian woman), Chuck
Roberson (Union soldier), Stanley Livingston (Prescott Rawlings).
Lincoln's Gettysburg Address (1973) [Charlton Heston]
The Faking of the President (1976) [William J. Daprato] Produced by Alan Abel,
Jeanne Abel, Alan Barinholtz. Written and directed by Alan Abel and
Jeanne Abel. Director of Photography: Arthur Albert. Film and Tape

Editors: Jeanne Abel, Roy Friedman, Ted Frasco, Rick Steiner, and Sonya Polonsky.
CAST: Marshall Efron (Donald Segretti), Alan Barinholtz (Ronald Ziegler), Robert Staats (G. Gordon Liddy), Richard M. Dixon (Richard Nixon).

The Lincoln Conspiracy (1977) Schick Sunn Classic Productions, Inc. [John Anderson]. Executive Producer: Raylan D. Jensen. Produced by Charles E. Sellier Jr. Directed by James L. Conway. Written by Jonathan Cobbler. Music: Bob Summers. Music Supervision: Don Perry. Cinematography: Henning Schellerup. Editing: Stan Siegel and Martin Dreffke. Historical Researcher: David W. Balsiger. Art Director: William Cornford. Production Manager: Cheryl Guarantiello. Production Coordinator: Leon Dudevoir. Assistant Director: Patrick Wright. Second Assistant Director: Jerry Fleck. Set Construction Supervisor: Jon Reeves. Script Supervisor: Pam Eddy. Location Manager: Rej Jackson. Assistant Cameraman: Paul Dillingham. Second Assistant Cameraman: Kim Marks. Gaffer: Glenn Schellerup. Best Boy/Gaffer: Stephen W. Gray. Set Dresser: Charles Bennett. Assistant Set Dresser: Mark Howard. Mixer/Recordists: Jan Brodin and Chris Leplus. Key Grip: Charles W. Wilde. Best Boy/Grip: Richard "Doc" Heavirland. Wardrobe: Cheryl Beasley. Assistant Wardrobe: Karen Kauffman. Seamstress: Ann Taylor. Makeup: Melanie Levitt. Assistant Makeup: Debra Rudy. Property Master: Fernando Celis. Special Effects: Mel Welch. Carpenters: Allan Terry, Doug Kramer, Dean Brown. Equipment Manager: Paul Thomas. Associate Editors: Steve Mark and Trevor Jolly. First Assistant Editor: Michael Sherman. Second Assistant Editor: Gary Krivacek. Sound Effects Editor: Michael Hilkene. Music Editor: Ken Johnson. Assistant Effects Editors: Les Udy and John Wilde. Security: Pete Liakakis and Tom Thornton. Still Photographer: Jay Hoey. Safety Officer: Bill Steinhauser. Stunts: Fernando Celis. Production Secretary: Vicki Garretson. Production Assistant: Carole Fontana. Film Runner: Steve Vandora. Location Accounting: Donna Sellier, Jamie Peterson, and Patricia Hassel. Secretary to the Producer: Lynette Gardner. Los Angeles Coordinator: Domenic Guarantiello. Casting: Samantha Monsour. Production Executive: Alan Pedersen. Equipment Systems by Cinemobile. Titles and opticals by Pacific Title. Rerecording by Producers Sound Service. Color by Technicolor. Narrated by Brad Crandall.
CAST: Whit Bissell (Senator John Connors), John Dehner (Colonel Lafayette Baker), Bradford Dillman (John Wilkes Booth), Fred Grandy (David Herold), James Green (Captain James William Boyd), Robert Middleton, Sonny Shroyer (Lewis Paine), Ken Kercheval, Len Wayland,

John Anderson as Abraham Lincoln and Bradford Dillman as
John Wilkes Booth in *The Lincoln Conspiracy* (1977).
Courtesy of Sunn Classic Pictures, Inc.

Ed Lupinski (Edwin Henson), Gregory J. Oliver (Representative George
Julian), Patrick Wright (Major Thomas Eckert), Frank Schuller
(Lieutenant Everton Conger), Wallace K. Wilkinson (Dr. Samuel Mudd),
Ben Jones (Samuel Arnold), Mimi Honce (Mary Surratt), Christopher
Allport (Michael O'Laughlin), Bill Dial (George Atzerodt), Charles Briggs
(Andrew Potter), Mark Harris (Luther Potter), J. Don Ferguson
(Lieutenant Luther Baker), Joe A. Dorsey (Lieutenant Edward P Doherty),
Billy Johnson (Senator Zachariah Chandler), Dick Callinan (Senator
Benjamin Wade), Maurice Hunt (Representative A. J. Rogers), Howard
Brunner (Louis J. Wiechmann), William Gribble (Captain Willie Jett),
Fred Buch (Captain D. H. Gleason), Ned Nartnett (General Christopher
Auger), William Travis (Senator George Boutwell), Paul Brown (Thomas
Caldwell), Bruce Atkins (John Parker), Larry Quackenbush (Harry Ford),
Ralph Flanders (Richard Garrett), Dan Fitzgerald (Sandford Conover),
Albert Smith (Ferryman), Doug Kaye (Lincoln's secretary), Ben Mayo
(Richard Montgomery), John Mackay (James Merritt), E. J. Andre
(Thaddeus Stephens).

Guardian of the Wilderness (1977) Schick Sunn Classics [Ford Rainey].
Executive Producer: Raylan D. Jensen. Produced by Charles E. Sellier Jr.
Directed by David O'Malley. Written by Casey Conlon. From a story by
Charles E. Sellier Jr. Cinematography: Henning Schellerup. Associate
Producer: James L. Conway. Production Executive: Art Stolnitz. Produc-
tion Manager: Cheryl Quarantiello. Production Coordinator: Jerry Fleck.
Editor: Sharron Miller. Assistant Director: David F. Oyster Jr. Production

John Wilkes Booth (Bradford Dillman, second from left) has
shaved off his distinctive moustache and is escaping into
Southern territory in *The Lincoln Conspiracy* (1977). This
docudrama explores the theory that Booth eluded capture and
that another man was killed in his place. This persistent historical
mystery was also covered in a Metro-Goldwyn-Mayer short from
1937 called *The Man in the Barn*.
Courtesy of Sunn Classic Pictures, Inc.

Supervisor: William Cornford. Special Effects: Doug Hubbard. Music
Supervision: Don Perry. Music conducted and composed by Bob Summers.
Second Unit Photography: Stephen W. Gray. Second Assistant Director:
Richard Boden. Assistant Cameraman: Paul Billingham. Second Assistant
Cameraman: Kim Marks. Art Director: Paul Staneli. Assistant Property
Master: W. Vosco Call Jr. Set Construction Supervisor: Jon Reeves. Gaffer:
Glenn Schellerup. Mixer-Recordist: Scott Terhark. Key Grip: Garlan W.
Wilde. Set Operations Grip: Michael Sherman. Boom Operator: Klay
Anderson. Wardrobe: Lee Sollenberger. Makeup: Julie Staheli and Mike
Bacarella. Script Supervisors: Tondea Kay Willis, Brenda Cobia. Still
Photographers: William Sellier and Craig Reese. Security: Mike Riedel.
Safety Officer: Howard Crittenden. Stunts: Wayne Bauer. Utah Film
Coordinator: Hal Schleuter. Production Secretary: Vicki Garretson.
Production Assistant: Carole Thomases. Unit Publicist: Jymme
Christensen. Research: Mary Thompson. Location Accounting: Donna
Sellier. Equipment Manager: Grady Daugherty. Los Angeles Coordinator:
Domenic Quarantiello. Casting: Susie McCarty. Carpenters: John
Mitchel, Alan Terry, and Richard W. Hayes. Wildlife Consultants: Steve
Martin, Jackie Martin, Ron Oxley, Mark Weiner, Jeff Haynes, Hubert

Wells, Helena Walsh, Vern Debord, George Toth. Wranglers: S Bar S Ranch, Tom Simpson and Dave Larson. First Assistant Editor: Gary Krivacek. Second Assistant Editor: John Wilde. Sound Effects Editor: Michael Hilkene. Assistant Effects Editor: Les Udy. Equipment Systems by F & B Ceco. Titles: Pacific Title. Rerecording: Producers Sound Service, Don Minkler, Howard Woolman, and Ray West. Color by Technicolor. "Yosemite Theme" performed by the Mike Curb Congregation.

CAST: Denver Pyle (Galen Clark), Ken Berry (Zachary Moore), John Dehner (John Muir), Norman Fell (Doctor), Jack Kruschen (Madden, surveyor), Prentiss Rowe (Forebes, surveyor), Cheryl Miller (Kathleen Clark), Don Shanks (Teneiya), Cliff Osmond (McCullough, limber foreman), Melissa Jones (Heather), Brett Palmer (Galen's grandson).

Two Idiots in Hollywood (1988) New World. [Richard Craycroft]. Produced by David Lancaster. Written and directed by Stephen Tobolowsky. Associate Producer: Ginny Nugent. Music: Stephen Tobolowsky. Cinematography: Robert Brinkmann. Costume Design: Carla De Govia. Production Design: Jack De Govia. Editing: Andy Blumenthal. First Assistant Camera: Joseph Antczak. Production Associate: Frederick Bailey. Script Supervisor: Susan Bierbaum. Grip: Afsaneh Bourtorabi. Second Assistant Camera: Katherine M. Butler. Production Coordinator: Cristen Carr. Assistant to Director: Joanne Wetzel Caverly. Sound Mixer: Peter Chaikin. Electrician: John Cheshire. Grip: Molly Cheshire. First Assistant Director: Matthew J. Clark. Production Manager: Lisa C. Cook. Production Assistant: Richard Craycroft. Set Decorator: Robert Franklin. Musical Director: Bert Good. Still Photographer: Gregory Grove. Gaffer: David Hayball. Second Assistant Director: Diana L. Hayes. Choreographer: Bonnie Oda Homsey. Art Director: John R. Jensen. Best Boy: Jonathan Kealey. Hairstylist/ Makeup Artist: Susan Jennifer Lipson. Boom Operator: Rob Scott. Construction Foreman: Bill Steis. Best Boy Grip: Michael Stocks. Property Master: Fred Van Baumann. Key Grip: Thaddeus Wadleigh.

CAST: J. B. McGrath (Murphy Wegg), Jeff Doucette (Taylor Dup), Cheryl Anderson (Marianne Plambo), Kat Sawyer-Young, Lisa Lack Robins (NBA casting secretary), Joe Clark (Joe Clark), Jenny Bourgeois (Lynn Jett), Wayne Winstead (barbershop quartet singer/judgehead #2), R. Wayne Kruse (judgehead #1), Kurtwood Smith (defense attorney), Budge Threlkeld (Dan Skink), William B. Steis (Wiler Weiner), Paul Koester (Mel Davis), M. C. Gainey (Sergeant Albert), Benjamin Jurand (NBA security guard/big men big women dancer), Ron Colizzo (Rupert

Roleridge), William Utay (Winn Kaalsen/Loupenis Jones), Charles Allen-Anderson (buffet chef #1/NBA security guard/big men big women dancer), Ritchie Montgomery (Perry White/Sgt. Rose), Bonnie Oda Homsey (Carla Tokenaga Dortmonger), Robert Darnell (Joc Jeremy), Ann Hearn (Morris Franklin/girl in ed. room), Joshua Levy (Skink's child), Scanlon Gail, Edward Anhalt (jury foreman), Phillip Ray Rolfe (man with poodle/big men big women dancer), Frederick Bailey (robot/nude chauffeur), Stephen Tobolowsky (prosecuting attorney), Thomas Callaway (T. Barry Armstrong), Joan Pirkle (Sandra), Bruce Wright (Todd Armstrong), Louise Baker, Carolyn English, Nancy Scher (actresses), Claire Malis (Indian juror), Carl Bressler (assistant to prosecutor), Jim Beaver (crying man), Rex Rotsko (barbecue singer), Ron Hoffman (barbecue singer), John Cox (barbecue singer), Jeff Murray (madman at trial), Hillarie Thompson (juror in red), Mary McCusker (hula juror), Wesley Pfenning (juror in black/woman dancing under tree), Tommy Bourgeois (man dancing under tree), Matthew Bourgeois (boy dancing under tree), Sunny Smith (cue card girl), Tony Campisi (propman), Katherine De Govia (actress), Gayna Shireen (statue of justice/female prisoner), Stephanie Lamotta (maid in hallway/big men big women dancer), David Kozubei (court stenographer), Brian Boyle (Puck), Joel Rudnick (dream barbecue father), Belita Moreno (dream barbecue mother), Matthew Rudnick (dream barbecue child), Laverne Thompson (big men big women dancer/female prisoner), Susan Youngblood (big men big women dancer/prison matron), Gregory Grove (big men big women dancer), Robyn Jacobs (big men big women dancer), Magenta (big men big women dancer), Kathleen Kelley (big men big women dancer), Joanne Wetzel Caverly (big men big women dancer), El Duce (male prisoner), Stan Yale (male prisoner), Ray Vernon (male prisoner), Reggie (male prisoner), C.C. Geno (female prisoner).

The Big Picture (1989) [Richard Blake]. Executive Producers: Richard Gilbert Abramson and William E. McEuen. Associate Producers: Richard Luke Rothschild and Michael Varhol. Associate Producer: Valen Watson. Directed by Christopher Guest. Written by Christopher Guest and Michael McKean. Story by Christopher Guest and Michael Varhol. Original music by David Nichtern. Cinematography: Jeff Jur. Costume Design: Karen Patch. Production Design: Joseph T. Garrity. Film Editing: Martin Nicholson. Set Dresser: G. Roger Abell. Grip: Ismael Araujo Jr. Casting: Nina Axelrod. Art Swing Gang: Todd Badalato. Assistant to Mr. Varhol: Debra Baumann. Adr Editor: Beth Bergeron. Negative Cutter: Lillian C. Best. Assistant to Mr. Guest: Patrick Billings. Casting Assistant:

Joel A. Blumenau. Music Editor: Sally Boldt. Craft Services: Suzi Bond. Boom Operator: Forrest Brakeman. Negative Cutter: Gary Burritt. Wardrobe: Kim Carleton. Foley Mixer: Greg Curda. Special Effects Coordinator: Gary D'Amico. Key Grip: J. Patrick Daily. First Assistant Director: Paul Deason. Electrician: Duane Dellamico. Construction Coordinators: Richard D. Galbraith, Ken Deubel III. Camera Operator: Don Devine. Assistant Sound Editor: Lily Diamond. Storyboard Artist: Andrea Diedrich. Rigging Gaffer: John Doherty. Supervising Sound Editor: Dody Dorn. Foley Editor: Michael Dressel. Sound Effects Recordist: John P. Fasal. Foley Editor: David Fechtor. Set Dresser: Richard A. Frisch. Assistant Production Coordinator: Damien Ganczewski. Electrician: George Gary. Sound Recordist: David Gertz. Extras Casting: Bess Gilbert. Sound Editor: Sarah Goldsmith. Location Manager: Barry Gremillion. Wardrober: Shari Griffin. Sound Editor: Kimberly Harris. Sound Assistant: Cynthia E. Hill. Dialogue Editor: John Hoeren. Production Sound Mixer: Jon Huck. Sound Rerecording Mixer: David J. Hudson. First Assistant Camera: Paul Hughen. First Assistant Film Editor: Tony Kadell. Adr Mixer: Doc Kane. Set Decorator: Jerie Kelter. Apprentice Sound Editor: Jonathan Klein. Dolly Grip: Dwight La Vers. Supervising Sound Editor: Blake Leyh. Music Recording Engineer: Laura Livingston. Art Lead Man: Robert Lucas. Horse Wrangler/Stunts: Richard Lundin. Title Designer: Burke Mattsson. Second Assistant Camera: Kelly E. McGowen. Electrician: Charles McIntyre III. Second Second Assistant Director: Keri L. McIntyre. Sound Rerecording Mixer: Mel Metcalfe. Art Swing Gang: Noel A. Middleton. Dog Trainer: Karl Lewis Miller. Set Dresser: Michael George Miller. Key Hairstylist: Gina Monaci. Rigging Gaffer: Kevin Myers. Still Photographer: Deana Newcomb. Assistant Sound Editor: Stephanie Ng. Grip: Charles "Chaz" Norcross. Production Assistant: Marshall Peck. Second Assistant Film Editor: Frederick Peterson. Assistant Location Manager: Martha Pilcher. Special Effects Assistant: David A. Poole. Sound Rerecording Mixer: Terry Porter. Electrician: Ronald J. Pure Jr. Wardrobe: Ellen Robinson. Unit Production Manager: Richard Luke Rothschild. Foley Walker: Joan Rowe. Best Boy Electric: John "Fest" Sandau. Music Scoring Mixer: Dennis S. Sands. Script Supervisor: Judith Saunders. Assistant Sound Editor: Janelle Showalter. Sound Editor: Frank Smathers. Special Effects Foreman: Ken Speed. Property Master: Philip Steuer. Production Coordinator: Nancy Rae Stone. Visual Effects: Mark Sullivan. Art Director: Pat Tagliaferro. Sound Editor: Kelly Tartan. Still Photographer: Suzanne Tenner. Electrician: Woogi Thomas. Foley Walker: Jerry

Trent. Gaffer: James R. Tynes. Second Unit Director: Michael Varhol. Best Boy Grip: Tom West. Key Makeup Artist: Lizbeth Williamson. Second Assistant Director: Kelly Wimberly. Editorial Trainee/Production Assistant: Diane Witter. Assistant Property Master: Bill Zullo.

CAST: Kevin Bacon (Nick Chapman), Emily Longstreth (Susan Rawlings), Michael McKean (Emmet Sumner), Jennifer Jason Leigh (Lydia Johnson), J. T. Walsh (Allen Habel), Kim Miyori (Jenny Sumner), Teri Hatcher (Gretchen), Dan Schneider (Jonathan Tristan-Bennet), Jason Gould (Carl Manknik), Tracy Brooks Swope (Lori Pressman), Don Franklin (Todd Marvin), Gary Kroeger (Mark), Alice Hirson (Mrs. Chapman), Grant Owens (Mr. Chapman), Fran Drescher (Polo Habel), Suzy Cote (Mindy Habel), Eddie Albert (M.C.), June Lockhart (Janet Kingsley), Stephen Collins (attorney), Roddy McDowall (judge), Robert Bauer (wounded soldier), Vladimir Skomarovsky (man in Nick's movie), C. W. Hemingway (Joey), Holly Fields (daughter), Yvonne Peattie (Mrs. Feldzar), Stan Ivar (Charlie), David Hayward (George), Caitlin Clarke (Sharon), Nancy Valen (Young Sharon), Wesley Pfenning (woman in cabin), John Cleese (bartender), Walter Olkewicz (Babe Ruth), Scott Coffey (waiter), Bruce Kirby (businessman), Richard Belzer (video show host), Tom Maier (building manager), Michael Jocum (pez people), Tim Landers (pez people), Martin Lund (pez people), Mike Miller (pez people), Novi Novog (pez people), Valen Watson (woman in restaurant), Jennifer Karr (woman in restaurant), Sue-Ann Leeds (woman in restaurant), Buddy Garion (man in restaurant), Jim Pollack (man in restaurant), Scott Williamson (restaurant manager), Victor Steinbach (Andres Vargiak), Arlene Lorre (Cleopatra), George Rogan (security guard/Nazi), Perla Walter (housekeeper), Pamela Morris (Cheryl), Lulie Newcomb (receptionist), Patty Howeth (woman with fridge), Beth Chamberlin (stewardess), Britta Wilson (stewardess), Suzee Slater (stewardess), Brad Zutaut (surfer), Matthew Eichler (piano player), Nadine Lenore Patterson (twin), Elliott Gould (lawyer), Martin Short (Nick's agent).

Bill and Ted's Excellent Adventure (1989) [Robert V. Barron]. Produced by Scott Kroopf, Michael S. Murphey, and Joel Soisson. Directed by Stephen Herek. Written by Chris Matheson and Ed Solomon. Original Music: David Newman. Cinematography: Tim Suhrstedt. Costume Design: Jill M. Ohanneson. Production Design: Roy Forge Smith. Film Editing: Larry Bock and Patricia Rand. Visual Effects Production Manager: Charles L. Finance. Animator: Kevin Kutchaver. Director of Photography, Second

Unit: Thomas Loizeaux. Location Accountant: Enzo Sisti. Music Editor: Tom Villano. Makeup Effects: Kevin Yagher.

CAST: Keanu Reeves (Ted "Theodore" Logan), Alex Winter (Bill S. Preston), George Carlin (Rufus), Tony Camilleri (Napoleon), Dan Shor (Billy the Kid), Tony Steedman (Socrates), Rod Loomis (Freud), Al Leong (Genghis Khan), Jane Wiedlin (Joan of Arc), Clifford David (Beethoven), Hal Landon Jr. (Captain Logan), Bernie Casey (Mr. Ryan), Amy Stock-Poynton (Missy/Mom), J. Patrick McNamara (Mr. Preston), Frazier Bain (deacon), Diane Franklin (Princess Joanna), Kimberley Kates (Princess Elizabeth), Will Robbins (Ox), Steve Shepherd (Randolf), Anne Machette (Buffy), Traci Dawn Davis (Jody), Duncan McLeod (bartender), John Clure (tattooed cowboy), Jim Cody Williams (bearded cowboy), Dusty O'Dee (old west ugly dude), Heather Pittman (Kerry), Ruth Pittman (Daphne), Richard Alexander (bowling alley manager), James Bowbitch (John the serf), John Karlsen (evil duke), Jeanne Hermine Herek (mother at waterslides), Jonathan Bond (waterslide attendant), Jeff S. Goodrich (music store salesman), Lisa Rubin (girl at mall), Marjean Holden (student speaker), Claudia Templeton (aerobic saleswoman), Carol Gossler (aerobic instructor), J. Donovan Nelson (mall photographer), Marcia Darroch (store clerk), Steven Rotblatt (police psychiatrist), Ed Solomon (stupid waiter), Chris Matheson (ugly waiter), Mark Ogden (Neanderthal #1), Ron Althoff (security guard), Tom Dugan (Neanderthal #2).

Civil War Diary (1990) [Kenneth Johnson]. Produced by Robert C. Peters. Directed by Kevin Meyer. Written by Kevin Meyer. Original Music: Alan Dermarderosian. Cinematography: James W. Wrenn. Film Editing: Rose Anne Weinstein. Production Design: James Smythe.

CAST: Todd Duffey (Jethro Creighton), Miriam Byrd-Nethery (Ellen Creighton), John Touchstone (Matt Creighton), Hollis McCarthy (Jenny Creighton), Pat Cochran (Bill Creighton), David Cloud (John Creighton), David Fritts (Tom Creighton), Stewart Skelton (Cousin Eb), Ben Stephenson (Shad), Robert Knott (Wortman), Mike Wiles (Burdow), Rex Linn (Jake), Dave Bennett (Roy), Michael T. McGraw (Ross Milton), Andy Sherman (Cousin Wilse), Bob Bennish (Sam Gardiner), Paul Hindman (Ed Turner), Scott Cordes (Dan Turner), Christopher E. Glaze (Union sergeant), Kenneth Johnson (older Jethro), Nolan Cispar (young Jethro), Deanne Yates (Mary Creighton), Joshua Smith (Jethro's snow double), Frank Kirtley (doctor), Becky Borg (Mary's voice), Jim Beckner (Union soldier), Scott Hughes (Union soldier), David Hyde Pierce (Union soldier), Stephen Pierce (Union soldier), Randy Anderson (Union soldier).

Doran Cart, Chad Dial, Aaron Raccine, John Mackey, Bob Talbot, Skip Merriman, Bill Broughton, Don Whitson, Max Maxon, Steve Hall, Charlie Riggs, Carlene Hale, Gail Higginbotham, Mona Talbot, Bettie Broughton, Chip Riggs, Gregg Higginbotham, Julie Sackman, William Sumnicht, Greg Jones, Hilliary Higginbotham, Cheryl Parvin (townspeople).

Bebe's Kids (1992) [Pete Renaday, voice only] Produced by Willard Carroll. Coproducer: David Robert Cobb. Executive Producers: Reginald Hudlin and Warrington Hudlin. Associate Producer: Lynne Southerland. Producer: Thomas L. Wilhite. Directed by Bruce W. Smith. Written by Robin Harris (album *Bebe's Kids*) and Reginald Hudlin. Original Music: John Barnes. Production Design: Fred Cline. Film Editing: Lynne Southerland. Character Animator: Stephen J. Anderson. Supervising/ Directing Animator: Lennie K. Graves. Visual Effects Animator: Adam Howard. Overseas Background Supervisor: Bill Kaufmann. Production Manager: Igor Khait. Music Editor: George A. Martin. Principal Characters Design: Bruce W. Smith. Executive Music Supervisor: Bill Stephney. Supervising Color Stylist: Brigitte Strother. Background Supervisor: Lucy Tanashian-Gentry. Production Assistant: Tyler Tharpe.

CAST: Faizon Love (Robin Harris), Vanessa Bell Calloway (Jamika), Wayne Collins Jr. (Leon), Jonell Green (Lashawn), Marques Houston (Kahill), Tone Loc (Pee Wee), Myra J. (Dorothea), Nell Carter (Vivian), John Witherspoon (card player #1), Chino "Fats" Williams (card player #2), Rodney Winfield (card player #3), George D. Wallace (card player #4), Brad Sanders (bartender), Reynaldo Rey (lush), Bebe Drake-Massey (barfly), Jack Lynch (Richie), Phillip Glasser (Opie), Louie Anderson (security guard #1), Tom Everett (security guard #2), Kerrigan Mahan (security guard #2/Fun World patrolman), Susan Silo (ticketlady/ saleswoman/nuclear mother/Rodney Rodent), Pete Renaday (announcer/ impericon/Tommy Toad), Rich Little (President Nixon), David Robert Cobb (Titanic captain), Barry Diamond (nuclear father/motorcycle cop), Stanley B. Clay, Michelle Davison, Judi M. Durand, Greg Finley, Maui France, Jaquita Green, Jamie Gunderson, J. D. Hall, Doris Hess, Barbara Iley, Daamen J. Krall, John Lafayette, Tina Lifford, Josh Lindsay, Arvie Lowe Jr., Devaughn Nixon, David Randolph, Noreen Reardon, Gary Schwartz, Cheryl Tyre Smith (additional voices).

Happy Gilmore (1996) [Charles L. Brame]. Executive Producers: Bernie Brillstein, Sandy Wernick, and Brad Grey. Produced by Warren Carr, Jack Giarraputo, and Robert Simonds. Directed by Dennis Dugan. Written by

Tim Herlihy and Adam Sandler. Original Music by Mark Mothersbaugh. Cinematography: Arthur Albert. Film Editing: Jeff Gourson. Casting: Joanna Colbert. Production Design: Perry Andelin Blake. Art Direction: Richard Harrison. Costume Design: Tish Monaghan. Hairstylist: Anji Bemben. Makeup: Lisa Robers. Unit Production Manager: Warren Carr. Assistant Director: Peter D. Marshall. Second Assistant Director: Wayne Bennett. Assistant Director, Second Unit: David W. Rose. Sound Rerecording Mixer: Chris David. Foley Artist: Doug Jackson. Foley Mixer: Mary Jo Lang. Digital Effects Producer: Tamara L. Watts. Stunts: Guy Bews, Jason Glass, Tom Glass, Corry Glass-Lowry, Alex Green, David Jacox, Ken Kirzinger, Michael Langlois, Mike Mitchell, Fred Perron, Fiona Roeske, Greg Schlosser, Dawn Stofer, Melissa R. Stubbs, Mike Vézina. Stunt Coordinator: Brent Woolsey. Dialogue Editor: Christopher Assells. Postproduction Supervisor: Robert Hackl. Coproduction Designer: William Heslup. Music Supervisor: Michelle Kuznetsky. Set Decorator: Mark Lane. Promotions Manager: Campbell McCubbin. Music Supervision: Jennifer Pyken and Mary Ramos. Property Master: Bill Thumm.

CAST: Adam Sandler (Happy Gilmore), Christopher McDonald (Shooter McGavin), Julie Bowen (Virginia), Frances Bay (Grandma), Carl Weathers (Chubbs), Allen Covert (Otto), Robert Smigel (IRS Agent), Bob Barker (himself), Richard Kiel (Mr. Larson), Dennis Dugan (Doug Thompson), Joe Flaherty (jeering fan), Lee Trevino (himself), Kevin Nealon (Potter), Vern Lundquist (announcer), Jared Van Snellenberg (Happy's Waterbury caddy), Ken Camroux (coach), Rich Elwood (assistant coach), Nancy McClure (Terry), Helena Yee (Chinese lady), William Sasso (mover), Dee Jay Jackson (mover), Ellie Harvie (registrar), Ian Boothby (guy on green), Andrew Johnston (crowd guy), Kim Restell (crowd girl), Fred Perron (Waterbury heckler), Helen Honeywell (crazy old lady), Paul Raskin (starter #1), William Samples (starter #2), John Shaw (Daniel Lafferty), Ted Deekan (auctioneer), John B. Destry (Zamboni driver), James Crescenzo (Shooters AT&T caddy), Brett Armstrong (Shooters tournament caddy), Peter Kelamis (Potter's caddy), Stephen Tibbetts (pro golfer), Edward Lieberman (pro golfer), Donald Macmillan (young Happy), Louis O'Donoghue (Happy's dad), Lisanne Collett (Happy's mom), Stephen Dimopoulos (Italian guy), Douglas Newell (starter #4), Frank L. Frazier (blue collar fan), David Kaye (reporter), Zachary Webb (batting kid), Simon Webb (doctor), Mark Lye (Mark Lye), Betty Linde (elderly woman), Dave

Cameron (reporter #2), Lou Kliman (reporter #3), Brent Chapman (official), Jessica Gunn (signed chest woman), Phillip Beer (Cowboy Joe), Fat Jack (Jack Beard), Michelle Holdsworth (babe on green), Ben Stiller (the orderly in the nursing home).

The King and I (1999) [See *Anna and the King of Siam* (1946)]

Anna (1999) [See *Anna and the King of Siam* (1946)]

Abraham Lincoln on Television

Abe Lincoln in Illinois, Act I (April 15, 1945) [Steven Courtleigh]
WNBT-NBC, New York. Produced and directed by Edward Sobol. Written by Robert E. Sherwood, based upon his play.
CAST: Alma Mansfield (Ann Rutledge), John Mckee, Vinton Hayworth, Mort L. Stevens, Mary Michaels.

Abe Lincoln in Illinois, Act II (May 20, 1945) [Steven Courtleigh]
WNBT-NBC, New York. Produced and directed by Edward Sobol. Written by Robert E. Sherwood, based upon his play. Assistant Director: Don Darey. Technical Director: Albert Protzman. Scenery: Robert Wade.
CAST: Wendel Phillips (William Herndon), Grandon Rhodes, Ralph Chambers, Vinton Hayworth, May Collins, Viola Frane, Lucille Fenton, Earl McDonald, Dorothy Emery, Kay Renard, Harry Bellaver.

Abe Lincoln in Illinois, Act III (May 27, 1945) [Steven Courtleigh]
WNBT-NBC, New York. Produced and directed by Edward Sobol. Written by Robert E. Sherwood, based upon his play. Assistant Director: Don Darey. Technical Director: Albert Protzman. Scenery: Robert Wade.
CAST: Wendel Phillips (William Herndon), Grandon Rhodes, Ralph Chambers, Vinton Hayworth, May Collins, Viola Frane, Lucille Fenton, Earl McDonald, Dorothy Emery, Kay Renard, Harry Bellaver.

Perry Como's Chesterfield Supper Club (November 19, 1949) [Raymond Massey]

Ken Murray Show (February 8, 1950) [Raymond Massey]

PULITZER PRIZE PLAYHOUSE
Abe Lincoln in Illinois (October 20, 1950) [Raymond Massey]
ABC Television Network. Supervised by Edgar Peterson. Directed by Alex Segal. Based upon the play by Robert M. Sherwood.
CAST: Betty Field (Mary Todd Lincoln)

Mr. I. Magination
Host: Paul Tripp. Book, lyrics, and staging by Paul Tripp. Music composed and conducted by Ray Carter. Story by Paul Tripp. Settings by Kathleen Ankers. Directed by Herbert Hirschman. Produced by Norman and Irving Pincus.
CAST: Ruth Enders, Ted Tiller, Donald Harris, Ed Fuller

NASH AIRFLYTE THEATER
A Kiss for Mr. Lincoln (February 22, 1951)
CBS Television Network. Nash Airflyte Theater. Executive Producer: Tom Hicks. Produced and directed by David Pressman. Adapted by Alvin Sapinsley. Based on a story by Louise Kennedy Mabie. Music: Jacques Press. Settings: Samuel Leve. Costumes: Paul de Pont. Host: William Gaxton.
CAST: Richard Greene (Henry Kenneth), Grace Kelly (Mrs. Kenneth), Bruce Gordon (Mr. Murdoch), Sarah Floyd (Maid), Sarah Cunningham (Mrs. Murdoch).

AMERICAN WIT & HUMOR #9
Lincolnholmes Incident: A Folktale (1952) [Royal Dano]
March of Time. Produced by Parsonnet Studios. Produced and directed by Marion Parsonnet.
CAST: Thomas Mitchell (Host and Narrator), Gene Lockhart (Oliver Wendell Holmes).

AMERICAN INVENTORY
The Election of Abraham Lincoln (May 18, 1952) [Crahan Denton]
NBC-TV, Chicago. Executive Producer: Bill Hodapp. Produced and directed by Ben Park. Production Supervisor: Walter Schwimmer. Written by Doug Johnston. Based on a radio script by Carl Haverlin. Music by Joseph Gallicchio and the Orchestra. Announcer: Hugh Downs.
CAST: Geraldine Kay (Mary Todd Lincoln), Maurice Copeland

(Herndon), Fred Smith, Ward Ohrman, Arthur Peterson, Stan Gordon (John Jennings), Vera Ward, Les Spears, Jim Johnson, Clifton Utley.

OMNIBUS
Mr. Lincoln (1952) [Royal Dano]
TV-Radio Workshop. A Division of The Ford Foundation. Produced by Richard de Rochemont. Directed by Norman Lloyd. Written by James Agee. Director of Photography: Marcel Rebiere. Assistant Director: George Ackerson. Script Clerk: Sascha Laurance. Assistants to the Producer: Stanley Kubrick, Gaetano Buscemi, and Gerald Weiler. Film Editor: Morrie Roizman. Business Office: Frederick Edelstein and Ruth Takamo. Research: Rita Vandivert. Art Direction: Herbert Andrews and Trew Hocker. Costumes: Jules Racine. Makeup: Fred Ryle. Chief Property Man: William Plunien. Narrated by Martin Gabel.
PART ONE: *The End and the Beginning* (November 16, 1952)
CAST: Royal Dano (Lincoln), Crahan Denton (Tom Lincoln), Marian Seldes (Nancy Hanks), Allen Nourse (Secretary Stanton), Richard Purdy (Alexander Gardner), Joanna Roos (Mary Todd Lincoln), Doris Rich (Aunt Peggy).
PART TWO: *Nancy Hanks* (November 30, 1952)
CAST: Marian Seldes (Nancy Hanks), Crahan Denton (Tom Lincoln), Blanche Cholet (Sally Bush Johnston Lincoln), Otis Reed Jr. (young Abe), Alice Brewer (young Sarah).
PART THREE: *Growing Up* (December 14, 1952)
CAST: Crahan Denton (Tom Lincoln), Blanche Cholet (Sally Bush Lincoln), George Mitchell (Teacher), James Broderick (Jake Cameron), Joe A. Driskill (Josiah Crawford).
PART FOUR: *New Salem* (January 11, 1953)
CAST: Joanne Woodward (Ann Rutledge), Harry Mehaffey (Bowling Green), Jack Warden (Jack Armstrong), James Agee (Jack Kelso), Raymond Roseberry (Mentor Graham), John Liggett (James Rutledge).
PART FIVE: *Ann Rutledge* (February 5, 1953)
CAST: Joanne Woodward (Ann Rutledge), Harry Mehaffey (Bowling Green), Jack Warden (Jack Armstrong), John Liggett (James Rutledge), Bettie Ward (Hannah Armstrong).

HALLMARK HALL OF FAME
Woman with a Sword (February 10, 1952) [Henry Sharp]
NBC Television Network. NBC Production Supervisor: Douglas Coulter.

Produced and directed by William Corrigan. Adapted for television by H. Philip Minus. Based on the story by Hollister Noble. Technical Director: Bob Hanna. Audio Engineer: Lincoln Mayo. Scenery: James Russell. Costumes: Saul Bolasni. Lighting: Jack Fitzpatrick. Associate Director: Paul Lammers. Production Assistant: Marilyn Evans. Presenting for Hallmark Cards: Lee Vines. Host: Sarah Churchill.

CAST: Jayne Meadows (Anna Ella Carroll), Douglass Montgomery (Lemuel Evans), Robert Simon (Captain Scott), Howard Wierum (General), Casey Walters (Major Denning), Sandy Kenyon (Dale Duncan), Richard Shankland (Nicolay).

WESTINGHOUSE STUDIO ONE
Abraham Lincoln (1952) [Robert Pastene]
Produced by Donald Davis and Dorothy Mathews. Directed by Paul Nickell. Written by David Shaw. Based on the play *Abraham Lincoln* by John Drinkwater (1919).

CAST: Judith Evelyn (Mary Todd Lincoln), James Dean (William Scott).

THE CAVALCADE OF AMERICA
One Nation Indivisible (1953) [Frank Ferguson]
E. I. du Pont de Nemours. Produced by Jack Chertok Productions. Produced by Jack Chertok. Directed by William J. Thiele. Teleplay: Warner Law. Film Editor: Frank Cappacchione.

CAST: Edgar Buchanan, Lyle Talbot, Fay Wray, Raymond Greenleaf.

YOU ARE THERE
The Capture of John Wilkes Booth (September 6, 1953)
CBS Television Network. Produced by Charles Russell. Directed by Sidney Lumet. Written by Leslie Slote. Host and Narrator: Walter Cronkite. CAST: David Stewart (John Wilkes Booth), Darren McGavin (Colonel), Richard Waring (Edwin Booth).

The Gettysburg Address (December 29, 1953)
CBS Television Network. Directed by Sidney Lumet. Written by Leslie Slote. Host and Narrator: Walter Cronkite.

HALLMARK HALL OF FAME
Lincoln's Little Correspondent (February 8, 1953) [Crahan Denton]
NBC Television Network. Devised and directed by Albert Mccleery. Adapted by Ellen and Richard McCracken. Based on the book by Hertha

Pauli. Story Editor: Ethel Frank. Musical Director: Jules Seidman. Scenic
Consultant: Richard Sylbert. Makeup: Vin Kehoe. Costumes: Guy Kent.
Audio Engineer: David Gould. Video Engineer: William de Lannoy.
Lighting Director: Lee Carlton. Technical Director: Robert Long.
CAST: Sarah Churchill (Narrator), Dorothy Peterson, Natalie Trundy,
Ellie Sommers, Charles Taylor, Edward Harvey, Elaine Ellis, Philippa
Bevans, Carl Harms, David White, Sondra Rogers, Pauline Myers.

KRAFT TELEVISION THEATER
The Thinking Heart—A Lincoln Biography (February 14, 1954) [Andrew
Duggan]
ABC Television Network. Teleplay by George H. Faulkner. Narrated by
Anthony Ross.

FIRESIDE THEATER
Joe Giordano and Mr. Lincoln (March, 1954)
Frank Wisbar Productions. Associate Producer: Sidney Smith. Director of
Photography: Benjamin Kline, A.S.C. Story and teleplay by Elwood
Ullman. Produced and directed by Frank Wisbar. Supervising Editor:
Holbrook N. Todd, A.C.E. Editor: Roy V. Livingston, A.C.E. Assistant
Director: Maurice Vaccarino. Sound Engineer: Phil Mitchell. Sound:
Ryder Sound Service.
CAST: Argentina Brunetti (Anna), Mario Siletti (Joe), Peter Price
(Dominic), Gloria Talbot (Tina), Frank Yaconelli (Nick).

Flame and Ice (1955) [Jason Robards]

THE CHRISTOPHER PROGRAM
Lincoln Speaks for Himself (1955) [Reed Hadley]
Jack Denove Productions, Inc. Produced by Jack Denove. Directed by
Alvin Ganzer. Lincoln material compiled by Robert Stevenson. Production
Design: Ernst Fegte. Photography: Fred Gately, A.S.C. Assistant Director:
Kenneth Walters. Supervising Editor: Stan Rabjohn. Property Master: Ken
Walton. Wardrobe: Joe Dimmitt. Set Decorator: John Macneil. Makeup:
Ted Coodley. Music Supervisor: Josef Zimanich. Host: Danny Thomas.

TV READER'S DIGEST
How Chance Made Lincoln President (February 9, 1955)

SCREEN DIRECTORS PLAYHOUSE

Lincoln's Doctor's Dog (1955) [Robert Ryan]

KRCA-TV. Filmed by Hal Roach Studios for Eastman Kodak (JWT). Directed by H.C. Potter. Teleplay by William R. Cox. Original Story: Christopher Morley. Camera: James Wong Howe. Film Editor: George E. Luckenbacher. Sound: Jack Goodrich and Jel Moss. Art Director: Charles F. Pyke. Host: H.C. Potter.

CAST: Charles Bickford (Doctor), Richard Long (Presidential aide), Willis Bouchey, Howard Wendell, Johnny Lee, Paul Keast, Mack Williams, John Craven, Dennis King Jr.

STAR PERFORMANCE THEATER

A Kiss for Mr. Lincoln (February 3, 1955)

Official Films Presentation. Executive Producer: Don W. Sharpe. Produced and directed by Roy Kellino. Screenplay: Irvin W. Phillips. Based on a story by Louise Kennedy Mabie. Editorial Supervisor: Bernard Burton. Director of Photography: George E. Diskant, A.S.C. Production Supervisor: Lloyd Richards. Story Editor: Coles Trapnell. Art Director: Duncan Cramer. Edited by Samuel E. Beetley, A.C.E. Assistant Director: Jack Sonntag. Makeup Artist: Karl Herlinger.

CAST: Joanne Dru (Delight Kenneth), Robert Cornthwaite (Henry), Dick Foran (Mr. Murdock), Kristine Miller (Mrs. Murdock), Mary Treen (Madeline, the maid).

YOU ARE THERE

The Emancipation Proclamation (1955) [Jeff Morrow]

CBS Television Network. Produced by James Fonda. Directed by Bernard Girard. Written by Howard Rodman. Suggested by a chapter in the book *Abraham Lincoln: The War Years* by Carl Sandburg. Production Supervisor: Walter Blake. Production Manager: Sidney Van Keuren. Director of Photography: Ed Fitzgerald. Film Editor: James D. Ballas. Art Director: William Ferrari. Assistant Director: Richard Dixon. Set Decorations: Rudy Butler. Sound: Phil Mitchell and Joel Moss. Costumes: Norma. Makeup: Jack P. Pierce. Hairstylist: Carmen Dirigo. Host and Narrator: Walter Cronkite. Filmed at Hal Roach Studios, Culver City, California.

CAST: Robert E. Simon (Reverand Sunderland), Denver Pyle (Captain Canfield), Russ Conway (Colonel Neibling), Robert Karnes (the Sergeant), Jester Hairston (Thornton), Amos Reese (Private Thomas Long), Howard

Wendell (William Seward), News Reporters: Harry Marble, Harlow Wilcox, Todd Hunter.

ROBERT MONTGOMERY PRESENTS
Good Friday, 1865 (February 6, 1956)

NBC Television Network. Neptune Productions. Executive Producer: Robert Montgomery. Directed by Perry Lafferty. Sets: Syrjala. Teleplay by John Lewellen. Based upon the autobiography *I Saw Booth Shoot Lincoln* by William J. Ferguson. Host and Narrator: Robert Montgomery.

CAST: Michael Allen (Billy Ferguson), William A. Lee, Charles Aidman, Anne Seymour, John Griggs, Leslie Woods, Mitchel Agruss, Walter Kinsella.

The Day Lincoln Was Shot (February 11, 1956) [Raymond Massey]

CBS Television Network. A Paul Gregory Theater Production. Produced for television by Gregory Associates, Inc. Executive Director for Special Productions: Harry Ackerman. Directed by Delbert Mann. Written by Denis and Terry Sanders and Jean Holloway. Based on the book by Jim Bishop. Art Direction: Robert Tyler Lee. Technical Director: Bob Colvin. Set Decorator: Buck Henshaw. Broadcast live in color.

CAST: Charles Laughton (Narrator), Jack Lemmon (John Wilkes Booth), Lillian Gish (Mary Todd Lincoln), Billy Chapin (Tad), Raymond Bailey (Stanton), Fay Roope, Bill Phipps, Ainslie Pryor, Herbert Anderson (army doctor), Charles Nolte, Paul Bryar, Richard Du Bois, Bill Schallert (Frederick Seward), Mark Herron, William Benedict (actor in Ford's Theater), Roy Engel, Doug Odney, Doris Lloyd, Shirley Mills, Jack Raine.

M-G-M PARADE
Man in the Barn (March 7, 1956)

ABC Television Network. Show #26. Hosted by George Murphy. This half hour television program contained the following: Judy Garland singing "On the Atchison, Topeka and the Santa Fe" from the film *The Harvey Girls* (1946); "The Trophy Room" in which George Murphy previewed a scene from the upcoming M-G-M film *Meet Me in Las Vegas* (1956), starring Cyd Charisse and Dan Dailey; "The Man in the Barn" (1937), a story about the death of John Wilkes Booth, written and narrated by Carey Wilson; a scene from *The Yearling* (1946), starring Gregory Peck, Jane Wyman, and Claude Jarman Jr.

Abraham Lincoln's Heavenly Crisis (1957)
WBZ-TV, Boston. Written by George E. Moynihan.

THE TWENTIETH CENTURY-FOX HOUR
Young Man from Kentucky (February 8, 1957) [Tom Tryon]
CAST: Ann Harding, Marshall Thompson.

Abe Lincoln in Illinois (1957)
CAST: Patricia English (Ann Rutledge)

Meet Mr. Lincoln (February 11, 1959)
NBC Television Network. Produced and directed by Donald B. Hyatt.
Written by Richard Hanser. Music: Robert Russell Bennett. Editor: Silvio
D'Alisera. Narrator: Alexander Scourby. Announcer: Thomas Mitchell.

Lincoln: The Young Years (1959)

DUPONT SHOW OF THE MONTH
The Lincoln Murder Case (February 18, 1961) [Drummond Erskine]
Dupont. CBS-TV, New York. Produced by David Susskind. Directed by
Alex Segal. Written by Dale Wasserman. Based on the book *The Web of
Conspiracy* by Theodore Roscoe. Host and Narrator: Alexander Scourby.
CAST: Luther Adler (Stanton), Roger Evan Boxhill (John Wilkes Booth),
Carl Don, James Hickman, James Patterson, Andrew Prince, Lonny
Chapman.

OUR AMERICAN HERITAGE
Not in Vain (April 1, 1961) [Raymond Massey]
NBC-TV, New York. Produced by Mildred Freed Alberg. Directed by Jack
Smight. Written by Richard Goldhurst. Narrator: Lowell Thomas.
CAST: Royal Beal, Harrison Dowd, Gerald Hiken, Joseph Mccauley, Paul
Tripp.

Young Abe Lincoln (June 7, 1961) [Darrell Sandeen]
WNEW-TV, New York. Produced by Arthur Shimkin. Written by Richard
N. Bernstein and John Allen. Music by Victor Ziskin. Lyrics by Joan Javits.
CAST: Judy Foster (Ann Rutledge), Lou Cutell, Joan Kilbrig.

Life of Lincoln (February 21, 1962)
WSB-TV, Atlanta. Produced and Directed by Gy Waldron.
Written and Narrated by Norman Shavin.

HALLMARK HALL OF FAME

Abe Lincoln in Illinois (February 5, 1964) [Jason Robards]
NBC Television Network. A Compass Production. Hallmark Cards.
Produced and directed by George Schaefer. Adapted for television by
Robert Hartung. Based on the play by Robert E. Sherwood. Reproduced by
the Kinephoto Process. Videotaped in Color Settings: Warren Clymer.
Costumes: Noel Taylor. Lighting: Alan Posage. Audio: James Blaney. Video:
Walter Werner. Makeup: Bob O'Bradovich. Stage Managers: Dick
Auerbach and Norman Hall. Production Assistant: Joyce Meckler. Graphic
Artist: Stas Pyka. Music Supervisor: Phebe Haas. Associate Director:
Adrienne Luraschi. Technical Director: O. Tamburri. Unit Manager: Bruce
Bassett. For Compass Productions, Inc.: Sybil Trubin, Joan H. Frank,
Gordon R. Wynne Jr., and John E. Friend. Associate Producer: Robert
Hartung.
CAST: Kate Reid (Mary Todd), James Broderick (Joshua Speed), Hiram
Sherman (Judge Bowling Green), Douglas Watson (Ninian Edwards), Burt
Brinckerhoff (William Herndon), Roy Poole (Seth Gale), Staats Cotsworth
(Crimmin), Mildred Trares (Ann Rutledge), William Hansen (Mentor
Graham), James Congdon (Jack), Don Gantry (Jasp), Nan McFarland
(Nancy Green), Joan Hotchkis (Elizabeth Edwards), Toni Darnay (Aggie
Gale), Jack Bittner (Stephen A. Douglas), Tom Slater (Robert Lincoln),
Casey Peters (Willie Lincoln), Harry Ellerbe (Harrick), Frederic Tozere
(Sturveson).

THE TIME TUNNEL

The Death Trap (1966) [Ford Rainey]
ABC Television Network. Twentieth Century-Fox Television, Inc. An Irwin
Allen Production in Association with Kent Productions, Inc. Executive in
Charge of Production: William Self. Written by Leonard Stadd. Directed
by William Hale. Story Editor: Arthur Weiss. Associate Producer: Jerry
Briskin. Music: Robert Drasnin. Music Supervisor: Lionel Newman.
Production Supervisor: Jack Sonntag. Production Associate: Hal Herman.
Unit Production Manager: Bob Anderson. Postproduction Supervisor:
George W. Swink. Art Directors: Jack Martin Smith and Ridger E. Maus.
Set Decoration: Walter M. Scott and Norman Rockett. Assistant to the

Producer: Paul Zastupnevich. Film Editor: Axel Hubert. Special Photographic Effects: L. B. Abbott, A.S.C. Makeup Supervision: Ben Nye. Hair Styling Supervision: Margaret Donovan. Production Coordinator: Les Warner. Supervising Sound Effects Editor: Don Hall Jr. Sound Effects Editor: Robert Cornett. Postproduction Coordinator: Robert Mintz. Color by Deluxe. Assistant Director: Ted Butcher. Supervising Music Editor: Leonard A. Engel. Music Editor: Sam E. Levin. Theme: Johnny Williams. CAST: Scott Marlowe (Jeremiah), R. G. Armstrong (Pinkerton), Tom Skerritt (Matthew), Christopher Harris (David). Series regulars: James Darren (Dr. Tony Newman), Robert Colbert (Dr. Doug Phillips), Whit Bissell (Lieutenant General Heywood Kirk), John Zaremba (Dr. Raymond Swain), Wesley Lau (Army Master Sergeant Jiggs).

Lincoln's Last Day (April 17, 1968)
WMAL-TV, Washington D.C. Produced and directed by Jerry Johnson. Written by Herb Rosen. Narrated by Harry K. Smith. Lincoln's words read by Senator Everett Dirksen.

STAR TREK
The Savage Curtain (March 7, 1969) [Lee Bergere]
NBC Television Network. A Paramount Production in Association with Norway Corporation. Executive Vice President in Charge of Production: Douglas S. Cramer. Produced by Gene Roddenberry. Directed by Herschel Dougherty. Teleplay: Gene Roddenberry and Arthur Heineman. Story: Gene Roddenberry. Associate Producers: Edward K. Milkis and Gregg Peters. Story Consultant: Arthur H. Singer. Theme Music: Alexander Courage. Additional Music: Fred Steiner. Art Director: Walter M. Jeffries. Director of Photography: Al Francis. Film Editor: Bill Brame. Unit Production Manager: Gregg Peters. Assistant Director: Gene Deruelle. Set Decorator: John M. Dwyer. Costumes created by William Ware Theiss. Photographic Effects: Vanderveer Photo Effects. Sound Effects Editor: Douglas H. Grindstaff. Music Editor: Richard Lapham. Rerecording Mixer: Gordon L. Day, C.A.S. Production Mixer: Carl W. Daniels. Script Supervisor: George S. Hutter. Recorded by Glen Glenn Sound Co. Casting: Joseph D'Agusta. Makeup Artist: Fred B. Phillips. Hairstylist: Pat Westmore. Gaffer: George H. Merhoff. Head Grip: George Rader. Property Master: Irving A. Feinberg. Special Effects: Jim Rugg. CAST: William Shatner (Captain James T. Kirk), Leonard Nimoy (Mr. Spock), Deforest Kelly (Dr. Leonard McCoy), James Doohan (Engineer

Montgomery Scott), George Takei (Lieutenant Sulu), Nichell Nichols
(Lieutenant Uhura), Ensign Chekov (Walter Koenig), Phillip Pine
(Colonel Green), Daniels Dement (Zora), Barry Atwater (Surak), Nathan
Jung (Genghis Khan), Robert Herron (Kahless), Arell Blanton (Lieutenant
Dickerson), Phil Adams (Shatner's stunt double), Bill Catching (Bergere's
stunt double), Gary Eppers (Atwater's stunt double), Jerry Summers
(Pine's stunt double), Bob Orrison (Nimoy's stunt double), Troy Melton
(Jung's stunt double), Janos Prohaska [costume] and Bart Larue [voice]
(Yarnek).

APPOINTMENT WITH DESTINY
They've Killed President Lincoln! (1971) [Joseph Leisch Jr.]
 NBC Television Network. A David L. Wolper Production. Executive
Producer: Warren V. Bush. Produced and directed by Robert Guenette.
Written by Robert Guenette and Theodore H. Strauss. Director of
Photography: Adam Giffard. Associate Producer: Paul Asselin. Film
Editor: John E. Link II. Sound: Curt Wittig. Musical Director: Jack Tillar.
Assistant Director: Diane Asselin. Costumes: Pat Segnan. Makeup: Lillian
Brown. Film and Still Research: Frances Guenette. Assistant Editor: Larry
Saltzman. Production Coordinator: Linda Ackerman. Postproduction
Supervisor: George Frederick. Supervising Sound Editor: Charles L.
Campbell. Sound Editor: Colin C. Mouat. Production Supervisor: Conrad
Holzgang. Host and Narrator: Richard Basehart. Historian: Bruce Catton.
CAST: Robert Leonard (John Wilkes Booth), Robert Prosky (Secretary of
War Edwin Stanton), Jill Eichenberry (Anne Surratt), Richard Bauer
(Colonel Porter), Mark D'Angelo (Samuel Chester), Brian Donohue
(bartender), Morris Engle (Gideon Welles), Michael Fairman (Major
Eckert), Grayce Grant (Asia Booth Clark), Dorothea Hammond (Mary
Lincoln), Donald Hotten (Charles Dana), Gregg Nickerson (Robert
Lincoln), Richard Sanders (Dr. Leale), Donegan Smith (Captain Gleason),
Cynthia Thomas (Laura Keene), Michael Tucker (General Grant), Peter
Vogt (Hotel Clerk), Liesel Flashenberg, Tom Kocherry, Carol Marney,
Claire Melly, and George Wilson (cast of *Our American Cousin*).

The Grate Mans Wiskurs (1971) [Dennis Weaver]
 A Universal Studios Production. Produced by Adrian Scott. Directed by
Philip Leacock. Written by John Paxton. Based on the play *The Great Man's
Whiskers* by Adrian Scott (1947). Director of Photography: John F. Warren,
A.S.C. Original music by Earl Robinson. Songs: "The Wilderness Man"

and "Things That Go Bump in the Night" by E.Y. Harburg (lyrics) and Earl Robinson (music). Art Director: George Webb. Set Decorations: John McCarthy and James M. Walters Sr. Unit Manager: Joseph E. Kenny. Assistant Director: Jack Doran. Film Editor: John Elias. Music Supervision: Stanley Wilson. Sound: David H. Moriarty. Color Coordinator: Robert Brower. Color by Technicolor. Titles and Optical Effects: Universal Title. Editorial Supervision: Richard Belding. Wardrobe Supervisor: Robert Ellsworth. Makeup: Bud Westmore. Hairstylist: Larry Germain.

CAST: Dean Jones (James Cooper), Beth Brickell (Catherine Winfield), Cindy Eilbacher (Elizabeth Cooper), John Hillerman (Major Underwood), Charles Lane (Philbrick), John McGiver (Andrew Hogan), Harve Presnell (Ballad Singer), Isabell Sanford (Ella), Ann Sothern (Margaret Bancroft), Richard Erdman (Somerby), Nicole Meggerson (Pearl), Maudie Prickett (Miss Albright), Woodrow Chambliss (Mr. Paddleford), Alvin Hammer (Mr. Whatley).

THE AMERICAN HERITAGE
Lincoln: Trial by Fire (1974) [John Anderson]

A David L. Wolper Production. Executive Producer: Warren V. Bush. Production Supervisor: Conrad Holzgang. Produced and directed by Ed Spiegel. Written by Ted Strauss. Photography: William Hartigan. Production Manager and Assistant Director: Harry F. Hogan III. Editor: Peter Johnson. Sound: Richard Wagner. Makeup: Robert Westmoreland. Production Stylist: Kent Gibson. Gaffer: William Brauniger. Production Associate: Faye Hogan. Assistant Editor: John Farrell. Postproduction Supervisor: Phillips Wylly. Production Coordinator: James Mohlmann. Production Assistant: Sara Lukinson. Director of Production Services: Christine Foster. Rerecording: Ryder Sound Services, Inc. Music Editing: Nieman-Tillar Associates. Sound Effects: Intent International. Negative Cutting: Elva Fraser. Narrated by Cliff Robertson. Historian: Bruce Catton.

CAST: Larry Lewman (General George McClellan), James O'Neill (Secretary of State Seward), Robert Prosky (Secretary of War Stanton), Bryan Clark (General Kearny), Norman Fitz (Frederick Douglass), Richard Sanders (Minister Adams), Mark Hammer (Senator Wade), Max Wright (Horace Greeley), Doug Roberts (Corporal Mitchell), Neal Ford (soldier), Ed Spiegel (Gustavus Fox).

Sandburg's Lincoln (1974–76) [Hal Holbrook]
PART ONE: *Mrs. Lincoln's Husband* (October 6, 1974)
A Wolper Production. Executive Producer: David L. Wolper. Produced and directed by George Schaefer. Associate Producer: William Beaudine Jr. Production Supervisor: Conrad Holzgang. Written by James Prideaux. Based on the book *Carl Sandburg's Abraham Lincoln*. Director of Photography: Howard Schwartz, A.S.C. Film Editor: James T. Heckert. Art Directors: Warren Clymer and George Troast. Set Decorator: Joanne Macdougall. Costume Designer: Noel Taylor. Music: Lyn Murray. Makeup: Charles Schram. Casting: Ramsay King. Sound Mixer: Glenn Anderson. Hairdresser: Mary Keats. Continuity: Dorothy Aldrin. Assistant to the Producer: Adrienne Luraschi. Manager Production Operations: Phillips Wylly. Assistant Director: Don Torpin. Production Coordinator: Bryant Henry. Postproduction Supervisor: George Taylor. Lincoln Research: Louise Cooper. Production Services: Christine Foster. Assistant Editor: Chuck Montgomery. Vice President Creative Affairs: Warren V. Bush. Postproduction Services: Neiman-Tillar Associates. Rerecorded by Ryder Sound Services, Inc.
CAST: Sada Thompson (Mary Todd Lincoln), Roy Poole (Salmon P. Chase), John Beal (Senator Fogelson), Michael Cristofer (John Nicolay), William Lemassena (Senator Remley), Davey Davison (Emily Helm), Melinda Fee (Kate Chase), James Carroll Jordan (Robert Lincoln), Michael-James Wixted (Willie Lincoln), William Lanteau (Mr. Richards), John Levin (Tad Lincoln), Jon Lormer (Senator Sutton), Anne Seymour (Mrs. Livingston).
PART TWO: *Sad Figure Laughing* (February 12, 1975)
A Wolper Production. Executive Producer: David L. Wolper. Produced and directed by George Schaefer. Associate Producer: William Beaudine Jr. Production Supervisor: Conrad Holzgang. Written by Jerry McNeely. Based on the book *Carl Sandburg's Abraham Lincoln*. Director of Photography: Howard Schwartz, A.S.C. Film Editor: James T. Heckert. Art Directors: Warren Clymer and George Troast. Set Decorator: Reg Allen. Costume Designer: Noel Taylor. Music: Lyn Murray. Makeup: Charles Schram. Casting: Ramsay King. Sound Mixer: Glenn Anderson. Hairdresser: Mary Keats. Continuity: Dorothy Aldrin. Assistant to the Producer: Adrienne Luraschi. Manager Production Operations: Phillips Wylly. Assistant Director: Don Torpin. Production Coordinator: Bryant Henry. Postproduction Supervisor: George Taylor. Lincoln Research: Louise Cooper. Production Services: Christine Foster. Assistant Editor:

Geoffrey Rowland. Vice President Creative Affairs: Warren V. Bush. Postproduction Services: Neiman-Tillar Associates. Rerecorded by Ryder Sound Services, Inc.

CAST: Sada Thompson (Mary Todd Lincoln), Elizabeth Ashley (Kate Chase), Roy Poole (Salmon P. Chase), Severn Darden (Gideon Welles), Normann Burton (General Grant), Michael Ivan Cristofer (John Nicolay), Bert Freed (Edwin Stanton), James Carroll Jordan (Robert Lincoln), Jon Cedar (captain), Booth Colman (Samuel Pomeroy), Charles Macaulay (Jay Cooke), Bartlett Robinson (senator), Gene Tyburn (carpenter).

PART THREE: *Prairie Lawyer* (April 7, 1975)

A Wolper Production. Executive Producer: David L. Wolper. Produced and directed by George Schaefer. Associate Producer: William Beaudine Jr. Production Supervisor: Conrad Holzgang. Story by Emmet Lavery. Teleplay by: Irene and Louis Kamp. Based on the book *Carl Sandburg's Abraham Lincoln*. Director of Photography: Howard Schwartz, A.S.C. Film Editor: James T. Heckert. Art Directors: Warren Clymer and George Troast. Set Decorator: Joanne Macdougall. Costume Designer: Noel Taylor. Music: Lyn Murray. Makeup: Charles Schram. Casting: Ramsay King. Sound Mixer: Charles Lewis. Hairdresser: Mary Keats. Continuity: Dorothy Aldrin. Assistant to the Producer: Adrienne Luraschi. Manager Production Operations: Phillips Wylly. Assistant Director: Don Torpin. Production Coordinator: Bryant Henry. Postproduction Supervisor: George Taylor. Lincoln Research: Louise Cooper. Production Services: Christine Foster. Assistant Editor: Chuck Montgomery. Vice President Creative Affairs: Warren V. Bush. Postproduction Services: Neiman-Tillar Associates. Rerecorded by Ryder Sound Services, Inc.

CAST: Robert Foxworth (John Stuart), Catherine Burns (Mary Owens), Richard A. Dysart (Judge Davis), Walter McGinn (Stephan Douglas), Paul Fix (Judge Thomas), James Greene (Henry Truett), Martine Bartlett (Kitty Cavan), Gerald Hiken (Urquhart), Michele Marsh (Mary Todd), Iggie Wolfington (William Butler),

PART FOUR: *The Unwilling Warrior* (July 24, 1975)

A Wolper Production. Executive Producer: David L. Wolper. Produced and directed by George Schaefer. Associate Producer: William Beaudine Jr. Production Supervisor: Conrad Holzgang. Written by Jerome Lawrence and Robert E. Lee. Based on the book *Carl Sandburg's Abraham Lincoln*. Director of Photography: Howard Schwartz, A.S.C. Film Editor: James T. Heckert. Art Directors: Warren Clymer and George Troast. Set Decorator: Joanne Macdougall. Costume Designer: Noel Taylor. Music: Lyn Murray.

Makeup: Charles Schram. Casting: Ramsay King. Sound Mixer: Glenn Anderson. Hairdresser: Mary Keats. Continuity: Dorothy Aldrin. Assistant to the Producer: Adrienne Luraschi. Manager Production Operations: Phillips Wylly. Assistant Director: Don Torpin. Production Coordinator: Bryant Henry. Postproduction Supervisor: George Taylor. Lincoln Research: Louise Cooper. Production Services: Christine Foster. Assistant Editor: Chuck Montgomery. Vice President Creative Affairs: Warren V. Bush. Postproduction Services: Neiman-Tillar Associates. Rerecorded by Ryder Sound Services, Inc.

CAST: Sada Thompson (Mary Todd Lincoln), Ed Flanders (General McClellan), Lloyd Nolan (William Seward), David Huffman (Elmer Ellsworth), John Randolph (Simon Cameron), Normann Burton (General Grant), Michael Ivan Cristofer (John Nicolay), Robert Emhardt (General Scott), Frank Maxwell (General Weitzel), Brendan Dillon (Allan Pinkerton), John Chandler (the assassin), John Levin (Tad Lincoln), Ron Hajek (cavalry man), Peter Hobbs (congressman).

PART FIVE: *Crossing Fox River* (January 12, 1976)

A Wolper Production. Executive Producer: David L. Wolper. Produced and directed by George Schaefer. Associate Producer: William Beaudine Jr. Production Supervisor: Conrad Holzgang. Written by Loring Mandel. Based on the book *Carl Sandburg's Abraham Lincoln*. Director of Photography: Howard Schwartz, A.S.C. Film Editor: Jerry Taylor. Art Directors: Warren Clymer and George Troast. Set Decorator: Joanne Macdougall. Costume Designer: Noel Taylor. Music: Lyn Murray. Makeup: Charles Schram. Casting: Ramsay King. Sound Mixer: Charles Lewis. Hairdresser: Mary Keats. Continuity: Dorothy Aldrin. Assistant to the Producer: Adrienne Luraschi. Manager Production Operations: Phillips Wylly. Assistant Director: Don Torpin. Production Coordinator: Bryant Henry. Postproduction Supervisor: George Taylor. Lincoln Research: Louise Cooper. Production Services: Christine Foster. Assistant Editor: Geoffrey Rowland. Vice President Creative Affairs: Warren V. Bush. Postproduction Services: Neiman-Tillar Associates. Rerecorded by Ryder Sound Services, Inc.

CAST: Sada Thompson (Mary Todd Lincoln), Beulah Bondi (Sarah Bush), Richard Dysart (Judge Davis), John Randolph (Simon Cameron), Whit Bissel (William Seward), Michael Ivan Cristofer (John Nicolay), James Carroll Jordan (Robert Lincoln), Lee Bergere (William Herndon), Robert Casper (Leonard Swett), Wally Engelhardt (Lamon), Doug Henderson

(Judd), John Levin (Tad Lincoln), Michael-James Wixted (Willie Lincoln), Bill Quinn (Mr. Ashmun).

PART SIX: *The Last Days* (April 14, 1976)

A Wolper Production. Executive Producer: David L. Wolper. Produced and directed by George Schaefer. Associate Producer: William Beaudine Jr. Production Supervisor: Conrad Holzgang. Written by Philip Reisman Jr. Based on the book *Carl Sandburg's Abraham Lincoln*. Director of Photography: Howard Schwartz, A.S.C. Film Editor: Jerry Taylor. Art Directors: Warren Clymer and George Troast. Set Decorator: Joanne Macdougall. Costume Designer: Noel Taylor. Music: Lyn Murray. Makeup: Charles Schram. Casting: Ramsay King. Sound Mixer: Glenn Anderson. Hairdresser: Mary Keats. Continuity: Dorothy Aldrin. Assistant to the Producer: Adrienne Luraschi. Manager Production Operations: Phillips Wylly. Assistant Director: Don Torpin. Production Coordinator: Bryant Henry. Postproduction Supervisor: George Taylor. Lincoln Research: Louise Cooper. Production Services: Christine Foster. Assistant Editor: Geoffrey Rowland. Vice President Creative Affairs: Warren V. Bush. Postproduction Services: Neiman-Tillar Associates. Rerecorded by Ryder Sound Services, Inc.

CAST: Sada Thompson (Mary Todd Lincoln), Normann Burton (General Grant), Michael Ivan Cristofer (John Nicolay), James Carroll Jordan (Robert Lincoln), Bert Freed (Edwin Stanton), Edward Bell (Frederick Seward), Jack Collins (Congressman Cory), Dennis Fimple (Private Yarrow), John Levin (Tad Lincoln), Peter Brocco (Cabinet member), John Kennedy (Cabinet member), David Hayward (soldier).

HALLMARK HALL OF FAME
The Rivalry (1976) [Arthur Hill]

Produced by Walt Defaria. Directed by Fielder Cook. Based on the play by Norman Corwin (1957). Adapted by Donald Carmorant and Ernest Kinoy.
CAST: Charles Durning (Stephen Douglas), Hope Lange (Adele Douglas).

HOLLYWOOD TELEVISION THEATER
The Last of Mrs. Lincoln (1976)

KCET-TV. Executive Producer: Norman Lloyd. Produced and directed by George Schaefer. Written by James Prideaux. Art Director: Roy Christopher. Set Decorator: Beulah Frankel. Assistant Art Director: James Shanahan. Music: Lyn Murray. Lighting Design: Tom Schamp. Costume Design: Noel Taylor. Casting: Sam Christensen and Melnick/Holstra.

Technical Director: Cal Slater. Associate Director: Adrienne Luraschi. Production Assistant: Janet Oswald. Audio: Gerald Zelinger. Camera: Barry Brown, Wayne Orr, Jack Reader. Video: Richard J. Ward. Videotape Editor: Terry Pickford. Property Master: Charles Whitmore. Scenic Artist: Liz Matus. Scenic Construction: Paul Rouleau. Lighting Director: Ken Dettling. Stage Manager: Mike O'Gara. Makeup: Maurice Stein, S.M.A. Miss Harris' Hair Styles: Ray Iagnocco. Hairstylist: Barbara Ronci. Graphic Artist: Keith Collins. Unit Manger: David Livingston. Main Title: Saul Bass. Main Title Theme: Jerry Goldsmith. Supervisory Producer: George Turpin.

CAST: Julie Harris (Mary Todd Lincoln), Robby Benson (Older Tad), Michael Cristofer (Robert Lincoln), Patrick Duffy (Lewis Baker), Jack Furlong (Porter), Linda Kelsey (Mary Harlan), Kurtis Lee (boy in park), Macon McCalman (attendant), Priscilla Morrill (Elizabeth Edwards), Denver Pyle (Senator Austin), Ford Rainey (Ninian Edwards), Jay M. Riley (man in park), Billy Simpson (younger Tad), Royce Wallace (Lizzie Keckley), Kate Wilkinson (Mrs. McCullough).

The Captains and the Kings (1976) [Ford Rainey]

Directed by Douglas Heyes and Allen Reisner. Original Music: Elmer Bernstein. Cinematography: Isidore Mankofsky. Supervising Sound Editor: Roger Sword.

CAST: Sian Barbara Allen (Cara Leslie), Ray Bolger (R. J. Squibbs), Philip Bourneuf (Father Scanlon), Neville Brand (O'Herlihy), Blair Brown (Elizabeth Healey), John Carradine (Father Hale), Katherine Crawford (Moira/Mary Armagh), Beverly D'Angelo (Miss Emmy), Severn Darden (Plover), Cliff De Young (Brian Armagh), Peter Donat (Clair Montrose), Robert Donner (wounded Texan), Patty Duke Astin (Bernadette Armagh), Charles Durning (Ed Healey), Ann Dusenberry (Ann-Marie), Henry Fonda (Senator Enfield Bassett), George Gaynes (Orestes Bradley), Stefan Gierasch (Gannon), Missy Gold (Mary Armagh as a child), Tracey Gold (Rosemary Armagh), Celeste Holm (Sister Angela), John Houseman (Judge Chisholm), David Huffman (Sean Armagh), Burl Ives ("Old Syrup"), Clifton James (Governor Skerritt), Richard Jordan (Joseph Armagh), Linda Kelsey (Peg), Perry King (Rory Armagh), Sally Kirkland (Aggie), Terry Kiser (Courtney Wickersham), Patrick Laborteaux (Young Rory), Sean McClory (Boland), Vic Morrow (Tom Hennessey), Barbara Parkins (Martinique), Joanna Pettet (Katherine Hennessey), William Prince (Jay Regan), Bill Quinn (Dr. Harris Herbert), Pernell Roberts

(Braithwaite), Jane Seymour (Marjorie Chisholm Armagh), Cynthia Sikes (Claudia Desmond Armagh), Ann Sothern (Mrs. Finch), Jenny Sullivan (Honora Houlihan), Ken Swofford (Captain Muldoon), Robert Vaughn (Charles Desmond), Mills Watson (Preston), Byron Webster (William Jennings Bryan), John de Lancie, William Gordon, Ted Gehring, William Bryant, Bernard Behrens, George Berkeley, Elizabeth Cheshire, Richard Herd, Harvey Jason, John Dennis Johnston, Joe Kapp, Martin Kove, Connie Kreski, James O'Connell, Barbara Morrison, Roger Robinson, Sandy Ward, Jack Stryker, George Skaff.

Abe Lincoln: Freedom Fighter (1979) [Allen Williams]
Schick Sunn Classic Productions, Inc. Executive Producer: Charles E. Sellier Jr. Executive in Charge of Production: James L. Conway. Directed by Jack B. Hively. Teleplay by Malvin Wald and Jack Jacobs. Story by Tom Chapman. Stunt Coordinator: James M. Halty. Associate Producer: Stan Siegel. Director of Photography: Stephen W. Gray. Music Theme: Bob Summers. Music: Andrew Belling. Music Supervision: Don Perry. Production Manager: Morris Chapnick. Production Executive: Elliot Friedgen. Film Editor: Trevor Jolly. Production Designer: Paul Steheli. Postproduction Supervisor: Jim Bryan. Casting: McLean/Ebbins/Mansour. First Assistant Director: Jefferson Richard. Camera Operator: Kim Marks. Sound: Rod Sutton. Associate Art Director: Paul Nibley. Wardrobe Mistress: Pat Wareing. Makeup Artist: Dennis Marsh. Script Supervisor: Patricia Motyka. Business Coordinator: Kimberly Avery. Construction Supervisor: Dean Brown. Special Effects: Harry Woolman. Gaffer: Glen Schellerup. Key Grip: Bruce Hamme. Music Editor: John Mick. Sound Effects Supervisor: Richard Adams. Dialogue Director: Norman Schwartz. Dialogue Editor: Robert Dadashian. Transportation Director: Tam Halling. Extras Coordinator: Lou Edwards. Construction Coordinator: Terry Haskell. Titles and Graphics: Pacific Title. Created by Charles E. Sellier Jr. and James L. Conway. Host: Walker Edminston (as Mark Twain). Filmed on location in Utah.
CAST: Whit Bissel (Judge Clark), Andrew Prine (Luke Bolton), Brock Peters (Henry Young), Caitlin O'Heaney (Nancy), Charles Bloom, Michael Bennett, David Chambers, William Kezele, Chay Leseur, Beverly Howard, Oscar Rowland, Michael Rudd.

HALLMARK HALL OF FAME
Mister Lincoln (February 9, 1981) [Roy Dotrice]
A coproduction of KCET-TV Los Angeles and WGBH-Boston. A Time-Life Production. Produced by David Susskind. Associate Producer: Terry Lee. Directed by Gordon Rigsby. Directed for the Stage by Peter Coe. Associate Director: Barry Greensfield. Technical Director: Art Guth. Lighting Director: Jack Malick. Makeup: Joe Cranzano. Audio: Bernie Zuck. Audio Assist: Richard Bedard. Production Assistant: Judy Glass. Video: Tom Guadarrama. Camera: Ed Buffman, Peter Blank, Jim Covello, Ken McCaleb. Utility: Howard Rowenzweig. Production Manager: John Micale Jr. Videotape Editors: Michael Biondi, Max Curtis. Videotape Recording: K. C. Millard, Richard Sens. Lighting for the Stage: Allan Stichbury. Set Designer: David L. Lovett. Theater Manager: John Wilbur. A Production of Citadel Theater, Edmonton, Canada. Recorded at Ford's Theater, Washington, D.C.

The Blue and the Gray (1982) [Gregory Peck]
CBS Television Network. Columbia Pictures Television. A Larry White and Lou Reda Production. Executive Producer: Larry White. Co-Executive Producer: Lou Reda. Produced by Hugh Benson and Harry Thomason. Directed by Andrew V. McLaglen. Teleplay by Ian McLellan Hunter. Story by John Leekley and Bruce Catton. Based in part on *Reflections on the Civil War* by Bruce Catton (Doubleday & Company). Director of Photography: Al Francis, A.S.C. Music: Bruce Broughton. Film Editors: Fred A. Chulack, A.C.E., and Bud Friedgen, A.C.E. Art Directors: Ross Bellah and Gary A. Lee. Associate Producers: Jon C. Anderson and John Leekley. Co-Executive Producer: Jack Arbib. Unit Production Manager: Jon C. Anderson. First Assistant Director: Jonathan Giles Zimmerman. Second Assistant Directors: Douglas F. Dean and Paul Magwood. Mr. Peck's Makeup by Leo Lotito Jr. Key Makeup by Zoltan Elek. Makeup: Tom Miller. Hairstylist: Lee Crawford. Costume Designer: Grady Hunt. Wardrobe Supervisor: Jim Tyson. Women's Costumer: Loraine Dawson. Men's Costumers: Tye Osward and Ron Rynhart. Set Decorators: Audrey Blasdel-Goddard and David Horowitz. Casting Executives: Meryl O'Loughlin and Fran F. Bascom. Casting Director: Patricia Mock. Music Editors: Erma E. Levin and Gene Feldman. Sound Effects Editing: Echo Film Service. Rerecording Mixers: Vern Poore, C.A.S., Andy Macdonald, C.A.S. and Tom E. Dahl, C.A.S. Sound Mixer: Mary Bolger. Camera Operators: Ralph Gerling and Jim Estridge. Special

Effects: Russell Hessey. Casting Asociate: Vivian Levy. Casting—Arkansas: Susan Jo Brown and Marsha Patterson. Sketch Artist: Jan Gosnell. Matscene effects by Effects Assoc. Inc. and Jim Danforth. Main title designed by Bill Millar. Title Drawings: Mentor Huebner. Optical Effects: Modern Film Effects. Script Supervisor: Doris Grau. Production Coordinator: Helen Conklin. Wrangler Boss: Dick Webb. Stunt Coordinator: Billy Burton. Property Master: John Sexton. Gaffer: Jim Lott. Key Grip: Bud Howell. Supervising Construction Coordinator: Hank Stonecipher. Construction Coordinator: Gene Robles. Transportation Captain: John Woodward. Location Auditor: John Janisch. Liaison Manager—Arkansas: Floyd Bohannan. Technical Advisor: Cal Kinzer. Balloons provided by Balloon Excelsior, Inc. Balloon Technical Advisor: Brent Stockwell. Color by Metrocolor. Filmed entirely on location in Arkansas.

CAST: John Hammond (John Geyser), Stacy Keach (Jonas Steele), Kathleen Beller (Kathy Reynolds), Colleen Dewhurst (Maggie Geyser), Rip Torn (General Ulysses S. Grant), Robert Vaughn (Senator Reynolds), Bruce Abbott (Jake Hale Jr.), Diane Baker (Evelyn Hale), Paul Benedict (Arbuthnot), Lloyd Bridges (Ben Geyser), Sterling Hayden (John Brown), Warren Oates (preacher/Major Welles), Walter Brooke (General Herman Haupt), Rory Calhoun (General George Meade), Janice Carroll (Mary Todd Lincoln), Fredric Cook, David Doyle (Phineas Wade), Julia Duffy (Mary Hale), Dan Shor (Luke Geyser), Robin Gammell (Jacob Hale Sr.), David W. Harper (James Hale), William Wellman Jr. (Union officer), Maggie Wellman (prostitute), Julius Harris (swamp preacher), Alex Harvey, Gregg Henry (Lester Bedell), Michael Horton (Mark Geyser), Cooper Huckabee (Matthew Geyser), John Dennis Johnston (Lieutenant Hardy), Brian Kerwin (Malachy Hale), William Lucking (Captain Potts), Charles Napier (Major Harrison), Royce D. Applegate (1st cell reporter), Gerald S. O'Loughlin (Sergeant O'Toole), Walter Olkewicz (Private Grundy), Geraldine Page (Mrs. Lovelace), Gregg Palmer (Bull Run Colonel), Penny Peyser (Emma Gayser), Veronica Redd, Duncan Regehr (Captain Randolph), John Rolloff (Secretary of War Stanton), Sara Rolloff (kissing girl), Robert Symonds (General Robert E. Lee), John Vernon (Secretary of State Seward), Donna Wallace (Nurse Butler), Noble Willingham (cavalry general on balloon field), Paul Winfield (Jonathan Henry), Peter von Zerneck (Prussian general), James Carroll Jordan, George Petrie, David Rounds, Warwick Sims, Christopher Stone, Fred Stuthman, Patrick Swayze.

Gregory Peck in a cameo role
in *The Blue and the Gray*
Courtesy of 20th Century-Fox

VOYAGERS
The Day the Rebs Took Lincoln (1982) [John Anderson]
    NBC Television Network. Created by James D. Parriott. Produced by Jill
    Sherman. Directed by Bernard McEveety. Written by Robert James.
    CAST: Jon-Erik Hexum (Phineas Bogg), Meeno Pelluce (Jeffrey Jones),
    Alexa Hamilton (Jane Phillips), Alex Hyde-White (Charles Dickens),
    Robert Phalen (Sykes), Gerald Hiken (Fagin), Rachel Bard (Mary Todd
    Lincoln), Donald Durrell (Bates), Alex Daniels (guard), Ross Evans
    (officer), Ray Colbert (rebel), Nicky Katt (Artful Dodger), Melissa Ann
    Fuller (Nancy), Cameron Dye (Steve), Glenn Morrissey (Lincoln's guard),
    Karen Dotrice (Marion), Ross Evans (gate guard), Julian Barnes, Suki
    Goodwin.

Police Squad! (1982) [Rex Hamilton]
    ABC Television Network. Produced by Jim Abrahams, Robert K. Weiss,
    David Zucker, Jerry Zucker. Directed by Jim Abrahams, Reza Badiyi, Georg
    Stanford Brown, Joe Dante, Paul Krasny, David Zucker, Jerry Zucker.
    Original Music: Ira Newborn.
    CAST: Leslie Nielsen (Detective Frank Drebin), Alan North (Captain Ed
    Hocken), Ed Williams (Ted Olson, scientist), William Duell (Johnny the
    Snitch), Peter Lupus (Officer Nordberg).

North and South (1985) [Hal Holbrook]
    ABC Television Network. Warner Bros. Television. A David L. Wolper
    Production. Executive Producers: David L. Wolper and Chuck McLain.

Abraham Lincoln on Television

Produced by Paul Freeman. Directed by Richard T. Heffron. Developed for television by Douglas Heyes. Music by Bill Conti. Written for television by Patricia Green. Based on the novel by John Jakes. Director of Photography: Stevan Larner, A.S.C. Film Editors: Scott Eyler, A.C.E., and Michael Eliot, A.C.E. Production Designer: Arch Bacon. Executive Script Consultant: Patricia Green. Unit Production Manager: Mike Salamunovich. First Assistant Director: Skip Cosper. Second Assistant Director: Douglas Dean III. Second Assistant Director: Josh McLaglen. Location Auditors: Kenneth D. Lee and Don Shelley. Music Editing: Stephen A. Hope, S.M.E., and Jay Alfred Smith. Sound Effects Editing: Lon Tinsley. Assistant Editors: Michael Cipriano, Richard McCullough, and Leon Garbers. Women's Costume Supervisors: Joie Hutchinson and Vicki Sanchez. Men's Costume Supervisor: Pat McGrath. Hairstylist: Virginia Darcy. Makeup Artist: Alan Fama, S.M.A. Mr. Holbrook's Makeup: Dick Smith. Script Supervisor: Alleen N. Hollmann. Production Sound: Richard Wagner. Set Decorator: Chuck Korian. Property Master: Earl W. Hunton. Camera Operator: Owen Marsh. Key Grip: Charles Morgan. Gaffer: Bob Farmer. Construction Coordinator: Richard J. Bayard. Production Executive: Mark Wolper. Dialect Coach: Robert Easton. Historian/ Technical Advisor: Ray Herbeck. Stunt Coordinator: Fred Lerner. Location Casting by Liz Keighley and Shari Rhodes. Casting by Phyllis Huffman and Jennifer Jackson Part. Drawings by Sandy Dvore. Titles and opticals by Pacific Title.

CAST: Kirstie Alley (Virgilia Hazard), Patrick Swayze (Orry Main), Lesley-Anne Down (Madeline Fabray), Morgan Fairchild (Burdetta Halloran), Elizabeth Taylor (Madam Conti), Robert Mitchum (Patrick Flynn), John Anderson (William Hazard), William Arvay (Whitney Smith), Lee Bergere (Nicholas Fabrey), Georg Stanford Brown (Grady), David Carradine (Justin Lamotte), Johnny Cash (John Brown), Philip Casnoff (Elkanah Bent), Olivia Cole (Maum Sally), Michael Crabtree (Galen Devere), Jonathan Frakes (Stanley Hazard), Genie Francis (Brett Main), Tony Frank (Salem Jones), Wendy Fulton (Isabel Hazard), Terri Garber (Ashton Main), Erica Gimpel (Semiramis), Cary Guffey (Young Billy Hazard), Robert Guillaume (Frederick Douglass), David Harris (Priam), Mert Hatfield (ironworker), Gene Kelly (Senator Charles Edwards), Wendy Kilbourne (Constance Flynn Hazard), Jim Metzler (James Huntoon), Tuck Milligan (Smith Dawkins), Mark Moses (General Grant), Ron O'Neal (William Still), William Ostrander (Forbes Lamotte), James Read (George Hazard), James Rebhorn (Major Anderson), Mitch Ryan (Tillet Main),

Jean Simmons (Clarissa Main), Lewis Smith (Charles Main), David Ogden Stiers (Congressman Sam Greene), John Stockwell (Billy Hazard), Inga Swenson (Maude Hazard), David Weaver (Preston Smith), Forest Whitaker (Cuffey).

North and South, Book II (1986) [Hal Holbrook]
ABC Television Network. Warner Bros. Television. A David L.Wolper Production. Robert A. Papazian Production. Executive Producer: David L. Wolper. Produced by Robert A. Papazian. Directed by Kevin Connor. Developed for television by Douglas Heyes. Teleplay by Richard Fielder. Based on the novel *Love and War* by John Jakes. Director of Photography: Jacques Marquette, A.S.C. Music by Bill Conti. Associate Producers: Stephanie Austin and Mark Wolper. Film Editors: Eric Sears and David Saxon, A.C.E. Production Designer: Joseph R. Jennings. Casting: Mary West, C.S.A., and Ross Brown, C.S.A. Production Manager: Hal Galli. First Assistant Director: Robert Jones. Second Assistant Director: Josh McLaglen. Third Assistant Director: Alice Blanchard. Costume Designer: Robert Fletcher. Second Unit Director/Stunt Coordinator: Joe Dunne. Assistant Art Director: Sandy Veneziano. Women's Costume Supervisor: Dodie Shepard. Men's Costume Supervisor: Bud Clark. Makeup Artists: Jack Petty and Rod Wilson. Mr. Holbrook's Makeup: Dick Smith. Hairstylist: Yolanda Toussieng. Script Supervisor: Dell Ross. Production Sound: Charles T. Knight. Set Decorator: Joe Mitchell. Property Master: Bill Macsems. Special Effects: Russ Hessey. Camera Operator: John Kiser. Key Grip: Robert J. Babin. Gaffer: Bill Tenney. Construction Coordinator: Cal Divalerio. Editors: Eric Boyd Perkins, John W. Carr, Susan Heick. Assistant Editors: Alec Smight and Kathleen Jo Skide-Elliot. Music Editors: Stephen A. Hope and James D. Young. Sound Editing: James Troutman & Associates. Historical/Technical Advisor: Ray Herbeck Jr. Location Manager: Star Price. Location Auditors: Kenneth D. Lee and Don Shelley. Main Title Design: Sandy Dvore. Titles and Opticals: Pacific Title.
CAST: Kirstie Alley (Virgilia Hazard Grady), Bonnie Bartlett (General's wife), Charles Boswell (Hughes), Lloyd Bridges (Jefferson Davis), Michael Burgess (Jim), Harry Caesar (Joseph), David Carradine (Justin Lamotte), Philip Casnoff (Elkanah Bent), Michael Champion (Detective Haller), John Cornejo (Union cavalryman), Mary Crosby (Isabel Hazard), Lesley-Anne Down (Madeline Fabray Lamotte), Billy Drago (rat), Michael Dudikoff (Lieutenant Rudy Bodford), Robert Englund (deserter), Linda

Lincoln (Hal Holbrook) is angry and frustrated over his
generals' lack of action in *North and South: Book II* (1986).
Courtesy of Warner Bros. Television

Evans (Rose Sinclair), Morgan Fairchild (Burdetta Halloran), Jonathan
Frakes (Stanley Hazard), Genie Francis (Brett Main Hazard), Tony Frank
(Salem Jones), Terri Garber (Ashton Main Huntoon), Burton Gilliam
(Corporal Strock), Erica Gimpel (Semiramis), Gary Grubbs (Lieutenant
Pickles), Clu Gulager (General Philip Henry Sheridan), Lee Horsley (Rafe
Beaudeen), James Houghton (Lieutenant Pell), Whip Hubley (Lieutenant
Stephen Kent), Rosanna Huffman (Mrs. Reilly), Wendy Kilbourne
(Constance Flynn Hazard), Eb Lottimer (Northern Lieutenant), Nancy
Marchand (Dorothea Dix), Kate McNeil (Augusta Barclay), Jim Metzler
(James Huntoon), James Morrison (Bradley), Wayne Newton (Major
Thomas Turner), James Read (George Hazard), Leon Rippy (Sanders),
Bumper Robinson (Michael), William Schallert (General Robert E. Lee),
Jean Simmons (Clarissa Main), Kurtwood Smith (Colonel Hiram Berdan),
Lewis Smith (Charles Main), Arlen Dean Snyder (General William
Tecumseh Sherman), Parker Stevenson (Billy Hazard), James Stewart
(Miles Colbert), David Ogden Stiers (Congressman Sam Greene), Ray
Stricklyn (Colonel Wade Hampton), Patrick Swayze (Orry Main), Inga
Swenson (Maude Hazard), Jack Thibeau (Mr. Morgan), Harvey Vernon
(Colonel Hart), Forest Whitaker (Cuffey), Anthony Zerbe (General
Ulysses S. Grant), Olivia de Havilland (Mrs. Neal).

Dream West (1986) [F. Murray Abraham]

Executive Producer: Chuck McLain. Produced by Hunt Lowry. Directed
by Dick Lowry. Written by Evan Hunter. Based on the novel by David

Nevin. Original Music: Fred Karlin. Cinematography: David Eggby. Production Design: Linda Pearl. Film Editing: Byron "Buzz" Brandt and Jack Fegan. Property Master: Guy Barnes. Second Assistant Director: Jeanne Caliendo. Technical Advisor: Bret Culpepper. Swing: Sean E. Markland.

CAST: Richard Chamberlain (John Charles Fremont), Alice Krige (Jessie Benton Fremont), Claude Akins (Tom Fitzpatrick), John Anderson (Brigadier General Brooke), Mel Ferrer (Judge Elkins), Burton Gilliam (Martineau), Jeff Allin (blonde man), George American Horse, Erich Anderson, Lee Bergere, Dan Biggers, Anna Bjorn, Cecile Callan (Nicole), Bill Campbell (Lietenant Gaines), Michael Crabtree (second man on trek 5), James Cromwell (Major General Hunter), Carole Davis, Joe Dorsey, Jeff East (Tim Donovan), René Enríquez (General Castro), Michael Ensign (Preuss), Terrence Evans (Farmer), Jonathan Frakes (Lieutenant Gillespie), Stefan Gierasch (Trenor Park), William Glover, Jim Grimshaw, Richard Hamilton (General Murdoch), Will Hare (Dr. McClain), John Harkins (Secretary of State George Bancroft), Barton Heyman, Gayle Hunnicutt (Maria Crittenden), Joe Inscoe, Ben Johnson (Jim Bridger), Dennis King (Francis Blair), Stephen Lee, Robert Lussier, Joaquín Martínez, Matt McCoy (Louis Freniere), George McDaniel (Colonel Mason), Cameron Mitchell (Commodore Robert Stockton), Kip Niven (Senator John Crittenden), Jerry Orbach (John Sutter), Randal Patrick (Carvalho), John Quade (Big Fallon), Hansford Rowe, Timothy Scott (Ezekial Merrit), G. D. Spradlin (General Steven Watts Kearny), Buck Taylor (Egloffstein), Rip Torn (Kit Carson), Fritz Weaver (Senator Thomas Hart Benton), Noble Willingham (President James Polk), Anthony Zerbe (Bill Williams), Lee de Broux (Provost), Helen Floyd, Cathryn Purdue, Jay Louden, Kelly Yunkerman, George Bazaldua.

Gore Vidal's Lincoln (March 27–28, 1988) [Sam Waterston]
NBC Television Network. Chris/Rose Productions and the Finnegan/Pinchuk Co. Executive Producers: Sheldon Pinchuk, Bill and Pat Finnegan. Produced by Bob Christiansen and Rick Rosenberg. Directed by Lamont Johnson. Written by Ernest Kinoy. Based upon the novel by Gore Vidal. Music composed and conducted by Ernest Gold. Cinematography: William Wages. Film Editor: James Oliver. Production Designer: Paul Peters. Costume Design: George L. Little. Casting: Donna Isaacson, C.S.A., and John Lyons, C.S.A. Unit Production Manager: Bruce L. Shurley. First Assistant Director: Jerry Grandey. Second Assistant Director:

Eric Wall. Sam Waterston's and Mary Tyler Moore's Costumes Designed by Joseph J. Aulisi. Costume Designer: George Little. Associate Producer: David Roessell. Additional Casting: Eleanor Cooke. Property Master: Robert Visciglia. Set Decorator: Lynn Smartt. Makeup Consultants: Vince Callaghan and Coree Lear. Hairstylists: Kevin Trahan and Sally Harper. Set Dressers: Joe Conway and Cathy Mckenney. Costumes: Dennis Fill, Vicki Graff, Melinda Howard, and Dan Chichester. Camera Operator: Edwin Myers. First Assistant Camera: Lee Blasingame. Second Assistant Cameras: Steve Mattson and Gerald Lewandowski. Sound Mixer: James D. Hawkins Jr. Script Supervisor: Connie Collins. Assistant Art Director: Gershon Ginsburg. Chief Lighting Technician: Joe Clayton. Best Boy Electric: Rick Anderson. Key Grip: Billy Sherrill. Best Boy Grip: Robert Shuford, Jr. Boom Technician: Shirley Libby. Special Effects: B. Russell Hessey. Production Controller: Lori-etta Taub. Production Auditor: Cary Weddington. Assistant Auditors: Dawn Dareus and Cindy Hornickel. Production Coordinators: Margaret E. Fannin and Tara Perry. Assistant to Executive Producers: Phyllis Watkins. Assistant to Producers: Claire Spencer. Location Managers: Jane Word and Charles T. Baxter. Transportation Coordinator: Fred Robbins. Construction Coordinator: Steve Hagberg. Technical Advisor: Mark Greenough. Choreographer: Gwendolyn Gwenn. Office Assistants: Michael Reed and Jane Urbanczyk. DGA Trainee: Debra Kent. Stunt Coordinator: Jimmy Medearis. Livestock Coordinator: Nita Long. Extra Casting: Grey Images and Pavana Kaine. Payroll Services: Elite Payroll and Jeff Behlendorf. Extra Payroll: Bon Bon International, Inc. and Academy Systems, Inc. Caterer: Transamerica Catering, Inc. Music Editing: Segue Music. Supervising Music Editor: Jim Harrison. Rerecording and Sound Effects Editorial: Todd-Ao/Glen Glenn Sound. Supervising Sound Editor: David Hankins. Rerecording Sound Mixers: Andrew D'Addario, Dean Okran, C.A.S., and Weldon Brown. Assistant Editor: Lisa Bianco. Electronic Laboratory Services provided by Pacific Video, Inc. Daily Film Processing: CFI. Lenses and Panaflex Camera by Panavision.

CAST: Mary Tyler Moore (Mary Todd Lincoln), Richard Mulligan (Secretary of State Seward), Deborah Adair (Kate Chase), Tom Brennan, Gregory Cooke, Steven Culp (John Hay), Ruby Dee (Elizabeth Keckley), Jerome Dempsey, Jeffrey Demunn, Jon Devries, George Ede, Robin Gammell, James Gammon (General Ulysses S. Grant), Thomas Gibson (Sprague), Tim Guinee, David Leary, Cleavon Little, John McMartin, Patrick Rowe, John Houseman (General Scott), James Anklam (telegraph operator #1), Bev Appleton (office seeker #2), Joe Ayres (singing soldier), Greg Baber (Henry), Coby Batty (Earle), Charles Thomas Baxter (staff captain), Joshua Billings (assistant manager), Roy Butler (southern congressman #3), Dick Cheatham (staff officer), Bill Chorney (Pinkerton), Ray Collins (office seeker #5), Ritchie Copenhaver (Captain Holmes), Del Driver (Thompson), Glenn Faigen (John Wilkes Booth), Bill Falkenstein (plenipotentiary), Kevin Grantz (office seeker #3), Fay Greenbaum (Mrs. Ord), Dick Harrington (Stewart), Rick Hite (Speaker Hickman), J. Michael Hunter (office seeker #1), Karen Hutcheson (Julia Grant), Edward James Hyland (Editor Forney), Philip Hyland (young soldier), Helen Jervey (Mrs. Laury), Colonel Marion Johnson (Blair), Lee Lively (General Wood), Jim Lowell (southern congressman #2), Tom Mason (southern congressman #1), John Mingus (Governor Curtin), Kevin Murry (hotel clerk), Patrick Coe McCluskey (Willie Perham), Harry McEnerny (Leland Grover), R. Max Ramsey (manservant), Adrian Rieder (Fred Grant), Stephen Rudin (telegraph operator #2), Alan Sader (Sickles), Michael Schauer (barkeep), Bob Schindler (sergeant), Troy Sweeney (Tad Lincoln), Richard Travis (Nicolay), Rick Warner (staff colonel), Paul Welch (Willie Lincoln), Phil Whiteway (glove salesman), Tom Width (surgeon).

Ironclads (1991) [James Getty]

Turner Network Television. Rosemont Productions Limited. Executive in Charge of Production: Ira Marvin. Produced by David A. Rosemont. Coproducer: Norman Rosemont. Directed by Delbert Mann. Teleplay: Harold Gast. Story: James Retter. Music composed and conducted by Allyn Ferguson. Cinematography: William Wages. Costume Design: Noel Taylor. Production Design: Joseph Jennings. Film Editing: Millie Moore, A.C.E. Director, Miniatures Unit: Martin Gutteridge. Paramedic: Anthony Harbour. First Assistant Directors: Don Roberts and Mark McGann. Second Assistant Directors: Bart Rowe and Johanna Jensen. Second Second Assistant Director: Joseph Brad Kluge. Unit Production Manager: Ira Marvin. Casting: Julie Hughes, C.S.A., and Barry Moss, C.S.A. Art Director: Charles Butcher. Set Decorator: David Ensley. Hair Designer: Vicki Phillips. Makeup Artist: Judy Ponder. Camera Operator: Robert Horne. Camera Assistant: Ian Dodd. Gaffer: Joe Clayton. Best Boy: Rick Anderson. Historical Consultant: Ray Herbeck. Cannoneer: Roger Ragland. Choreographer: Gwendolyn Glenn. Property Master: Kelly Farrah. Construction Coordinator: Richard Blankenship. Location

Manager: Kirk Poore. Production Accountant: Deborah Hebert. Production Coordinator: Christopher Starke. Script Supervisor: Connie Barzaghi. Key Grip: Billy Sherril. Best Boy: Eddie Evans. Dolly Grip: Michael Fedack Production Assistant: Jennie Turner. Producer's Secretary: Sandra Reid. Rosemont Productions Controller: Camille Pollack. Primary Production Illustrator: Mentor Huebner. Special Effects Coordinator: Matt Vogel. Key Effects Assistant: Joel P. Blanchard. Stunts Coordinator: Phil Nelson. Costume Supervisor: Michael Boyd. Sound Mixer: Ken Ross. Boom Operator: Jeff Norto. Transportation Manager: J. T. Lannen. Wrangler: Doug Sloan.

Second Unit: Cinematographer: Arthur Wooster. Camera Assistant: Jeffrey Lane. First Assistant Director: Nick Prince. Second Assistant Director: Michael Ingber. Script Supervisor: Becca Poulos. Gaffer: Russell Parsons. Best Boy: David Shannon. Key Grip: Ron Goldsmith. Dolly Grip: Skelly Cummings. Hair Designer: Taylor Knight. Makeup Artist: Leslie Fuller. Extras Casting: Isabel Cramer.

Miniature Unit: Miniature effects produced and created by Martin Gutteridge. Photographed by Paul Wilson, A.S.C. Models and miniature effects designed, constructed, and operated by Effects Associates Limited. Associate Film Editor: Bob Kagey. Assistant Editors: Lareine Johnson and Lucyna Wojiechowski. Negative Cutter: Glenn Suffern. Audio Postproduction: Larson Sound Center. Supervising Sound Editor: Burton M. Weinstein. Music Editor: Lori Slomka. Rerecording: Tim Philben, Scott Millan, and George R. Groves Jr.

CAST: Virginia Madsen (Betty Stuart), Alex Hyde-White, Reed Diamond, Philip Casnoff, E. G. Marshall (Joseph Smith), Fritz Weaver (John Ericsson), Leon B. Stevens (Captain Franklin Buchanan), Kevin O'Rourke (Lieutenant Joe Smith Jr.), Joanne Dorian (Blossom), Beatrice Bush (Opal), Conrad McLaren (Secretary of the Navy Gideon Welles), Burt Edwards (Secretary of War Edwin M. Stanton), Phil Whiteway (Commander Davis), Carl Jackson (Cletus), Marty Terry (Mrs. Coyt), Chistopher Northup (Spencer Brown), Joan Demarrais (Mrs. Fletcher), Michal Leamer (Ella Mae), Roy Lind (Secretary Mallory), George Baber (Sergeant Collins), Michael Costello (Engineer Ramsey), J. Michael Hunter (Lieutenant Simms), Michael Stanton Kennedy (Pilot Patten), Gayle Turner (Quartermaster Williams), Duke Lafoon (Seaman Yates), Andy Park (Captain John Worden), George Kelly (Lieutenant Samuel Green), Ford Flannagan (Ensign Keeler), Mark Ransom Eis (Seaman

Stodder), Joel Abel (Captain Van Brunt), Tom Width (Lieutenant Austin Pendergrast), Ernie Dunn (Ensign Stone).

The Perfect Tribute (1991) [Jason Robards]
Directed by Jack Bender. Based on the story by Mary Raymond Shipman Andrews.
CAST: Lukas Haas (Benjamin Blair), Campbell Scott (Carter Blair), Katherine Helmond (farm woman), Ed Flanders (Warren), José Ferrer (Edward Everett), Daniel Davis (Governor Curtin), Richard Jenkins (Blair), Laurie Kennedy (Mrs. Blair), Dakin Matthews (Dr. Thomas), Bruce McGill (Lamon), Scott Paulin (Wills), James Sutorius (Shelby), Jeanne Tripplehorn (Julia), James Donadio (Alexander), Haynes Brooke (Jonas), Amy Bryson (Victoria), Robert C. Treveiler (Hay), Ed Grady (Doctor Stone), Susie Hall (Indiana Mother), Andrew Winton (Tad Lincoln), Eric Petz (dying boy), Fred Dollar (Confederate sergeant), James Michael McDougal (southern engineer), Michael H. Moss (Yank), Billy Ray Reynolds (company captain), Jim Peck (Seward), Rebecca Wackler (Miss Everett).

Tad (1996) [Kris Kristofferson]
The Family Channel. Chris/Rose Productions, Inc. Executive Producer: James M. Dowaliby. Produced by Bob Christiansen and Rick Rosenberg. Co-Producer: Daniel Schneider. Directed by Rob Thompson. Written by Ernest Kinoy. Original Music: George S. Clinton. Director of Photography: Frank Prinzi. Production Design: Bill Malley. Film Editing: Paul Dixon, A.C.E. Postproduction Supervisor: Tina Threadgill. Stand-in for Kris Kristofferson: Aaron Michael Lacey. Casting: Meryl O'Loughlin, C.S.A., and Jackie Margey, C.S.A. Unit Production Manager: Daniel Schneider. First Assistant Director: Bradley M. Gross. Second Assistant Director: Peter Choi. Executive in Charge of Production for the Family Channel: Bob Chmiel. Production Executive: Jerry Cardwell. Costume Designer: Jo Ynocencio. Location Casting: Tracy Kilpatrick. Assistant Art Director: Mark J. Shively. Set Decorator: Donald Elmblad. Lead Person: Ray Fisher. On Set Dresser: Cliff Eubank. Set Dressers: Chris Arias, Arthur Wood III, Dabney Carr, and Matt Miley. Property Master: Richard Mazzochi. Assistant Property Master: Tommy Estridge. Key Hairstylist: Sally Harper. Key Makeup Artist: Bob Harper. Hair/Makeup Artist: Lee Ann Brittenham. Additional Hair: Gregor T. Young. Historical Advisors: Mark Greenough and Dick Cheatham. Sound Mixer: Walter Anderson.

Boom Operator: Michael Patillo. Cable Person: Chris Jones. Camera
Operator: Phil Detiker. First Assistant Camera: David S. Tuttman. Second
Assistant Camera: N. G. Ranger. Additional Second Assistant Camera:
Tyger Belton and Lee Fiedler. Costume Supervisor: Catharine Fletcher.
Men's Costumer: Michael Nations. Women's Costumers: Ann Lytle and
Katherine Karbowski. Assistant to the Costume Designer: Kathlene
Mobley. Cutter/Draper: Gray Hunter. Stitcher: Dennisse Kane. Wardrobe
Production Assistant: Bradley Garett. Location Manager: John Crowder.
Assistant Location Manager: Lenny Brisendine. Location Assistant: John
McSweeney. Script Supervisor: Dawn C. Dreiling. Production
Coordinator: Nathan C. Harding. Assistant Production Coordinator:
Rebecca Gibson. Production Accountant: Norma Smith. Assistant
Production Accountants: Derek Smith and Michelle Thomas.
Postproduction Accountant: Stephen J. Bokmiller. Gaffer: Felix Rivera.
Best Boy Electric: Jay Kemp. Electricians: Mike Flinn, Todd Ranson, and
Bob Spencer. Key Grip: Tom Barrett. Best Boy Grip: Charles A. Harris.
Dolly Grip: Skelly Cummings. Grips: Kent Eanes and Greg Martin. Special
Effects Coordinator: Bob Vasquez. Special Effects Foreman: Kathleen
Tonkin. Transportation Manager: J. T. Lannen. Transportation Captain:
Gerald L. Sidwell. Construction Coordinator: J. T. Woods. Construction
Foreman: Thomas Mentzer. Scenic/Signwriter: Susan Golsarry. Legal
Affairs: Lou Sakoff. Studio Teacher: Barbara Mannlein. Animal Wranglers:
Nita Long-Mawyer and Thomas M. Mawyer. Craft Service: Linda Bassett.
Caterer: Unique Catering. Chef: Henry Burrell. Location Casting
Assistant: Chris Baldwin. Set Production Assistants: Julie P. Adams and
Gayle Gilberto. Office Production Assistants: Mary Matthews and Brian
Davidson. Assistant to Mr. Thompson/Mr. Christiansen: Liz Fowler.
Postproduction Supervisor: Tina Threadgill. Assistant Editor: Richard J.
Rossi. Apprentice Editor: Jeffere Ferris. Negative Cutter: Glenn Suffern.
Sound Editing: Echo Films, Inc. Supervising Sound Editors: Joe Melody.
Dialogue/ADR Editor: Rusty Beith. Music Editor: Marty Weresky.
Rerecorded at Four Media Company. Rerecording Mixers: Bob Harman,
Wayne Artman, and Nick Alphin. Voice Casting: Barbara Harris. Titles and
Opticals: F-Stop, Inc. Color by CFI. Lighting and Grip Equipment by
Hollywood Rentals, Inc. Camera cranes and dollies by Chapman.
CAST: Bug Hall (Tad Lincoln), Jane Curtin (Mary Todd Lincoln), Jean
Louisa Kelly (Julia Taft), Kieran Mulroney (Robert Lincoln), Tyler Long
(Willie Lincoln), Billie Worley (Elmer Ellsworth), Joanne Pankow (Tad's
nurse), Muse Watson (Tom Pendel), Margo Moorer (Elizabeth Keckley),

Ed Gale (General Stratton), Jesse James Locorriere (Nicolay), Colonel Jim Allen (Edward), Ed Grady (Seward), Mark Garber (Hay), Alan Sader (Cameron), David Califf (Chase), Carl Jackson (Cudjo), Arthur Bridgers (Bud), Christopher Jones (Holly), Ralph Wilcox (Watts), Jim Grimshaw (general), James Bradfield (minister), George Kelly (Bixby), Karen Osburn (lady singer), Blaque Fowler (band leader), Kweli Leapart (servant), Jay Ross (man #1), Gregory Miller (man #2), Michael Mattison (steamboat colonel), Andy Lynch (boy urchin), R. J. Chmiel (Aladdin), Roger Simmons (Genie), Josh Keaton (Older Tad).

The Day Lincoln Was Shot (1998) [Lance Henriksen]
   Robert Greenwald Productions. Turner Network Television. Executive Producer: Robert Greenwald. Producer: Thomas John Kane. Supervising Producer: Philip K. Kleinbart. Associate Producer: Elizabeth Selzer. Directed by John Gray. Written by John Gray and Tim Metcalfe. Based on the book by Jim Bishop. Original Music: Mark Snow. Cinematography: Ron García. Costume Design: Michael T. Boyd and Cynthia Brenner. Production Design: Roy Forge Smith. Film Editing: Scott Vickrey. Sound Rerecording Mixer: Wayne Artman. Key Makeup Artist: Vivian Baker. Script Supervisor: Maxine Bergen. Construction Coordinator: Richard Blankenship. Key Costumer: Jennifer J. Cacavas. Music Editor: Dana Campbell. Music Editor: Jeff Charbonneau. Foley Artist: Tim Chilton. Lead Scenic: Mike Clark. Gaffer: Peter Clarson. Sound Editor: Bob Costanza. Location Manager: Mark Cottrell. Sound Editor: Rick Crampton. Set Designer: David Crank. Extras Casting: Maxann Crotts. Transportation Coordinator: Tyler C. Daum. Camera Operator: Sean Doyle. Production Coordinator: Carrie Durose. Sound Mixer: Mary H. Ellis. Property Master: Kelly Farrah. First Assistant Director: Dick Feury. Boom Operator: Bill Fibben. Production Assistant: Abe Forman-Greenwald. Foley Mixer: Tommy Goodwin. Sound Supervisor: Michael Graham. Second Second Assistant Director: Jay Guerra. Historian, Lincoln Assassination: William Hanchett. Sound Rerecording Mixer: Robert L. Harman. Assistant Hairstylist: Bob Harper. Hairstylist: Robert Harper. Key Hairstylist: Sally J. Harper. ADR Voice Casting: Barbara Harris. Casting; New York: Olivia Harris. Casting; Washington, D.C.: Benita Hofstetter. Casting: Richmond, VA: Helen Jervey. Sound Editor: Anton Holden. Stunt Coordinator: Shawn Howell. Still Photographer: Doug Hyun. Adr Editor: Kristi Johns. Casting Associate: Mindy Johnson. Sound Rerecording Mixer: Frank Jones. Unit Production Manager:

Dann Florek is a dim-witted, sex-obsessed Abe Lincoln in *The Secret Diary of Desmond Pfeiffer* (1998). *Courtesy of Paramount Pictures Television*

Thomas John Kane. Second Assistant Director: Jeff Kay. Best Boy: Jay Kemp. Assistant Makeup Artist: Rachel Kick. Lead Man: Andy Krish. Casting: Wendy Kurtzman. Sound Supervisor: Joseph Melody. Second Assistant Camera: Tim Metivier. Costume Supervisor: Stanley Moore. Production Supervisor: Doug Nicely. Historian, Lewis Paine: Betty J. Owensby. Set Decorator: Marthe Pineau. Historical Advisor: Brian Pohanka. Art Director: Michael Rizzo. Foley Artist: Jill Schachne. Special Effects Coordinator: Michael Schorr. Head Wrangler: Doug Sloan. First Assistant Camera: Michael C. Stailey. Sound Editors: Richard S. Steele, Lou Thomas, Robert Webber. Head Taylor: Jeff Transki. Assistant Production Coordinator: Caleb Womble. Key Grip: Dennis Zoppe.

CAST: Rob Morrow (John Wilkes Booth), Donna Murphy (Mary Todd Lincoln), Jean Louisa Kelly (Lucy Hale), Wil Wheaton (Robert Todd Lincoln), Titus Welliver (Lewis Paine), Jaimz Woolvett (David Herold), Jeremy Sisto (Fredrick Seward), Kirk B. R. Woller (George Atzerodt), John Pleshette (Secretary of State Seward), Gregory Itzin (crook), Adam Lamberg (Tad Lincoln), John Ashton (Ulysses S. Grant), Eddie Jones (Secretary of War Stanton), Nancy Robinette (Mary Surratt), Doug O'Lear (Doctor Leale), Sean Baldwin (Major Rathbone), Mercedes Herrero (Clara Harris), Jason Bowcutt (John Surratt), Marty Lodge (Parker), Tom Quinn (James Ford), Michael Noel (Doctor Mudd), Gary Wheeler (Lieutenant Bolton), Bob Supan (Burke, Booth's photographer), Tim Carlin (Gardner, Lincoln's photographer), Martha Thimmesch (Senator's wife), Dan De

Paola (Ned Spangler), Scott Rinker (Nicolay), Bob Child (Lieutenant Doherty), Kevin Murray (Harry Hawk), O'Mara Leary (Laura Keene), Jacqueline Jones (Mrs. Mountchessington), Meike Ter Poorten (Augusta), Jon Tindle (Safford), John Healey (senator), Brad Waller (cop), Melvin L. Cauthen (Bell), Jerry Laylon Ojeda (young man in ballroom), David Bryan Jackson (Louis the clerk), Terry Wells (man at Surrat house), Joseph Eubanks (older black man in Richmond), Carter Jahncke (man in bar), Richard Pilcher (Kirkwood bartender), John Lescault (Attorney General Speed).

The Secret Diary of Desmond Pfeiffer (1998) [Dann Florek]
UPN Network. Paramount Pictures Television. Executive Producers: Barry Fanaro and Mort Nathan. Producer: Marcia Govons. Directed by Matthew Diamond. Original Music: Rich Eames and Scott Gale. Cinematography: George La Fountaine. Editor: Mike Wilcox. Casting: Richard Casaletta. Sound: Richard Masci. Casting: Greg Orson.
CAST: Chi McBride (Desmond Pfeiffer), Max Baker (Nibblet), Christine Estabrook (Mary Todd Lincoln), Kelly Connell (Ulysses S. Grant), Cindy Ambuehl (Mona), Terry Kiser (Stonewall Jackson).

Theatrical, Radio, and Miscellaneous Works about Abraham Lincoln

(Note: While it is neither desirable nor possible to provide credits for each of the works listed here, the casts and crews of some of the more significant productions are provided.)

Ahab Lincoln (1861) by Stephen Franks Miller. Dramatic Poem.

The Irrepressible Conflict (1862) by S. D. Carpenter. Play.

The Administration Telegraph, or How It Is Done for Metropolitan Record (1863). Play.

King Linkum the First: A Musical Burletta (1863) John Hill Hewitt. Performed at the Concert Hall, Augusta, Georgia, February 23, 1863. Play.

The Royal Ape (1864) (author unknown). Play.

The Lost "Spade" or the Grave Digger's Revenge (1864) by The Happy Democratic Family. Play.

Lincoln's Aufgang Gluck und Ende (His Beginning, Greatness, and End) (1866) by Edward Reulon. German Play.

The Play of Destiny (1867) by Stephen W. Downey. Play.

The Sixteenth President (1871) by William Bush. Play.

A National Drama from the Beautiful World (1872) by C. E. Keith and Co. Play.

The Tragedy of Abraham Lincoln (1876) by Hiram D. Torrie. Scottish Play.

Madame Surratt (1879) by J. W. Rogers. Play.

John Wilkes Booth, or The National Tragedy (1880) by William A. Luby. Play.

Abraham Lincoln (1886) by Col. J. W. Bryant. Play.

Theatrical, Radio, and Miscellaneous Works about Abraham Lincoln

Love is Eternal (1895) by Ruth Sergel. Play.
Abraham Lincoln in the White House, also known as *Lincoln* and
Honest Abe (1906) by Benjamin Chapin. Play.
    CAST: Benjamin Chapin and Caroline Harris.
Abraham Lincoln (1911) by Martin L. D. Bunge. Play.
Abraham Lincoln—Rail Splitter (1912) by Constance D'Arcy Mackay. Play.
Abraham Lincoln (1914) by Mary Hazleton Wade. Play.
The Son of Democracy (ca. 1915) by Lucille Ann Chapin.
Lincoln and Humanity (1916) by Walter M. Zink. Play.
The Qualities of Washington, Lincoln and Humanity (1916) by Walter M. Zink.
    Play.
The Masque of the Titans of Freedom (1918) by William Chancy Langdon. Play.
The Copperhead (1918) by Augustus E. Thomas. Play.
Abraham Lincoln (1919) by John Drinkwater. Play. First presented at the
    Birmingham Repertory Theater where Drinkwater was director and
    producer, in October, 1919, with William J. Rea in the title role. It opened
    in February 1920 at the Lyric Theater, London; this production also starred
    Rea. Its first New York production occurred at the Cort Theater on
    December 15, 1919, produced by William Harris Jr. with Frank McGlynn
    Sr. playing the title role. McGlynn also appeared in a revival ten years later,
    beginning October 21, 1929, at the Forrest Theater in New York. The
    revival was also produced by Harris and the cast included Gerald Cornell
    as Seward, Alfred Moore as Gideon Wells, and Albert Phillips as General
    Grant.
Solemn Pride (1919) by George R. Leighton. Play.
Abraham Lincoln: God's Gift to the Ages (1919) by A. Donald Upton. Play.
The Mantle of Lincoln (1922) by Test Dalton. Play.
Transfusion (1923) by W. W. Davies. Play.
Abraham Lincoln's Pardon (1924) by Marie Irish. Play.
Washington and Lincoln Celebrations (1924) by Marie Irish. A collection of
    eleven short plays.
Abraham Lincoln and the Little Bird (1925) by Emma L. Johnston and Madelene
    D. Barnum. Play.
A Child of the Frontier (1925) by Elma E. Levinger. Play.
A Present for Mr. Lincoln (1925) by Elmer E. Levinger. Play.
The Haunted Biographer (1927) by Gamaliel Bradford. Play.
The Spirit of Ann Rutledge: A Drama of Abraham Lincoln in Four Acts
(1927) by Harold Winsor Gammons. Play. From Gammons's foreword to the
    published edition: "This play was first presented by my pupils of Central

High School, Scranton, Pa. The first professional performance was given by the WGY Players of Schenectady, NY, when Ten Eyck Clay played the part of Lincoln and Miss Rosamond Greene, the part of Ann Rutledge."

Abe Lincoln Comes Home (1928) by Louise Van Voorhis Armstrong. Play.

Abraham Lincoln (1928) by Herman Ludke. German Play.

Black Congo (1928) by Olive M. Price. Play.

Captain Lincoln's Way (1928) by Rea Woodman. Play.

The Old History Book (1928) by Louise Van Voorhis Armstrong. Play.

When Lincoln Went Flat Boating From Rockport, Indiana (1930) by Bess V. Ehrman. Pageant.

Abraham Lincoln (1931) by Clarence M. Gallup. Play.

Lincoln's Days of Destiny (1931) by Margaret M. Cheany. Pageant.

Lincoln and the Pig (1931) by Edgar Caper. Play.

Abe's First Fish (1932) by Alice Johnstone Walker. Play.

A Birthday Present for Lincoln (1932) by Dorothy C. Allan. Play.

If Booth Had Missed (1932) by Arthur Goodman. Play.

The Strength of Abraham Lincoln (1932) by Agnes Curtis.

Short Plays from the Life of Lincoln (1933): *Ann Rutledge, A Scene in the Rutledge Tavern,* and *A Scene in the White House* adapted from *The Soul of Ann Rutledge* by Bernie Babcock.

New Salem Days by Lucy Burton

Grampa Tells about Lincoln by Phyllis Marschall

Turning Points by Perry Boyer Corneau

Abraham Lincoln—A Pageant by Anne Deiss Fielden

Houses Divided by Marion Holbrook

Massa Linkum's Sojer by Margaret Parsons

At Old Vincennes by Ruth Reno Smith

Her Name was Ann by Anna Jane Harwell

In 1864 by Vida R. Sutton

Abraham and the Ages by Jean Milne Gower

The Tree Inclined by Grace Dorcas Ruthenburg

These Savages by Ashley Miller

Honest Abe (1934) by Madelene D. Barnum. Play.

Lincoln Reckons Up (1934) by Henry Bailey Stevens. Play.

The Soul of Ann Rutledge (1934) by Miss Bernie Babcock. Based on her novel of the same title. Play.

Prologue to Glory (1936) by E. P. Conkle. Play.

Abe Lincoln (1937) by Greville Lewis. British Play

Abe Lincoln in Illinois (1937) by Robert E. Sherwood. Play.
Presented by the Playwrights' Company-Maxwell Anderson, S. N. Behrman, Sidney Howard, Elmer Rice, and Robert E. Sherwood-at the National Theater, Washington, D.C., on October 3, and at the Plymouth Theater, New York City, October 15, 1938, with the following cast and crew: Staged by Elmer Rice. Settings by Jo Mielziner. Stage Manager: Elmer Brown. Assistant Stage Manager: John Triggs.
CAST: Frank Andrews (Mentor Graham), Raymond Massey (Abraham Lincoln), Adele Longmire (Ann Rutledge), George Christie (Ben Mattling), Arthur Griffin (Judge Bowling Green), Lewis Martin (Ninian Edwards), Calvin Thomas (Joshua Speed), Harry Levian (Trum Cogdal), Howard da Silva (Jack Armstrong), Everett Charlton (Bab), David Clarke (Fergus), Kevin Mccarthy (Jasp), Herbert Rudley (Seth Gale), Lillian Foster (Nancy Green), Wendell K. Phillips (William Herndon), May Collins (Elizabeth Edwards), Muriel Kirkland (Mary Todd), Augusta Dabney (the Edwards' maid), Howard Sherman (Jimmy Gale), Marion Rooney (Aggie Gale), Hubert Brown (Gobey), Albert Phillips (Stephen A. Douglas), Lex Parrish (Willie Lincoln), Lloyd Barry (Tad Lincoln), John Payne (Robert Lincoln), Iris Whitney (the Lincolns' maid), Frank Tweddell (Crimmin), John Gerard (Barrick), Thomas F. Tracey (Sturveson), Harry Levian (Jed), Glenn Coulter (Kavanaugh), Everett Charlton (Major). Soldiers, Railroad Men, Townspeople: Allen Shaw, Phillip Caplan, Wardell Jennings, Dearon Darney, Harrison Woodhull, Robert Fitzsimmons, Joseph Wiseman, Walter Kapp, Melvyn Dinellie, Bert Schorr, Ora Alexander, Richard Allen, Bette Benfield, Dorothy Greeley, David Hewes, Alfred Jenkins, George Malcolm, Mckinley Reeves, Elizabeth Reller, Lotta Stawisky, Ann Stevenson.
Abe Lincoln in Illinois—1963 revival
Staged by Stuart Vaughan. Presented by T. Edward Hambleton and Norris Haughton. Scenery and Lighting by Peter Wexler. Costumes by Alvin Colt. Music by George Fischoff. Production Stage Manager: Frank Gero. At the Anderson Theater.
CAST: Hal Holbrook (Abe Lincoln), Eileen Fulton (Ann Rutledge), James Kenny (Judge Bowling Green), John Hetherington (Ninian Edwards), Herbert Nelson (Joshua Speed), David Ford (Jack Armstrong), Dulcie Cooper Brown (Nancy Green), Jake Dengel (William Herndon), Bette Henritze (Mary Todd), Jack Bittner (Stephen A. Douglas).
Abe Lincoln in Illinois—1994 revival
Directed by Gerald Gutierrez. Sets: John Lee Beatty. Lighting: Beverly

Emmons. Music: Robert Waldman. Costumes: Jane Greenwood. Lincoln Center Theater, Vivian Beaumont.

CAST: Sam Waterston (Abe Lincoln), Lizbeth Mackay (Mary Todd Lincoln), David Aaron Baker (William Herndon), David Huddleston, Robert Westenberg, Robert Joy, Marissa Chibas, Nesbitt Blaisdell, Brian Reddy, Ann McDonough, Barton Tinapp.

Prologue to Glory: A Play in Eight Scenes Based on the New Salem Years of Abraham Lincoln (1938) by E. P. Conkle. Play.

Thirty Minutes with Lincoln (1938) by H. L. Bland. Play.

Washington and Lincoln (1938) by WPA. A collection of short plays.

Young Lincoln (1938) by Wilbur Braun. Play.

Easy Plays for Lincoln's Birthday (1939):

    Thanks to Abe by J. M. McMullen

    New Salem Days by Lucy Barton

    Houses Divided by Marion Holbrook

    In Boston, 1864 by Alice J. Walker

    Mr. Lincoln and the Little Girl by Alice J. Walker

    At the White House by Alice J. Walker

    For Lincoln's Birthday (author unknown)

    Lincoln Sort of Fellow (author unknown)

    On a Plantation (author unknown)

Lawyer Lincoln (1939) by Betty Smith and Chase Webb. Play.

Lincoln's Last Soliloquy (1939) by Henry Thomas. Play.

Nor Long Remember (1939) by Harold G. Hoffman. Play.

North Star (1939) by Jacob Bentkover. Play.

The Shot That Missed Lincoln (1939) by Channing Pollock. Play.

Cradle of Glory (1940) by Marie McNett. Play.

Just Call Me Abe (1940) by Clarence C. Johnson. Play.

Out of the Wilderness (1940) by WPA. Play.

President Lincoln (1940) by Earl Hobson Smith. Play.

One Who Came to Gettysburg (1941) by Robert Knipe. Play.

When Abe Kept Store (1942) by Bronsen Blake. Play.

And There Were Voices (1943) by Robert Kuipe. Play.

The Boy Abe (1943) by Betty Smith. Play.

Mrs. Bixby Gets a Letter (1943) by Elmer Gertz. Play.

Abe Lincoln's Story (1944) by Carl Haverlin and H. Bedford-Jones. Play.

The Man Who Taught Lincoln (1945) by Bernard Reines. Play.

A China-Handled Knife: A One Act Play About Young Abe Lincoln (1946) by E. P. Conkle. Play.

Theatrical, Radio, and Miscellaneous Works about Abraham Lincoln

The Great Man's Whiskers (1947) by Adrian Scott. First presented as a Workshop. Run-Through at the Actor's Lab, Hollywood, California, on June 30, 1947. Directed by Phil Brown. Designer and Stage Manager: Ralph Delauney. Lighting: Jack Hyam. Assistant Stage Manager: George Buchanan. Play.
The Washington Years: A New Play about Abraham Lincoln (1947) by Nathan Sherman. Play.
Cradle of Glory: A Drama in Three Acts (1948) by Marie McNett. Play.
Indiana Abe: A Comedy-Drama in Three Acts (1948) by J. Langdon Daly. Play.
Lincoln, el Lenador (the Woodcutter) (1948) by Celso Pomero, Pelaez. Spanish Play.
The Lawyer of Springfield: A Play in One Act (1948) by Ronald Gow. Play.
Mr. Lincoln's Whiskers: A Play in One Act (1948) by Adrian Scott. Play. The published version of Scott's *The Great Man's Whiskers.*
Mary, the Wife of Abraham Lincoln (1949) by Frank P. Breckinridge. Play.
Abe Lincoln, Our Friend (1951) by Lillian Griffin and the Fifth Grade of the North Shore Country Day School, Winnetka, Illinois. Play.
Forever This Land (1951) by Kermit Hunter. Play.
Marked Corners: A Three Act Play about Young Abraham Lincoln (1954) by Francesca Falk Miller. Play.
Lincoln's Secret Messenger-Boy Detective to a President: A Historical Play (1955) by Charlotte Chorpening. Play.
Love is Eternal: A Play in Three Acts (1955) by Ruth Perry. Play. Based on the book by Irving Stone. Concerning the romance and marriage of Abraham and Mary Todd Lincoln.
Mary the Wife (1955) by Frank P. Breckenridge. Play.
The Rivalry (1957) by Norman Lewis Corwin. A drama about the Lincoln-Douglas debates. Play. The original cast consisted of Raymond Massey (Lincoln), Martin Gabel (Stephen A. Douglas), and Agnes Moorehead (Mrs. Adele Douglas).
One Love Had Mary (1958) by Princine M. Calitri. Play.
The Instructor: Playlets (1959):
  Lincoln and the Emancipation Proclamation (1940) by Lois C. Andrews
  Abe Lincoln in Indiana (1942) by Ethel Wiley Stallings
  Lincoln's Life in Music and Pantomime (1948) by Ruth Harris Tyson
  The Gettysburg Address (1950) by Lawrence R. Root
  A Boy Begins to Wonder (1953) by Mary Nygaard Peterson
  A Day with President Lincoln in 1863 (1954) by Mary Nygaard Peterson
  I Knew Abe (1955) by Eleanor Marie Walker
  Modiste to Mrs. Lincoln (1958) by Marion Wefer

Lincoln Secrets (1957) by Alice L. Carmodeys

The Lincolns Heed the Call of the Frontier (1959) by Mary Nygaard Peterson

The Last of Lincoln: A Play in Six Scenes (1959) by Mark Van Doren. Play.

The Last Days of Lincoln (1959) by Mark Van Doren. Sound recording. Recorded on April 28, 1959, in the Coolidge Auditorium at the Library of Congress in Washington D. C.

The Golden Prairie (1960) by Kermit Hunter. Pageant.

Long, Long Ago (1960) by Edward R. Janjigian, MD. Play.

Out of the Wilderness (1960) (author unknown). Pageant.

Not in Vain (1961) by Richard Goldhurst. Play.

The Boy from Pigeon Creek (1961) (author unknown)

Thunder on the River (1961) by Kermit Hunter. Pageant.

Abe Lincoln of Pigeon Creek (1962) by William Edward Wilson. Play.

Lincoln (1963) by Dr. Jerome Head. Dramatic Poem.

Lincoln and Douglas: Years of Decision (1964) by Elise Bell. Sound Recording. A dramatization, with music and sound effects, adapted from the Landmark book of the same title by Regina Z. Kelly (New York, Random House, 1954). Enrichment Records Erl 111.

The Lost Speech (1966) by Sara Greeley. Play.

Mrs. Lincoln (1969) by Thomas Cullinan. Play.

Heritage: An American Folk Tale about the Lincoln Women. (1971) by P. J. Barry. Sound Recording.

    CAST: Joan Penn (Nancy Hanks), Marguerite McNeil (Sarah Bush Johnston), Nanci Addison (Ann Rutledge), Geraldine Teagarden (Mary Todd).

The Last of Mrs. Lincoln: A Play in Two Acts (1973) by James Prideaux. Play.

A Lincoln: A Play in Two Acts (1974) by Bill Stonebarger. Play.

Hidden Springs or Abe Grew Strong in Indiana: A Play in Four Acts with Prologue and Epilogue (1974) by Lela Kern Richmann. Play.

President Lincoln: Opera in Four Acts and Nine Scenes (1976) by Sam Raphling. Opera.

Mister Lincoln: A Drama in Two Acts (1982) by Herbert Mitsgang. Play.

One Land, One Nation (1987) by Mabel Johnson. Play.

Abraham Lincoln, the Complete Politician (1990) by William L. Huganir. Play.

The Prairie Man (1992) by Steven Porter. Play.

A Day in June (1992) by Helen Lewis. Sound Recording. An historic reeneactment of the wedding of Thomas Lincoln and Nancy Hanks on the bicentennial of the event. Recorded June 13, 1992, in Springfield, Kentucky.

Note: The dates, and some of the authors, of the following works are unknown.

Abe Lincoln and the Little A. D. (date and author unknown). Play.
Abe Lincoln—A Musical Play (date unknown) by Minar Dorey. Play.
Abe Lincoln: New Salem Days (date unknown) by Charlotte B. Charpening. Play.
Abraham Lincoln (date unknown) by F. S. Hereford. Play.
Abraham Lincoln (date unknown) by Franz A. F. Schmake. Play.
Abraham Lincoln or The Rebellion (date and author unknown). Play.
Abraham Lincoln's First Case (date unknown) by Delle Oglesbee Ross. Play.
The Abraham Lincoln Story (date unknown) by Walter E. Owen. Play.
The Day That Lincoln Died (date unknown) by Prescott Warren and Will Hutchins. Play.
Following Lincoln's Footsteps (date unknown) by Hellen Maurene Cotts. Play.
The Heart of Lincoln (date and author unknown). Play.
If Lincoln Were with Us Today (date and author unknown) Play.
La vie et la Morte D'abraham Lincoln (date unknown) by M. Reuter. French Play.
The Lincoln Memorial (date and author unknown). Play.
Lincoln as a Young Clerk (date unknown) by Frances O'Ryan and Anna Wynne O'Ryan. Play.
A Man of the People (date unknown) by Thomas Dixon. Play.
The New Salem Days (1941) (author unknown). Play.
The Rise and Fall of the Confederate States (date unknown) by Dr. C.W. Seldon. Play.
The Woman Lincoln Loved (date unknown) by George Truman Carl. Play.

Index

Index

in *Dramatic Life of Abraham Lincoln, The*, 6, 22–24, 33, *41*
Birth of a Nation, The, 15, 35, 102, 161, 176
    controversy over, 167–171
Blondell, Joan, 103
Blue and the Gray, The, 7, 8, 16, 19, 70, 89, 92–95
Blue Bird, The, 109
Boles, John, 153
Bondi, Beulah, *82*, 86
Booth, John Wilkes, 21, 27, 54, 115, 116, 131, 154, 162, 172
Brady, Mathew, 1, 159, 169
Brickell, Beth, 75
Brotherhood Crusade, 107, 108
Bull, Charles Edward, 39, 40, 137
Bush, Sarah. *See* Lincoln, Sarah Bush
Bush, W. Stephen, 40, 41, 141

Captains and the Kings, The, 112
Carlin, George, 105
Carroll, Janice, 92
Casey, Bernie, 104
Cavalcade of America, The, 55
Chapin, Benjamin, 11, 30, 41, 101, 102, 130, 131, 165, 188
    profile of, 139–149
Cheyenne Autumn, 39
Christopher Program, The, 7
Clifford, Ruth, 22, 23
Cohan, George M., 103
comedies about Lincoln. *See also* miniseries about Lincoln; movies, biographical; theatrical productions
    Bebe's Kids, 106
    Big Picture, The, 106
    Bill and Ted's Excellent Adventure, 104
    Blue Bird, The, 109
    Captains and the Kings, The, 112
    Guardian of the Wilderness, 112
    Happy Gilmore, 104
    Phantom President, The, 103
    Police Squad, 103
    "Savage Curtain" episode of *Star Trek*, 112–114
    Secret Diary of Desmond Pfeiffer, The, 106, 107, 108
    Stand-In, 102, 103
    Time Tunnel, 110
    Two Idiots in Hollywood, 104
Copperhead, The, 3
Corey, Jeff, 12, *13*

Court Martial, 35, 49
Craig, Nell, 24
Crisis, The, 35, 36, 37, 38
Crossing Fox River, 82
Cycle of Lincoln Plays, The, 142

Dana, Leora, 89
Dano, Royal, 24, 57
    in *Mr. Lincoln*, 60, *61*, 62
Day Lincoln Was Shot, The, 49, 161, 162
Dean, James, 16
Dee, Ruby, 26
Denton, Crahan, 11, 64, *65*, 74
directors/producers/playwrights. *See also individuals' names*
    Adrian Scott, 74
    Al Rockett, 31
    Benjamin Chapin, 11
    D. W. Griffith, 11
    David L. Wolper, 5
    Frank Woods, 169
    George Schaefer, 78
    Harold Winsor Gammons, 20
    Hermann Luedke, 122
    James Agee, 11
    John Drinkwater, 15
    John Ford, 1
    John Hill Hewitt, 117
    Lament Johnson, 5
    Lew Ayres, 153
    Norman Corwin, 163
    Norman Lloyd, 59
    Phil Rosen, 43
    Ralph Ince, 19
    Ray Rockett, 31
    Robert E. Sherwood, 10
    Sam Raphling, 122
    Stanley Kubrick, 58
    Thomas Ince, 28
    William N. Selig, 38
Douglas, Stephen A., 10, *24*, 35, 45, 51, 163, 185, 187
Dramatic Life of Abraham Lincoln, The, 6–7, 11, 22, 23, 24, 31, 33, 41–45, 49, 130, 174
Drane, Sam D., 35, 38, 39
    in *Crisis, The*, 36, 37
Drinkwater, John, 15, 20, 55, 122–128, 131, 150, 151, 177
Duggan, Andrew, 55, 56
Durning, Charles, *79*, 163

Index

Index

Index